THE CORN LAWS AND SOCIAL ENGLAND

LONDON
Cambridge University Press
FETTER LANE

NEW YORK · TORONTO
BOMBAY · CALCUTTA · MADRAS
Macmillan

TOKYO
Maruzen Company Ltd

THE CORN LAWS AND
SOCIAL ENGLAND

By C. R. FAY

Reader in Economic History in the
University of Cambridge

CAMBRIDGE
AT THE UNIVERSITY PRESS
1932

PRINTED IN GREAT BRITAIN

To

THE EDITOR

OF

The Wealth of Nations

CONTENTS

Preface   *page* ix

Chap. I. The Significance of the Corn Laws in English
        History   1

    II. The Economics of the Corn Bounty, 1688–
        1765   12

   III. Policy in transition, 1765–1815   28

    IV. Digression upon the Corn Trade around 1800   44
        Article 1. The Miller and the Baker   44
        Article 2. The London Corn Market   52
        Article 3. Taking the Averages   62
        Article 4. Sale by Measure or Sale by
        Weight   68

    V. 1815 on Trial   78

   VI. The League and Repeal   88

 VII. The Effect of the Corn Laws on the Price of
        Corn, 1815–1846   109

VIII. Huskisson and Imperial Statesmanship   121

   IX. The Corn Laws and Social Thought   135

Appendix. Two Speeches of Sir Robert Peel   156
        Précis of Speeches   213

Index   217

ERRATA

p. 11, *l.* 22, *for* Hokham *read* Holkham

p. 13, *l.* 5, *for* (1700) *read* (1698–9)

p. 31, *l.* 7, *for* (1662) *read* (1663)

p. 54, *last line, for* c. 7 *read* c. 71

p. 70, *l.* 5, *for* (1820) *read* (1824)

p. 84, *l.* 1, *for* Dr Skene Smith *read* Dr Skene Keith

p. 154, *l.* 1, *for* Sir William Crooks *read* Sir William Crookes

PREFACE

NOW that it has been decided once again to tax or restrict the nation's bread, it seems not inappropriate to pass in review the circumstances under which in former times such taxes and restrictions were imposed and then repealed. In 1815, as to-day, Parliament feared the open taxation of foreign corn; and continued to fear it, despite the pronouncement, first of Ricardo and then of McCulloch, in favour of a fixed duty. In 1815 they got round the difficulty by a rigid scheme of alternative freedom and prohibition, so that between 1815 and 1828 it is literally true that there was no taxation of bread: instead, there were merely violent and disturbing restrictions on foreign supplies, which had evil repercussions on the export trade and on agriculture itself. In 1828 they still feared direct taxation, employing a sliding scale which appeared to promise free wheat when foreign supply was really needed. They had not thought of the wheat quota then. If they had known it, we may surmise that they would have employed it; because it supplies protectionists with an ingenious weapon for taxing food at the consumer's expense and in the same breath denying that they tax it at all. It would, however, be idle to pretend that the food problem of 1932 closely resembles that of 1842. We are not near to famine. Our need is an increase of industry and trade, which will bring an increase of employment. And if this can be ensured by imperial reciprocity, we are rich enough to pay the tax it may involve. The risk seems to be that by devices such as the quota we shall clog the course of commerce and involve ourselves in some of the hindrances and circumventions that clustered so thickly around the Corn Averages of an earlier day.

To those who may have read *Life and Labour in the Nineteenth Century* I may explain that the story of Corn Law Repeal there given was condensed from the MS. which forms Ch. VI here. I acknowledge permission to reprint the following:

Ch. I, first half (*Economic History Review*).

Ch. IV, Art. 1 (*Cambridge Historical Journal*).

Ch. IV, Art. 2 (*Journal of American Economic Association*).

Ch. IV, Arts. 3 and 4, and Ch. VII (*Economic Journal*).

I thank A. M. Blake of Magdalene College, Cambridge, for reading the proofs and making the index.

C. R. F.

1 *August* 1932

Here you have nothing to do but repeat the same old story over and over again, which comes as pat off the lips as a child's church catechism. "Infamous aristocracy"—"iniquitous"—"ruinous starvation"—"landlord-supporting tax"—"blasted Quarterly"—and all that sort of thing. Whatever is wrong, lay it to the corn tax,

HILLINGDON HALL

CHAPTER I

THE SIGNIFICANCE OF THE CORN LAWS IN ENGLISH HISTORY

I N GREAT BRITAIN corn connotes wheat; in North America, maize. But in strict language and in the schedules of the English corn laws corn embraces grain generally.

After 1660 as England became at once a great producer and consumer of wheat, the regulations affecting the imports, exports and internal conduct of the grain trade figured largely in legislation and executive orders. These laws and orders in council applied not only to wheat, but also to barley, oats, rye, beans and pease. The items other than wheat together occupy a much larger space in the duty schedules of the corn laws, but they attracted little attention from statesmen and commentators. One or other of them is occasionally mentioned in the evidence given before parliamentary committees by farmers or merchants who were interested in a particular grain; but, in the main, they were treated as etceteras to the leading cereal, the "noblest grain", as Edmund Burke once called it.[1] Indeed, the celebrated corn bounty act of 1688, in which a bounty was given to wheat, rye, barley and malt, took no cognisance of the minor crops—oats, beans and pease. In general, however, it was the purpose of the legislature to assign uniform treatment to all the grains by framing duty scales proportionate to the normal difference in their prices. It appears, however, that this intention miscarried in one significant instance. For the low duty point of the corn law of 1670, which was so high as to prevent the import of all other grains except at famine prices, was comparatively low for oats. Between 1697 and 1765 the imports of oats amounted to about two-thirds of the total imports of grain, and in 1757 the Royal Burghs of Scotland, where oats were the staple food, protested against the unfavourable treatment of British oats. It was a season of scarcity, and speaking for the consumers of towns, they were not asking for a bounty or

---

[1] "Thoughts and Details on Scarcity", 1795, in *Works*, ed. 1826, VII. 405.

protection, but for the removal of the high bonds exacted on coast-wise shipping which (they said) caused the oats of Northumberland to "be coopt up in the Hands of the Farmers without Sale, to the Detriment of the landed Interest, and Distress of the manufacturing Counties, which consume Oats in Bread".[1]

The anomaly was removed by the act of 1773[2] to the extent of granting a bounty of two shillings per quarter on the export of oats; of which Adam Smith spoke with a disapproving "but". This law (he was arguing), in that it opened the home market at lower prices, stopped the bounty earlier and admitted corn for re-export duty free, "seems evidently an improvement upon the ancient system.

"But by the same law a bounty of two shillings the quarter is given for the exportation of oats whenever the price does not exceed fourteen shillings. No bounty had ever been given before for the exportation of this grain, no more than for that of peas or beans".[3]

His statement in the last sentence is substantially correct, because though by two acts of 1707[4] a bounty was given on the export of oatmeal, the payments thereunder were trifling. But having been admitted to bounty, they were subjected, like wheat, to a maximum export price. Thus wheat under 44s. export with bounty, at or over 44s. export prohibited: oats under 14s. export with bounty, at or over 14s. export prohibited.

For the whole period from 1697 to 1801 the imports of oats into Great Britain were twelvefold the exports; whereas for other cereals, except pease and beans, there was a large balance of exports on the aggregate; of wheat, 7 million quarters; of barley and malt, 18 million; of rye, 1 million.[5]

Four-fifths of the oats came from Ireland, the main part to Liverpool for consumption in the manufacturing districts of the North. Yet little notice was taken of this in that classical

---

[1] C. Smith, *Corn Tracts*, I. 5 n.
[2] 13 George III, c. 43 (the general corn law of that year).
[3] *Wealth of Nations*, ed. Cannan, II. 45.
[4] 6 Anne, c. 8 (Scotland), c. 29 (England).
[5] Skene Keith, *The Farmers' Magazine*, August 1802. Cf. also tables in R. E. Prothero, *English Farming, Past and Present*, p. 452.

advertisement of Irish wants, the Corn Trade Report of 1813.[1]
The Commons Committee of 1813 argued at eloquent length that
Ireland, which had supplied one-third of England's corn imports for the last five years as against one-seventh for the previous
sixteen, was capable of supplying the whole in the future. In
this context corn included grain of all kinds. But the Report
does not make it clear that the main supply from Ireland was of
oats, while that from foreign countries was of wheat and flour.
A table of "corn" exports, compiled from the Custom House
books in the National Library, Dublin, reveals the true situation
between 1801 and 1823:[2]

Year	Wheat in Barrels	Other Grain in Barrels
1803	168,397	494,421
1813	334,886	1,058,325
1823	631,877	895,860

In 1813, of the total grain exports from Ireland, nearly the
whole went either to Great Britain or to the British army in the
Spanish Peninsula.

The reason for the desire of the Corn Committee of 1813 to
dress the Irish corn exports in a wheat setting is obvious. Wheat
was the national foodstuff. In the words of Charles Smith, the
author of the Corn Tracts, written in 1766: "It is certain that
bread made of wheat is become much more largely the food of
the common people since 1689 than it was before that time, but
it is still very far from being the food of the people in general".[3]
Taking the population of England and Wales at 6 millions, he
concludes that 3¾ millions ate wheat, at the rate of one quarter
per head per annum. Rye and barley bread competed with
wheaten bread in the Midlands of England and were consumed

[1] *Report of Committee (House of Commons) on the Corn Trade of the United
Kingdom* (1813).
[2] Given in A. E. Murray, *Commercial Relations between England and Ireland*,
p. 441.
[3] C. Smith, *Three Tracts on the Corn Trade and Corn Laws* (ed. 1766)
(*Supplement*, p. 182). The three tracts were (I) *Short Essay on the Corn Trade
and Corn Laws* (1758); (II) *Considerations on the Laws relating to the Importation and Exportation of Corn* (1759); (III) *Collection of Papers*, relating to
(II), together with *Supplement* (1766). The pagination of Tract III runs on
from Tract II at p. 93; and that of the Supplement from Tract III at p. 149.
"Three Tracts" is the heading of the title-page to Edition II. Tract III and
the Supplement are undated, but the figures in them extend to 1765 inclusive.

almost solely in Wales. It was observed in Parliament in 1772 that the scarcity among the poor of England could not be measured by the price of wheat because "the poor lived mainly upon rye and other grain and not solely upon fine wheat".[1] Oats, which were eaten only by horses in the South of England, formed a larger part of the people's food than either wheat or rye in the north Midlands, in the North of England, and in Scotland. For Great Britain generally the main use of barley was in the making of beer. Pease and beans, when not reserved for sailors and soup, were fed to negroes, horses and hogs;[2] for it was not until the 25th of March, 1807, that the port of Liverpool had to mourn the abolition of the African slave trade. Smith's figures are reproduced in Eden's *State of the Poor*. As he tells us at the end of his great work, published in 1797, Scotland in those days was eating its oatmeal called "crowdie", and the North of England its "frumenty" of barley and milk: while Lancashire, whose history has always been bound up with that of Ireland, was addicted to potatoes, "produced in much greater perfection in Lancashire than in other parts of England, so men say". The loaves of barley, rye and oats which were very common in the North of England were despised, says Eden, in the Midlands and South. The labourers of Notts ate rye bread under protest: "they have lost their rye teeth, as they express it". In Kent and Sussex they had grown so luxurious that they thought brown bread "purgative and relaxing". And he gives other interesting distinctions of drink and dress.

In an able article by Dr Skene Keith in 1802, we get a glimpse of the position of the nation's food supply a few years later.[3] "Nearly twice as many persons now eat wheaten bread as formerly consumed this species of corn." By "formerly" the reverend doctor seems to mean not more than fifty years ago at the outside. In 1802, when he wrote, the rivalry of oaten bread in Scotland and of barley bread in England had declined. "Now the great proportion of the inhabitants subsist chiefly on wheat; and in plentiful years a considerable quantity has been

---

[1] *Parliamentary History of England*, XVII. 461.
[2] Cf. Smith, *Corn Tracts, Supplement*, p. 202.
[3] *The Farmers' Magazine*, Aug. 2, 1802.

used in the distillery." But it must be remembered that in the days of Charles Smith the counties north of the Trent contained little more than a quarter of the population of England, and even in 1800, despite the estimated addition of one-fifth of the population of Great Britain, the balance of population was still in the South. In the eighteenth century, even more than to-day, the citizens of London stood for the urban consumers as a class, just as the farmers of East Anglia and the South of England were the representative wheat farmers of the country; and because of their proximity to the capital they secured prompter attention to their grievances and interests. But after 1815 the North began to make itself heard; and when in 1838 a band of seven Manchester radicals founded the Anti-Corn Law Association, the agitation which they instigated was inspired and financed by the wheat-eating industrialists of the North. When the Anti-Corn Law League had achieved its purpose and obtained free trade in wheat, the English co-operative stores, whose wholesale centre was Manchester, consolidated the victory by establishing federal bakeries and mills at the leading ports of importation. Thus from 1660 to the present day the trade in wheat has been the trade in the staple food of a vocal part of the population.

But all bread made from wheat is not fine wheaten bread. The Standard Bread controversy, which the popular press advertised some years ago, was raised more than once in the eighteenth century in connection with the Assize of Bread. The controversy was most acute in periods of scarcity, in 1756–8, 1772–4, 1795 and 1800. In the interests of nutrition and economy Parliament endeavoured to popularise bread made of the whole produce of the wheat. This was the "Standard Parliamentary Whole Meal Bread", which figured in so many pamphlets and reports of the time. But Parliament was putting itself in opposition to the practice of millers and the taste of the public. The millers found it to their interest to divide the grain differently, converting the inner portions only into flour and supplying the bakers with no other sort. The pollards and bran, which remained over, were used as cattle feed or made into coarse bread for the very poor. In 1800 the London bakers assured Parliament that "scarcely any Bread is consumed in the metropolis but that which is made from the fine Wheaten Flour; that attempts have been made in times of scarcity to introduce a coarser species of bread into use, but without success; and that in their opinion the high price of bread would be considered, by the lower classes of people, as a small evil, when compared with any measures which would have the effect of compelling them to consume a bread to which they have not been accustomed".[1]

The fondness for new bread (it was estimated that the Londoners ate half of their bread on the day it was baked) made the waste still greater. But in spite of legal prohibition and the heroic example of their betters, the "lower classes of people" refused to change. Even the paupers insisted on white bread. Arthur Young lamented that "throughout a great part of the kingdom the general assistance given to the poor is by Money, Bread, or Flour, all three being almost equally an encouragement to the consumption of wheat".[2] He and his friends sang the praises of soup-kitchens with a fervour which was shared by all but those who were invited to eat the soup. Government prohibited the export of rice and encouraged with advances of money the herring fisheries round the Firth of Forth.[3] But the people declined rice and fish as obstinately as the famine-stricken rice-eaters of India of a later age declined the cartloads of Government wheat. Nor was their prejudice altogether senseless; for they were clinging instinctively to a standard of life higher than that betokened by the substitutes which were offered to them, and neither they nor their betters knew anything of vitamins.

Essential foodstuffs are a nation's life-blood, just as the means of transportation are its arteries. Therefore any measure of State which concerns the supply of these two things reaches far into the national life. The series of corn laws, like that of the navigation laws, is long and complex and the mastery of their detail is wearisome, but both series are always more than a chronicle of variations in scales of duty or enumerations of prohibited goods. Both have a history in a sense that the wine

[1] *Committee (H. of C.) on the Assize and Making of Bread* (1800). Evidence.
[2] *Ibid.*
[3] *Committee (H. of C.) on the High Price of Provisions. 2nd Report,* Dec. 1800.

duty or the soap duty excise has not. On the navigation laws was grounded the policy of national defence and the aspiration to command the seas. And the corn laws swayed to an even sterner stress. Producers' strength pulled one way and consumers' necessity the other. For wheat was a necessity of the poor, and agriculture was the symbol of productive strength at home. Cotton and wool were also objects of national concern; but cotton was an upstart, and more wool meant more sheep, and more sheep had hitherto meant fewer husbandmen. By contrast the smiling wheatfields with their human labour always on or about them were a precious boon for which England, like other wheat-raising nations, thanked the Divine Providence; and therefore she took such measures as she could to keep them smiling. The Divine Providence stirs even philosophers to enthusiasm! Adam Smith places agriculture in authority over all other pursuits, but the economist in him worried the philosopher for justification, and produced untenable analysis concerning the different quantities of capitals and men which agriculture "sets in motion". "No equal capital puts into motion a greater quantity of productive labour than that of the farmer." For "nature labours along with man", and "not only his labouring servants, but his labouring cattle, are productive labourers".[1] But the wind and tide which sail the ships and the humble post-horse of the common carrier he does not include in the labour force of the merchant.

Thus much for the producer's stake in wheat. What of the consumer's? Inasmuch as a steadily increasing section of the population lived on wheat, the variations in its price affected them vitally. As Adam Smith says in his digression on the corn trade: "The laws concerning corn may everywhere be compared to the laws concerning religion. The people feel themselves so much interested in what relates either to their subsistence in this life, or to their happiness in a life to come, that government must yield to their prejudices, and, in order to preserve the public tranquillity, establish that system which they approve of. It is upon this account, perhaps, that we so seldom find a reasonable system established with regard to either of those two

[1] *Wealth of Nations*, I. 343.

capital objects".[1] And the labourers who could not earn a livelihood were, as a result of the poor law policy at the end of the eighteenth century, interested even more in the price of wheat. For their deficiency of wages was made up to them from the poor rates by a scale varying with the size of their family and the price of the gallon loaf of wheaten bread.

When the Gallon Loaf of Second flour, weighing 8 lb. 11 ozs. shall cost 1s.

Then every poor and industrious man shall have for his own support 3s. weekly..., and for the support of his wife and every other of his family, 1s. 6d.

So it was ordained at Speenhamland in 1795.[2]

Thus in England the great economic struggle between producer and consumer was fought out over the price of bread and the restrictions on the importation of wheat. The struggle coincided with, and was intensified by, the death struggle with the French Republic and Napoleon. It was the anger spot in the fight for free trade from the rise of Huskisson to the fall of Peel. The act of corn law repeal in 1846 marked the triumph of the consumer and the fulfilment in England of that hard fiscal saying: "Consumption is the sole end and purpose of all production".[3] The country gentlemen and farmers put up a good fight, but they collapsed before the brazen monotone of Cobdenism, "Monopoly, landlords' monopoly". Men forgot what the great free-trader had once said of them, that they were "to their great honour, of all people, the least subject to the wretched spirit of monopoly".[4]

"Nations", says Arthur Young, "figure by comparisons";[5] and in respect of the grain trade and grain trade regulation the experience of England differed profoundly from that of France. By 1660 in England the municipal policy of the Tudor age was passing into the glorified municipalism of the mercantile

---

[1] *Wealth of Nations*, II. 42.
[2] Bland, Brown and Tawney, *English Economic History, Select Documents*, p. 656.   [3] *Wealth of Nations*, II. 159.   [4] *Ibid.* I. 426.
[5] Arthur Young, *Travels in France 1787, 1788 and 1789* (ed. Bohn, 1892), p. 109.

system. The metropolitan pre-eminence of consuming London and its new rôle as an exporter of English-grown wheat set the seal on the transition. The continuous market, generated within the nation, and the wholesale merchants, through whom a continuous market operates, dominated English procedure henceforth. The presence of an export surplus veiled from popular suspicion the free play of competition in the internal trade and for this reason, if for no other, was worthy of encouragement. Only when famine was imminent did Panic clamour for a reversion to the discontinuity and *sauve qui peut* of the municipal age. But just because the market was continuous, supply was greater and famine was rare. The circle was a healthy one, as healthy in England as it was vicious in contemporary France.

In 1660, when Colbert was on the eve of power, there was at Bray in the Seine valley the beginnings of an organised wholesale market for the supply of Paris.[1] But elsewhere for the most part province fought province, producer fought consumer, one province banned export to another, and towns competed savagely for control of neutral hinterlands. We associate Colbert's name with the increase of regulation, and rightly in the sphere of the new industries fostered by him, but in the grain trade his work was a stage in the progress to greater freedom; for he sought to overrule local differences in the interest of France as an economic whole. He left to his successors an organisation and sources of information which should have produced a national uniformity, but did not. For right through the eighteenth century royal policy foundered on the obstruction of the provincial Parliaments, which continued to follow the ancient tradition of consulting the local safety first. By contrast, the internal policy of England was invincibly national. It was not imposed by government from above, being in the essence of the market relationships. The only over-lord was Adam Smith's Invisible Hand.

The corn-law policy of England down to 1815 centres around two episodes, the corn bounty of 1688 and the dip towards a regard for the consumer, evidenced in the legislation of 1772 and

[1] Cf. A. P. Usher, *History of the Grain Trade in France* (1400–1710), pp. 39–43, etc.

1773 anent the home and foreign trades respectively. The corn bounty was followed shortly by a half-century of falling prices, so that in the general opinion export and low prices were associated. Precisely the opposite occurred in France. At long last, under the new influence of Physiocracy, the central government nerved itself to declare for freedom of trade within the realm, 1763, and for free export to foreign parts, 1764. But prices now were rising; and it was not until Turgot came into power that the decree of 1775 put into execution the declaration of 1763. Necker, a strong opponent of exporting abroad, was a champion of internal freedom, but neither he nor the Government of the Revolution was able to enforce it against the popular resistance in seasons of scarcity. Moreover, up to the end of the eighteenth century local tolls and dues persisted in almost undiminished amount. The variety of weights and measures was bad enough in England, but in France it was fantastic: "Chaque ville, chaque bourg, chaque marché, chaque seigneur, chaque marchand même a sa mesure particulière".[1] So, too, with the export trade. Despite the general declaration of 1764, export was only permitted spasmodically between 1764 and 1800; and when after 1800 Napoleon regulated the export trade by licences, he was but continuing into war time the normal apparatus of the *Ancien Régime*.

The French in general (an export province like Brittany was different) disliked export abroad, because it so happened that the institution of free export was followed by rising prices, which were thought to be caused thereby. It is common knowledge that the system of land tenure evolved in eighteenth-century England was highly exceptional in the world as a whole. Equally exceptional was the rôle played by wheat in the economy of England. Wheat, characteristically, is a frontier crop, easy to grow on new land with a little capital; and this is its history as a crop in eighteenth-century Brittany, nineteenth-century Poland and twentieth-century Canada. The people of Brittany lived on chestnuts, black bread, barley and a little rye: and grew for export wheat and rye. In their poverty they exported. But

[1] J. Letaconnoux, *Les subsistances et le commerce des grains en Bretagne au XVIIIe siècle*, p. 348.

wheat during the time that it was being exported from England, say 1660–1760, was rapidly becoming the staple food-stuff of England; for England had the foreign trade to support a wheat diet. She could afford it, because she was growing rich by commerce and manufacture for overseas. She was as Holland was. But she had a corn-growing hinterland wider and more fertile than that of Holland (though, indeed, no better tilled); and therefore, while Holland by her good situation and the strength of her foreign trade was a great granary and mart for the exchange of Baltic corn with Mediterranean wines, England was sufficient to herself in corn and had a little over. Only by the end of the nineteenth century had her population so grown that she was become, like eighteenth-century Holland, a granary for the re-export of other countries' wheat, though quite incapable of feeding herself. In eighteenth-century Brittany the peasants fed the native population; while the granaries of the seigneurs, filled by rents in kind, were shipped abroad (and shipped abroad in defiance of royal prohibition, time and again). But in England landlords and substantial tenants evolved a permanent agriculture, in which they fed their own countrymen, and, while the surplus lasted, the near-by foreigner also. During the Napoleonic wars Coke of Hokham, as was truly said, saved England by a ploughshare, when the sword would have availed nothing. That an agriculture with this record should have achieved national unpopularity before fifty years had elapsed is a testimony to the pace of English industrialism and the shortness of the national memory. By 1846, when the corn laws were perishing in disgrace, France was slowly reaching the stage of productive skill which had made eighteenth-century England the banner country of agricultural progress. Thus, before plunging into industrialism England introduced the world to an agricultural revolution; and leaving it to the great continents to carry to maturity, she specialised herself to the complementary task of supplying the consumption, the capital and the commerce which made Canada,[1] New Zealand, Australia and the Argentine an economic possibility.

[1] For a fundamental chapter on the rôle of the staple exports in the economic development of Canada, see H. A. Innis, *The Fur Trade in Canada* (1930), chap. VI.

CHAPTER II

THE ECONOMICS OF THE CORN BOUNTY
1688–1765

T HE act of 1 William and Mary, c. 12 (1688), commonly and correctly termed the act of 1689[1], granted a bounty on the export of wheat at the rate of 5s. per quarter, when the home price per quarter was at or under 48s. The bounty remained on the statute book until 1814, but was of small importance after 1765, when England became on the balance an importing country. It was not the first corn law, being preceded by (a) acts restricting export, (b) a money act imposing a similar bounty, (c) acts imposing duties on import.

(a) Of these Lord Ernle writes: "In the reign of Philip and Mary, home-grown wheat could not be exported if home prices for wheat rose above 6s. 8d. per quarter, and for cheaper grains in proportion. This limit was raised by subsequent legislation. Thus the home price for wheat, at which exportation was prohibited, was raised in 1593 to 20s., in 1604 to 26s. 8d., in 1623 to 32s., in 1660 to 40s., in 1663 to 48s."[2] The rises before 1660 were in sympathy with the rising price of wheat. C. 13 of 22 and 23 Charles II (1670–1), amending the law of 15 Charles II, c. 7 (1663), allowed wheat to be exported without duty up to 48s. per quarter, and on payment of a poundage of 1s. per quarter at any higher price. There was no prohibition of export.

---

[1] William of Orange landed at Torbay on Nov. 5, 1688. William and Mary were proclaimed on Feb. 13, 1689. The first year of their reign, their first "regnal" year, as it is called, ran, therefore, from Feb. 13, 1689, to Feb. 12, 1690. On April 24, 1689, the King gave his assent to the "Act for encouraging the Exportation of Corn". Under the old style Feb. 13, 1689, was Feb. 13, 1688; and Feb. 12, 1690, was Feb. 12, 1689: because until 1752 the English legal year, in contrast with the practice of foreign countries and of Scotland, did not end until March 25. This was terminated by 24 Geo. II, c. 23, which at the same time corrected the error of 12 days in the Julian calendar.

Though passed in April 1689 the statute is listed in the Chronological Table of the Statutes of the Realm as I William and Mary, c. 12 (1688)—because the parliamentary session began in 1688, old style. In my references to statutes I have followed generally the notation of the Chronological Table.

[2] R. E. Prothero (Lord Ernle), *English Farming, Past and Present*, p. 143.

After the first of William and Mary the acts of 1670 and 1688 in conjunction provided the following regulation:

At or under 48s. per qr., bounty on export   5s. per qr.
Above   48s.   „   poundage on export 1s.   „

By 11 and 12 William III, c. 20, s. 4 (1700), entitled "an act for taking away the duties on the woollen manufactures, corn, grain, etc. exported", the poundage charge was abolished. Therefore, after March 30, 1700, there was no *statutory* restriction, or duty, on the export of grain at any price. But in periods of scarcity the bounty was suspended and export was prohibited by order-in-council.

(*b*) The Commons Committee on Agriculture of 1821 adverted in its Report to the bounty policy, which "more desultory in its application and more frequently interrupted by arbitrary interference prevailed under the Princes of the House of Stuart".[1] The statutory origin of the policy was c. 1, s. 37 of 25 Charles II (1672). The act is given in full in Keble's Statutes. The language of section 37 is almost identical with that of 1 William and Mary, c. 12, which was clearly modelled upon it. The bounty was in operation for about five years. "During each of the years 1675–6 and 1676–7 over £60,000 were paid out; and during the whole period...in the whole of England about £150,000."[2] To Mr Gras belongs the honour of recalling this act to the knowledge of modern historians. He says of it, "It supplies a link in the evolution of the export corn policy between the earlier laws, which merely allowed exportation (with or without restrictions) on the one hand and the bounty act of 1689 on the other".[3]

(*c*) The act of 12 Charles II, c. 4 (1660), which permitted the export of wheat at prices not exceeding 40s. per quarter, imposed also an import rate of 2s. per quarter when the price at the port of importation did not exceed 44s. per quarter and of 4d. when it exceeded 44s. This was the first statute of the century imposing duties on import. As the Committee of the Council on Trade observed in 1790: "As it appears by some

[1] *Report of Committee on the Agriculture of the United Kingdom*, p. 18.
[2] N. S. B. Gras, *The English Corn Market*, p. 253.
[3] *Ibid*. pp. 253–4.

ancient statutes not to have been lawful to carry corn out of the
Realm without the licence of the King, it may be collected from
others that it was generally lawful to import foreign corn into
this country: and from both these circumstances it may justly be
inferred that the legislature in ancient times was more solicitous
to provide for the plentiful subsistence of the People than to
encourage tillage within the Realm".[1] The act of 1660 was the
beginning of a series extending beyond the century. Thus the
act of 1663 (15 Charles II, c. 7) substituted 5s. 4d. for 2s. and
48s. for 44s. The act of 22 Charles II, c. 13 (1670), entitled "an
Act for the Improvement of Tillage", raised further the rates of
duty and the prices at which they came into effect:

On wheat, at prices not exceeding 53s. 4d. per qr. 16s. 0d. per qr.
    ,,   ,,   exceeding 53s. and not
                           above 80s. per qr.   8s. 0d.   ,,
    ,,   ,,   exceeding 80s. per qr.   4d.   ,,

An "Additional Act for the Improvement of Tillage" (1 Jas. II,
c. 19, 1685) instructed the justices to certify the current price to
the customs officials. These rates at these prices, thus certified,
were slightly augmented for revenue purposes from time to time
between 1670 and 1747; so that the rates ruling between 1747
and 1773 (when an important new law was passed) were:

On wheat, not exceeding 44s. per qr. 22s. 0d. per qr. (2nd high).
    ,,   44s. to 53s. 4d. per qr.   17s. 0d.   ,,   (1st high).
    ,,   53s. 4d. to 80s. per qr.   9s. 0d.   ,,   (1st low).
    ,,   exceeding 80s. per qr.   1s. 4d.   ,,   (2nd low).

It will be observed that there were now four rates, the single
high rate having been split up into a 2nd high and 1st high:

[1] *Report of* 1790, p. 14. The body of Lords Commissioners of Trade and
Plantations, commonly known as the Board of Trade, was instituted in 1696
and abolished in 1782. Its chief business was with the Plantations, and upon
the loss of the American colonies it was disbanded. In March 1784 the Privy
Council appointed a special Committee for Trade and Plantations, whose
chief business was with trade. Out of it developed the Board of Trade of the
nineteenth century. The full title of this special Committee was: Lords of the
Committee of Council appointed for the consideration of all matters relating
to Trade and Foreign Plantations. Its Report, or "Representation", of 1790
upon the present state of the law for regulating the Import and Export of
Corn, I refer to, here and later, as *Committee of the Council on Trade, Report of*
1790.

followed by a 1st low and 2nd low. This was a sliding scale in embryo. The act of 1670 has been termed "protective", "frankly protective";[1] and no doubt it was inspired by a new concern for the producer. But we may infer that it had little direct effect on the price of wheat from the following facts:

(1) The total of wheat imported between 1697 (the year when our figures begin) and 1773 was only about $1\frac{1}{2}$ million quarters, of which 1 million entered between 1765 and 1773.

(2) Between 1660 and 1765 Great Britain had normally an export surplus.

(3) In years of scarcity such as 1741, 1757–9, 1765–8, 1772–3 the import duties were suspended. Indeed it was only in these years and in the war periods of 1693–9[2] and 1709–10 that a price as high as 53s. 4d. (at which the 1st low duty came into effect) was reached.

The duties, however, were necessary to the maintenance of the bounty. For if wheat could have been imported free when the home price was below the bounty point of 48s. per qr., there would have been an inducement to import it (from another British port perhaps), in order to re-export it with bounty. (This, of course, was contrary to the intention of the law, and was provided against, e.g. in 14 Charles II, c. 11 (1662), an act for preventing Frauds and Abuses in His Majesty's Customs.) Even as it was, it sometimes paid merchants to export wheat to Holland under bounty, store it there at low interest, and re-import it at nominal rates in dear times. The dynamic side of the seventeenth- and eighteenth-century corn policy was the bounty; and it is by this that the wisdom of the whole must be judged. The corn bounty, Adam Smith suggests, was established at the instance of the country gentlemen from a mistaken sense of their real interest. It chiefly (he argues) benefited the corn merchant; "it is in this set of men, accordingly, that I have observed the greatest zeal for the continuance or renewal of the bounty".[3] Characteristically he criticises a class whose rôle, in general, he strongly applauded—"No trade

[1] Cf. W. Smart, *Economic Annals*, 1801–20, p. 91 and Prothero, *op. cit.* p. 143.
[2] This was also a period of currency disturbance and credit inflation.
[3] *Wealth of Nations*, II. 16.

deserves more the full protection of the law".[1]   Cunningham conjectures that in introducing this policy "the Whigs schemed to foster the agricultural interest, so that the landed men might be able to make [these] large contributions to the expenses of government, both local and national".[2]   But the policy, as we have seen, was not new; and therefore it would be better to say that seeking the support of the landed gentry and their acquiescence in the land tax, they renewed the experiment of the Stuarts in permanent political form.   Moreover, 1686 and 1687 were years of abundant harvests and high prices; and, in Tooke's judgment, "this low and declining state of prices produced, as usual on such occasions, considerable distress among the landed interest, and was, probably, the ground on which the celebrated Act of the 1st of William and Mary, granting a bounty on the exportation of corn, was passed".[3]

The effect of the bounty has been the object of keen controversy.   Charles Smith, the "ingenious and well informed" author of the Corn Tracts, warmly approved it, as did the majority of his generation.   Adam Smith in the next generation as strongly condemned it.   Cunningham approves it on economic and political grounds in general terms; while Mr E. Lipson in his *Economic History of England* (1931), vol. II. chap. III, submits Adam Smith's argument to a running critique, and Mr D. G. Barnes[4] in his monograph of 1930 finds Adam Smith's conclusions unhistorical and one-sided.

Certain facts are clear enough.   For the forty years before 1688 the level of prices was higher than in the period 1689–1765, when the bounty was normally in operation.   After 1765 the price of wheat was much higher and the bounty was rarely given.   How much, then, if any, of the fall of price, 1689–1765, was due to the bounty? What other effects, good or bad, had it? The problem is not easy.   For, as Tooke reminds us, "statements of historical fact, professing to be illustrative of particular conclusions on questions relative to prices and the circulation,

---

[1] *Wealth of Nations*, II. 28.
[2] *Growth of English Industry and Commerce*, II. 541.
[3] *Thoughts on High and Low Prices*, Part III. p. 12.
[4] D. G. Barnes, *A History of the English Corn Laws* 1660–1846 (Routledge, 1930).

unless guarded by a careful reference to the dates and an explanation of attendant circumstances, may be made subservient to the most distorted views".[1]

To Charles Smith the effect was clear and certain. "The matter under consideration is to enquire, *if the Bounty hath done any good*: now how can this be known, but by comparing the prices of Corn before and after it took place?"[2] "If we compare the average of the forty years immediately before that in which the Bounty took place, with the average of the whole time since, the difference appears still greater." (He had just given the average of 1595–1686 at £1. 18s. 0d.)

	£	s.	d.
"From 1646 to 1686 Average	2	0	11
„ 1686 to 1765 Average	1	13	2
Less for the last 79 years	0	7	9

and hereby the utility and good effects of the Bounty are manifested, in that Tillage hath been thereby so encouraged and improved as to make wheat cheaper at home and at the same time brings large sums into the Kingdom for the Corn exported...."[3] Its utility was "further proved in that, since its first establishment, the Parliament have not thought fit to suspend it, either in part or the whole, only four times, viz. in 1698, 1709, 1740, and 1757, which last suspension is still in force, and to continue to Christmas next".[4] These particular lines were penned in January 1759. Had he written in 1773, the significance of the exceptions would have been much greater: for by that time they were becoming the rule.

We should underrate our "very well-informed author", if we supposed him capable of the *post hoc propter hoc* fallacy in its crudest form. "It may", he said, "have happened by the number of the people being lessened, or by some other means, that the consumption of Grain in this Kingdom hath been so decreased, as that such cheapness should not at all, or at least not wholly, be attributed to the *imaginary* increased quantity of corn grown by the extension of Tillage, arising from, or rather

---

[1] *History of Prices*, III. Intro. 1.
[2] *Tracts on the Corn Trade and Corn Laws*, III. 230.
[3] *Ibid*. III. 106.   [4] *Ibid*. II. 73.

occasioned by, the encouragement given by such bounty."[1] He therefore instituted an enquiry into the consumption per head of the population in 1758 and the size of the population of England and Wales in 1688 and 1758. His conclusion was that in 1758 population was certainly not less and consumption per head undoubtedly greater. The fall of prices, not being due to decreased consumption, must therefore be due to the extension of tillage occasioned by the bounty. Between 1697 and 1765, indeed, the average annual export of wheat was less than one-nineteenth part of the annual growth. But this elicits from him admiration rather than suspicion, "And yet what prodigious benefit hath the Nation reaped from the Exportation!"[2]

Adam Smith, with his larger mind and a perspective improved by the lapse of years, exposed the hollowness of the prodigy. Charles Smith had reckoned the advantage of the bounty as the sum by which the value of wheat exported, plus "the savings in the price of Wheat eat at home",[3] exceeded the amount paid away in bounties, plus the value of the negligible imports. (The "savings" were the difference between the average prices over a period of years before and after 1689.) Adam Smith dressed the balance differently.

In years of plenty…the bounty, by occasioning an extraordinary exportation necessarily keeps up the price of corn in the home market above what it would naturally fall to. To do so was the avowed purpose of the institution. In years of scarcity, although the bounty is frequently suspended, yet the great exportation which it occasions in years of plenty, must frequently hinder more or less the plenty of one year from relieving the scarcity of another. Both in years of plenty and in years of scarcity, therefore, the bounty necessarily tends to raise the money price of corn somewhat higher than it otherwise would be in the home market….[4]

The corn bounty…, as well as every other bounty upon exportation, imposes two different taxes upon the people; first the tax which they are obliged to contribute, in order to pay the bounty; and secondly, the tax which arises from the advanced price of the commodity in the home market, and which, as the whole body of the people are the purchasers of corn, must, in this particular commodity, be paid by the whole body of the people.[5]

[1] *Tracts on the Corn Trade and Corn Laws*, III. 138–9.
[2] *Ibid*. III. 144–5.   [3] *Ibid*. III. 132.
[4] *Wealth of Nations*, II. 9.   [5] *Ibid*. II. 10.

Adam Smith attributed the fall to the currency. The declension of prices

must have happened in spite of the bounty, and cannot possibly have happened in consequence of it. It has happened in France, as well as in England, though in France there was not only no bounty, but, till 1764, the exportation of corn was subjected to a general prohibition. This gradual fall in the average price of grain, it is probable, therefore, is ultimately owing neither to the one regulation nor to the other, but to that gradual and insensible rise in the real value of silver, which, in the first book of this discourse, I have endeavoured to show has taken place in the general market of Europe, during the course of the present century. It seems to be altogether impossible that the bounty could ever contribute to lower the price of grain.[1]

Thomas Tooke accepts Adam Smith's line of criticism, but differs on a point of interpretation. He agreed that silver had appreciated relatively to wheat. But whereas Adam Smith held that the full effects of the new American silver on English prices had worked themselves out by 1640, so that the subsequent declension in the price of wheat was due mainly to a comparative scarcity of the metal, Tooke considered that Adam Smith put the date too soon and that in any case the money price of common day labour was a better criterion than corn. Between 1700 and 1765 this had risen in Great Britain. According to Adam Smith it was "the effect, not so much of any diminution in the value of silver in the European market, as of an increase in the demand for labour in Great Britain, arising from the great, and almost universal prosperity of the country".[2] According to Tooke, "the fall and the low range of the price of corn, while money was undergoing, however slowly, a depreciation, prove how powerful must have been the depressing circumstances operating upon the price of corn, to be sufficient, not only to prevent a rise corresponding with the diminished value of silver but to cause a tendency in the opposite direction".[3] These circumstances Tooke found in the exceptionally favourable series of

---

[1] *Wealth of Nations*, II. 9. Figures for Brittany (1699–1790) show a small rise in the price of wheat, 1700–40: a stationary or falling level, 1740–64: and thereafter notably higher prices, culminating in 1789–90 (J. Letaconnoux, *Les subsistances et le commerce des grains en Bretagne au XVIIIe siècle*, p. 130).

[2] *Wealth of Nations*, I. 200.   [3] *History of Prices*, I. 56.

seasons from 1715 to 1765, which was also the long period of low average price.

Recent research confirms the currency history of Adam Smith. "Between 1630 and 1640, or about 1636, the effect of the discovery of the mines of America in reducing the value of silver, appears to have been completed,"[1] he boldly wrote. On this Mr Earl Hamilton in his *American Treasure and Andalusian Prices* (based on the original price records of Seville), observes: "When Adam Smith, with the scanty material at his command, concluded that English prices did not commence to rise before 1570, that the price revolution ran its course by 1636, and that silver declined in value by two-thirds, he exercised uncanny powers of penetration".[2] We are entitled, therefore, to believe that as between Adam Smith and Tooke, the verdict is with the former. But in general they agree; and which ever be right, Charles Smith is counted out.

It was still open to the bounty champions to argue that the corn laws, taken as a whole and as a policy, served to steady the trade; and further that, though the bounty raised prices at times and for a time, it gave such a stimulus to agriculture as to lower the cost of production in the long run. I am not aware that the supporters of the policy in the eighteenth century ever pressed the second argument closely. But the Committee of the Council on Trade in 1790 did contend that the corn laws had diminished the vicissitudes of plenty and dearth; and the sentiment was anticipated and re-echoed by the pamphleteers. The Committee were quite alive to what we call the inelasticity of demand for wheat, Gregory King's estimate being common property, and readily appreciated in a period of rising prices. They understood that "a very small deficiency of the crop will raise the price in a very high degree",[3] and its converse. There-

---

[1] *Wealth of Nations*, I. 192.

[2] In *Journal of Economic and Business History*, vol. I. No. 1. p. 32 n.

[3] For King's estimate, see *Dictionary of Political Economy*, s.v. King, Gregory (1648–1712) and Marshall, *Principles* (8th ed.), p. 106. Cf. C. Smith, *op. cit.* I. 50: "Mr King, a very ingenious and accurate calculator... tells us that one-tenth of Defect in the Harvest will raise the price of corn about three-tenths above the common rate; that two-tenths of Defect will advance the price eight-tenths, and three-tenths Deficiency will advance it about one and five-tenths".

fore, they thought the farmer ought to be assured of a market for his occasional surpluses. Without an assurance such as the bounty offered, the farmer, owing to lower costs of production abroad, would never find a profitable outlet there, except in years of general scarcity when none could be spared from home.[1]

This line of thought runs through the open *Letter from Governor Pownall to Adam Smith* of 1776, which is a reasoned reply by the author of the law of 1773 to the strictures in the *Wealth of Nations* on colonial policy and the corn bounty. He writes as an admirer and a liberal, but he has a horror of paper currency, which, as Governor of Massachusetts, he had seen issued to excess and which, notwithstanding, Adam Smith appeared to condone. He contends that the state of progressive improvement brings, and in England had brought, a continued influx of riches, and this in its turn a continued rise of prices. But rent and wages lag behind, or, as he puts it, other commodities continue "*so to forerun* in the rise that the landed man and the labourer must be in a continued state of oppression and distress". He justifies the bounty as an offset to this; "it relieves the relative distress, which the acceleration of the inflowing of riches occasions to the land-worker". And he contends that the bounty policy, by its momentum, had encouraged "a succession of surpluses", which were put into the general commerce of Europe, but which, in the event of scarcity, were available at home—and effectually available since the passage of the law of 1773, which made importation easier.

We may admit the steadying effect of the bounty on the producer without accepting the larger proposition that the bounty reduced the price of wheat by improving the conditions of production. This could only follow if the conditions of agricultural production were those of strongly increasing return. Conceivably they were. Conceivably at that time a subsidy to production would have induced lower costs of production in the long run, as the result of extended production. But it is altogether improbable that the bounty was big enough to accomplish this. As Charles Smith himself admits, "It may be questioned f the Bounty, one time with another, pays freight, commission

---

[1] *Report of* 1790, p. 8.

and all other incident charges".[1] One further argument in favour of the bounty pertains to psychology. It is that farmers would have been discouraged and backward in enterprise if the Government gave them no proof of its good will. The argument is not bad, especially if it can be shown that agriculturists were burdened with extra taxes, to which the bounty might be considered an offset. For at this period they could not be adequately encouraged, like the manufacturers, by protective import duties. But the argument does not reach far. Ungrounded timidity and contrived optimism, though they may exert a momentary influence on prices, cannot effect a permanent change. And I venture to sum up the effect of the bounty by saying that it raised home prices and landlords' rents a little, cost the Treasury more than it could afford, kept the farmer in good heart and provided succeeding generations with abundant food for erroneous reasoning in speech, tract and treatise. If it is to be justified as a piece of policy, it must be on the ground that it was in keeping with the expedients of a mercantile age for the regulation and encouragement of desirable enterprise. It was as clumsy and as effective as the navigation laws and the Acts of Trade. The desired result followed, but other and less desired results accompanied it, which Adam Smith evaluated aright.

Mr Lipson quarrels with Adam Smith specifically as follows:

(1) "Adam Smith [in attributing the fall in corn to the rise in silver] neglected the possibility that the fall might have been due—apart from a succession of favourable seasons—to increased production arising from better technique, the consolidation of holdings, and the cultivation of the waste" (E. Lipson, *Economic History of England*, II. 456).

This is not so. Adam Smith is contending that "Whatever be the actual state of tillage, it renders our corn somewhat dearer in the home market than it otherwise would be in that state" (*Wealth of Nations*, II. 15). It was central to his whole position that he should have some view as to the conditions governing the state of tillage. This he set forth in the Digression on Silver, which is part of the long chapter, Book I. chap. XI,

---

[1] *Tracts on the Corn Trade and Corn Laws*, III. 132 n.

Of the Rent of Land. He there discusses the different effects of improvement on different sorts of raw produce:

The extension of improvement and cultivation, as it necessarily raises more or less, in proportion to the price of corn, that of every sort of animal food, so it as necessarily lowers that of, I believe, every sort of vegetable food. It raises the price of animal food; because a great part of the land which produces it, being rendered fit for producing corn, must afford to the landlord and farmer the rent and profit of corn land. It lowers the price of vegetable food; because, by increasing the fertility of the land, it increases its abundance. The improvements of agriculture too introduce many sorts of vegetable food, which, requiring less land and not more labour than corn, come much cheaper to market. Such are potatoes and maize... (I. 241).

Mr Lipson would have to persuade Adam Smith that the grant of a bounty was preferable to the removal of those privileges to trade and manufacture which made investment in agriculture less profitable than it otherwise would be (cf. *Wealth of Nations*, I. 354); and, since he believed in the natural order, there could be no doubt as to his preference.

(2) "He [Adam Smith] seems to overlook the consideration that farmers, deprived of the security which the subsidy on corn afforded them, might have been induced by the alternation of low and high prices to contract the arable area and lay the land down to grass.... To whatever extent the bounty served to keep the land under the plough, which would otherwise have gone out of cultivation, it must also have served to keep prices over a long period at a lower level" (Lipson, II. 457).

The first of these two statements contains a possibility, though a very slender one. It amounts to arguing that in the face of a constantly increasing demand for wheat at home, undisturbed by any threat of heavy supply from abroad, the farmers of Great Britain would have failed to develop that mixed farming which is the basis of a permanent agriculture and contains within itself a protection against price failure in one class of product.

The second is a *non sequitur*. It assumes that the stimulus to arable production more than cancelled out, through lower long-period costs, the addition in price which the bounty caused and was intended to cause. For this there is no shadow of proof.

(3) "The gain which the bounty brought to the farmer was greater stability of prices" (Lipson, II. 457): to which there is the footnote:

"Marshall, *Industry and Trade* (ed. 1920), pp. 749–50, considers that 'during the years 1773 to 1792 [when] the English corn trade was practically free to follow its own course...the price of wheat fluctuated less than during the preceding period'. But the record of wheat prices makes this doubtful. See the tables of prices in *Parliamentary Papers* (1898), LXXXV. 253–4".

I see them. They suggest that Mr Lipson's note might quite fairly be recast as follows:

"In the nineteen years from 1688 to 1707 the range of fluctuation in the average Eton price was wider and more violent than that in the annual average of England and Wales in the nineteen years between 1773 and 1792. It was also wider and more violent in 1753–72 than in 1773–92. *So far as the statistical evidence of these tables go*, it is not clear, *pace* Joshua Gee, that the bounty brought stability to the farmer".

(4) "It appears evident from the low range of prices that they [the earlier Corn Laws as a whole] did not make bread dearer, while the effect of the bounty was to keep land under the plough which might otherwise have been laid down to grass" (Lipson, II. 464).

Thus Mr Lipson closes his chapter and volume. Any stimulus by way of import restriction or export subsidy will, indeed, cause more land to be devoted to the assisted product than otherwise would be the case—other things being equal. But when Mr Lipson prefaces this innocuous afterthought with a sweeping pronouncement upon prices and when he calls this pronouncement "evident", then it is evident also that between him and Adam Smith the terms of debate do not exist.

The criticisms of Mr Barnes are rather more difficult to counter. One point, indeed, may be conceded forthwith. Adam Smith's "differentiation between the effect of a bounty on grain and other commodities is a difficult one to maintain", he urges.[1] This is true. For according to Adam Smith the money price of corn "regulates that of all other home-made commodi-

---

[1] D. G. Barnes, *History of the English Corn Laws*, p. 29.

ties. It regulates the money price of labour....It regulates the money price of all the other parts of the rude produce of land.... It regulates that of the materials of almost all manufactures.... It regulates that of manufacturing art and industry" (II. 11–12).

Corn has not in such fullness this unique regulative power. But argument in this direction was fundamental to classical political economy from Adam Smith to Mill, because they thought it explained the relation between population and produce. But this is Mr Barnes's minor count. The major has to do with the history. Adam Smith, it is suggested, is at the opposite end of the pole to Arthur Young and as one-sided as he. "Neither showed the slightest inclination to treat the bounty as a policy whose value depended upon conditions at the time of its application" (Barnes, p. 29). This seems to me hard both on Young and Adam Smith; and unfair to Adam Smith, if the analytical attack on the bounty in Book IV. chap. V is read side by side with the historical excursus of Book I. chap. XI, in which the bounty figures prominently.

According to Mr Barnes,

Both Smith and Young believed that the improvement in tillage was due to an event in 1689; the former ascribed it to securities forfeited by the revolution, and the latter to the bounty act of that date. Smith pointed out that the advocates of the bounty were guilty of the *post hoc* fallacy in insisting that, because the improvement in cultivation followed the bounty act, the law was responsible for the change. Yet he, himself, is guilty of the same fallacy when he holds that this improvement came as a result of the security perfected by the revolution of 1689 (p. 29).

But this does violence to the language of Adam Smith. What he said was,

That system of laws, therefore, which is connected with the establishment of the bounty, seems to deserve no part of the praise which has been bestowed upon it. The improvement and prosperity of Great Britain, which has been so often ascribed to those laws, may very easily be accounted for by other causes. That security which the laws in Great Britain give to every man that he shall enjoy the fruits of his own labour, is alone sufficient to make any country flourish, notwithstanding these and twenty other absurd regulations of commerce;

and this security was perfected by the revolution, much about the same time that the bounty was established (II. 42–3).[1]

He does not isolate the bounty. His quarrel is with the whole system of which it was a part. He did *not* say that "the improvement in tillage was due to an event in 1689": which, indeed, would have been ridiculous. In his great chapter IV of Book III, *How the Commerce of the Towns contributed to the Improvement of the Country*, and in numerous incidental references, he gives the many reasons for this improvement, both in England and Scotland; as well as the obstacles which it encountered through the impolicy of governments. Nor did he deny that the corn bounty, in itself, stimulated production. His position was that under a free trade, in which there were neither restrictions nor bounties, prices would have been lower, consumption greater and the real earnings of agriculture not less. There is nothing essentially unhistorical in this view. Mr Barnes's own history, however, is not above reproach.

"The population", he says, "increased by a million and a half between the years 1689 and 1765" (p. 30). This is hardly supported by recent revisions of the population estimates. Mr Talbot Griffith, e.g. in *Population Problems of the Age of Malthus* (1926), p. 18, gives for the population of England and Wales

Year	Millions
1700	5·8
1740	6·0
1750	6·2
1760	6·6

Between 1700 and 1740 population was nearly stationary. It was only after 1760 that the rapid increase occurred which brought the population to 9·1 millions in 1801. Then Mr Barnes

---

[1] It is well to remember that here, and not in a discussion of wage regulation, follows the famous sentence, "The natural effort of every individual to better his own condition, when suffered to exert itself with freedom and security, is so powerful a principle that it is alone, and without any assistance, not only capable of carrying on the society to wealth and prosperity, but of surmounting a hundred impertinent obstructions with which the folly of human laws too often incumbers its operations" (II. 43). But concerning wage regulation he writes, "Wherever the legislature attempts to regulate the differences between masters and their workmen, its counsellors are always the masters" (I. 143).

advances the view that owing to the imperfect communications of the late seventeenth century the corn surplus could not have been marketed inside England. But could not London and other towns have eaten more and better bread? Is corn really so difficult a commodity to market inland? Surely it was the much more serious difficulties of bringing raw materials in, and taking heavy or fragile manufactures out, that the new roads and canals surmounted. Suddenly, Mr Barnes appears to think, the hindrance ceased, so that the bounty was no longer necessary. For "after 1745 the turnpikes and, after 1760, the canals revolutionised the internal communications of England" (p. 31). This is the "catastrophic" Industrial Revolution with a vengeance. Mr Lipson would have something to say here.

But on another side of the bounty Mr Barnes has important observations, in which Adam Smith is not noticed. The great exports of 1748–51 exhausted the funds assigned to the payment of the corn debentures under the bounty scheme. These were the customs of tonnage and poundage, on which it transpired that the annuity of the South Sea Company had a prior legal claim. In 1749, therefore, the debentures went unpaid, and, as a makeshift, interest was allowed by a law of 1753[1] on unredeemed debentures. However, "the rapid decline in exports after 1752 relieved the government of an embarrassing problem" (p. 24). Adam Smith would have heartily applauded here. For, as he himself said, "In that single year [sc. 1749] the bounty paid amounted to no less than 324,176l. 10s. 6d. It is unnecessary to observe how much this forced exportation must have raised the price of corn above what it otherwise would have been in the home market" (I. 199–200).

In fine, neither Mr Lipson nor Mr Barnes undermine Adam Smith's analysis and history. The only way, indeed, he can perhaps be overthrown is that followed by Cunningham, when he commends as a whole the policy of Parliamentary Colbertism and sees in the corn bounty the agriculturist's share in the fruits of mercantile power. In that case it is not so much the economics as the politics of the corn bounty that is under review.

---

[1] 26 George II, c. 15. An act for allowing interest upon certain debentures for the bounty granted on the exportation of corn.

CHAPTER III

POLICY IN TRANSITION, 1765–1815

ECAUSE of England's island limits, the decade in which she launched the industrial revolution, say 1765–75, was also the decade in which she began to lean seriously, though as yet intermittently, upon foreign countries for a portion of her wheat supply. In five years of this decade the import of wheat was over 100,000 qrs.: in 1765 it was 104,000: in 1775, 560,000. In 1766, shortly after the edict permitting export from France, a Havre merchant writes to his English correspondent:

Enfin voilà donc un évenement arrivé qu'on n'auroit jamais pû croire, que la France, qui tous les ans recevoit de l'Angleterre une partie de Bléd et de farine, soit en état aujourd'huy de fournir ces mêmes vivres à ce pays reputé avec raison le grenier de l'Europe; il sort de nos ports une quantité considérable de Bléd et de farine pour l'Angleterre et pour l'Irelande; et après avoir été chargé de vendre ici ces marchandises, je puis être chargé d'en acheter et d'envoyer et c'est ce que je fais.[1]

Behind the immediate causes of harvest failure and major war lay the more abiding cause of an industrial population, now in rapid increase. It is estimated that the population of England and Wales rose from 6·2 millions in 1750 to 9·1 in 1801.[2] Therefore, despite the notable improvements in English agriculture, the home demand tended always and increasingly to outrun the home supply. On top of this was imposed (if we may accept the evidence of Tooke[3]) an exceptionally large number of unfavourable seasons in the last thirty-five years of the eighteenth century, 1765–1800, by the end of which period the country was locked in a twenty years' war. Harvest failure in England, it may be observed, tends to coincide with harvest failure in Northern Europe, which was then the chief source of import.

[1] Extract from *A Letter on the Flour Trade and Dearness of Corn*, by a person in business, 1766.
[2] G. T. Griffith, *Population Problems of the Age of Malthus*, p. 18.
[3] *History of Prices*, I. 82.

In respect alike of population, harvests and foreign relations the first half of the eighteenth century was more favourable to a low price of corn than the second half; and the price was much lower. Nevertheless the landed interest looked back with longing to the palmy days of the early eighteenth century. In the debates preceding the corn law of 1804, when war again overshadowed the land, the memory of the ancient policy looms through. We undervalue the importance which Parliament at that late season attached to the preservation and extension of the facilities for export, if we represent the act as one designed to confirm a protected class in their exploitation of the home market. Doubtless the preceding years of scarcity had increased landlords' rents and farmers' profits, but they were years also of popular discontent and feverish risk. The country, including the country gentlemen, longed for a return to quieter and better times, when the harvests should yield a moderate abundance, with a small surplus for export.

The corn law of 1773, the most important since that of 1 William and Mary, marks a transition in terms of the old hopes to a new and imperfectly appreciated state of affairs. It was followed by two other important laws, each conceived in the same mood and environment; and the formal changes effected may be presented in tabular form thus:

Wheat per quarter

1670 and 1688

Export. No prohibition at any price.
         Above 48s., poundage duty 1s.
         At or under 48s., 5s. bounty.

Import. Over 80s., 2nd low duty 4d.
         Above 53s. 4d. to 80s., 1st low duty 8s.
         53s. 4d. or under, high duty 16s.

1773

Export. At or above 44s., prohibited.
         Under 44s., 5s. bounty.

Import. At or above 48s., low duty 6d.
         Over 44s. to under 48s., 1st high duty 17s.
         Not over 44s., 2nd high duty 22s.

1791

Export. At or above 46s., prohibited.
   44s. to under 46s., export without bounty.
   Under 44s., export with 5s. bounty.
Import. At or above 54s., 2nd low duty 6d.
   50s. to under 54s., 1st low duty 2s. 6d.
   Under 50s., high duty 24s. 3d.

1804

Export. Above 54s., prohibited.
   Over 48s. to 54s., export without bounty.
   At or under 48s., export with 5s. bounty.
Import. At or above 66s., 2nd low duty 7½d.
   63s. to under 66s., 1st low duty 3s. 1½d.
   Under 63s., high duty 30s. 3¾d.

The act of 1773 came into force on January 1, 1774. Governor Thomas Pownall fathered it, and Edmund Burke gave it his grudging support. He disliked the departure from the time-honoured balance, but thought it was necessary for the avoidance of jealousy between the landed and commercial interests.[1] It terminated the bounty at 44s. instead of at 48s.: and (if comparison is made with the rates in force 1747–73)[2] it introduced the low nominal duty at 48s. instead of at 80s., and imposed the 1st high duty of 17s. at 44s. to 48s., instead of at 44s. to 53s. 4d. Moreover, it had no 1st low duty. When the price reached 48s., the duty fell from 17s. to 6d.

Thus it was a little less kind to the exporter and stepped in more quickly and more vigorously to protect the consumer by free importation, as prices rose. It presumed that 44s. to 48s. was the range at which the position would be one of equilibrium without need for the stimulation of sales to, or purchases from, abroad. Disturbance downward would be met by bounty and

---

[1] Cf. *Parliamentary History of England*, XVII. 480.
[2] As explained above, the import rates of 1670 were slightly augmented from time to time, down to this year. The 1747–73 import rates were:

   Exceeding 80s., 1s. 4d. (2nd low).
   Exceeding 53s. 4d. to 80s., 9s. (1st low).
   Exceeding 44s. to 53s. 4d., 17s. (1st high).
   Not exceeding 44s., 22s. (2nd high).

high duties, disturbance upward by suspension of export and free import. In the acts of 1791 and 1804 the 1st low duty was re-introduced and the 2nd high duty was dropped; so that in these two laws the critical figure is that at which, as the price rose, the heavy duty on import ceased. In the act of 1791 this was 50s., and in that of 1804, 63s. Significantly, the act of 1791 repealed so much of 15 Charles II, c. 7 (1662), as prohibited the buying of wheat to sell again and the laying it up in granaries when wheat exceeded 48s. the quarter; for by 1791 the price was uniformly higher than this.

To resume, in 1773 import was free (i.e. from all but a nominal duty of 6d.), when prices touched 48s. In 1791 it was substantially free, when prices touched 50s.; and in 1804 it was substantially free, when prices touched 63s. I say "substan-tially", because both in 1791 and 1804 the 1st low duties, which came into operation at these points, were really low (2s. 6d. and 3s. 0½d. respectively): so that it is permissible to say that, when these points were reached, import was substantially free. Further-more, in the act of 1791 lower rates were allowed to Ireland and the colonies; and this preference was continued to the colonies in all subsequent corn laws.

The framework of the corn laws was the point or points at which the rates of duty altered, and especially that at which the high duty ceased. These points were not altered between 1791 and 1804, but the duty rates themselves were periodically augmented by small percentages in conformity with fiscal in-creases elsewhere; and this accounts for the awkward rates of 1804. But the revenue which they yielded was slight; for nearly all imported wheat entered at one or other of the low rates, if not altogether free by special order.[1] Much more important to the Exchequer was the fact that after 1773 the bounty was rarely payable owing to the price being usually above the figure at which it lapsed. Even so it cost the Exchequer between 1774 and 1788 nearly £600,000. It was the loss of the bounty, rather than the influx of competing corn, which separated the

---

[1] 1792 was the last year in which England had an export surplus. The harvest of 1791 was excellent, the average price for 1792 was 43s., and the net export was 275,861 qrs.

new times from the old. The import duties yielded from 1800 to 1804 (all grains):[1]

Year	£	
1800	936	
1801	nil	[Free import and bounty on importation]
1802	1,786	
1803	30,398	
1804	17,692	

And from 1804 to 1815, the year in which duties were replaced by prohibition, the yield was equally negligible. For after 1804 the history of 1791–1804 was repeated. The upward extension of the export limits, of export itself from 46s. to 54s., and of export with bounty from 44s. to 48s., was the sop to tradition, but it was nullified by the fact that prices after 1804 always exceeded 63s., the point at which the high duty lapsed. The import duties were increased by fragments, but the proceeds were negligible because all the corn came in either at the nominal duty or on terms still more favourable. A special feature of the period was a small *ad valorem* duty on the export of corn, in line with that on other articles of merchandise. It was, of course, a war tax.

From facts we turn to interpretation. What was the policy underlying, or supposed to underlie, these changes? The Napoleonic age was of the opinion that 1773 marked a new departure and a departure which was in the nature of a reversal. According to the Corn Committee of 1813: "In 1765 and each of the seven following years, laws were made prohibiting the exportation of corn, and allowing the importation of corn duty-free; and in 1773 the act 13 George III, c. 43, was passed, which established a new system with regard to the corn laws...". From 1670 to 1765 "the several laws together formed a system for regulating the corn trade upon the principles of restraining importation and encouraging exportation". But since 1765, the system had proceeded on the opposite principle of encouraging importation and discouraging exportation by prohibition or limitation of the bounties. Under the former system "the prices were steady and moderate", under the latter "they

[1] *Customs Tariff* (1897), p. 258.

had progressively risen". Under the former Great Britain "not
only supplied herself but exported a considerable quantity of
corn": under the latter "she has not only not supplied herself,
but has imported vast quantities from foreign countries". Thus
there was a "strong coincidence of plenty and low prices with a
system of restricted importation, and of scanty supply and high
prices with the contrary system". It was expedient, therefore,
to recur to the principles abandoned in 1765.[1] The Chairman of
the Committee (Sir Henry Parnell) and his disciples learned by
rote this audacious piece of history and reproduced it in debate
with wearisome iteration.

Adam Smith had marked the change, but commended it.

The 13th of the present king c. 43 seems to have established a new
system with regard to the corn laws, in many respects better than the
ancient one, but in one or two respects perhaps not quite so good....
With all its imperfections, however, we may perhaps say of it what
was said of the laws of Solon, that, though not the best in itself, it is
the best which the interests, prejudices and temper of the times would
admit of. It may perhaps in due time prepare the way for a better.[2]

Finally, in February 1815, when a new and drastic law was in
the making, Malthus wrote:

The act of William, which gave the bounty, combined with the
prohibitory act of Charles II, was founded obviously and strikingly
upon the principle of encouraging exportation and discouraging
importation; the spirit of the regulations adopted in 1773, and acted
upon some time before, was nearly the reverse and encouraged importation and discouraged exportation. Subsequently, as if alarmed at
the dependence of the country upon foreign corn, and the fluctuations of price which it had occasioned, the legislature in a feeble act of
1791, and a rather more effective one in 1804, returned again to the
policy of restrictions. And if the act of 1804 be now left unaltered, it
may be fairly said that a fourth change has taken place; as it is quite
certain that to proceed consistently upon a restrictive system, fresh
regulations become absolutely necessary to keep pace with the progressive fall in the value of currency.[3]

These views are misleading through too great emphasis on
new purpose. They assign to purpose what belonged to events.

---

[1] Cf. *Corn Committee (H. of C.)*, 1813, *Report*, p. 6, and abstract in W. Smart,
Economic Annals, 1801–20, p. 376.   [2] *Wealth of Nations*, II. 44–5.
[3] *The Grounds of an Opinion on the Policy of restricting the Importation of
Foreign Corn, intended as an appendix to "Observations on the Corn Laws"*,
p. 43.

From 1670 to 1804 the purpose of the corn laws was unchanged. It was the dual one of preventing "grain from being at any time, either so dear that the poor cannot subsist, or so cheap that the farmer cannot live by growing of it".[1] And in 1790 the Committee of the Council on Trade reaffirmed this duality when they declared that corn was exceptional and that "in the management of this Trade Governments ought ever to have in view not only the Prosperity of the Trade itself and the interests of those concerned in it, but the subsistence of the people".[2] After 1765 Parliament was called upon to adjust an old policy to new conditions of demand and supply; and the law of 1773 was the result. For year after year, since 1765, it had been necessary to suspend the bounty, prohibit export and admit imports duty-free. But these supersessions of the law were distasteful to a constitutional people and disturbing to the fundamentals of policy, and this braced Parliament eventually to face the new situation. A high bounty limit with frequent suspensions was to be replaced by a low bounty limit with no suspensions, and the point of free import was reduced in the same way and with the same hope. To restore the equilibrium which the events of 1765–72 had overthrown was the purpose of the law of 1773. It was a continuation of the ancient policy in a way that was intended to meet new conditions, and not a conscious reversal of it.

The acts of 1791 and 1804 have the same significance. The points of free import were raised, and this *prima facie* is protection. But there was no embarkation upon, or stiffening of, or return to, a policy of protection in either of these acts, for in the interval, as Malthus observes, the price of wheat rose more than in proportion. The instruction of the legislature throughout was, "Feed the people, from home grown wheat if you can, but feed them". A clause in the act of 1791 specially enabled the King-in-Council to modify the act, if necessity should arise, and the power was availed of in every single year from 1793 to 1801. Stimulated to hopes of normality by the short peace, the legislature in 1804 again provided for new conditions. A fresh rise in the low-duty point was "demanded by the advance in the prices of labour and all other expenses"; and it was hoped that "when due encouragement is given to the agriculture of the country...

---

[1] C. Smith, *Tracts on the Corn Trade and Corn Laws*, II. 72.   [2] *Report*, p. 7.

the Product of the Grower of Corn in Great Britain will afford such regular and ample supply for the consumption of the Kingdom as to admit the repeal of that Power given to his Majesty's Privy Council without the danger of any detriment arising therefrom to the public ".[1] But once again hopes were disappointed. In no year between 1804 and 1814 was the average price of wheat as low as the point at which the high duty would come into effect. Therefore, *in toto* from 1791 to 1814 the statutory restrictions on importation were in practice either inoperative or in suspense. The one and only serious breach in corn-law policy from beginning to end came in 1815, on the termination of war, under apprehension of the ensuing peace. This law was defiantly protective, and differed both in principle and spirit from the legislation of the eighteenth century. It sought to fasten on a country at peace the protection furnished by a generation of war.

The train of events which led up to the law of 1815 is obscure. It is itself the concluding part of the emergency measures which began with the outbreak of the French Revolution in 1789. For all practical purposes the exceptions to normal policy then became the rule down to the peace of 1815; and these emergencies, first of revolution and then of war, must be reviewed in brief.

1789 was a foretaste of the war years to come. At Amsterdam, a free market for corn, the price rose to 62s. the quarter. The Municipality of Paris and the Government of corn-producing France gave bounties on importation; and other countries started public granaries. The English Government reacted to the alarm. Pitt refused Necker's anxious appeal for 20,000 sacks of flour (July 3, 1789), and Parliament supported him by passing temporary laws in 1789 and 1790, which forbade export at any price. This was to circumvent the reputed attempts of foreign merchants to release grain for export by depressing English prices to the point when export would be legal (i.e. below 44s.). In this atmosphere of *sauve qui peut* the act of 1791 was passed.

The enabling section in the act of 1791 ran: "The King-in-Council shall have power, when Parliament is not sitting, to

---

[1] *Report of the Committee on the Corn Trade*, May 1804.

prohibit the exportation for a limited time of corn, meal or flour, when the average price is higher than that at which the same sort of corn may be imported on the low duty; and in like manner to permit the import, at the lowest duty, of the same articles, whenever the average price...may be higher than that fixed for admission from foreign parts at the low duty". The power was taken, but it was not enough when acute scarcity was added to serious war.

In the beginning of 1795 the Government entertained a project of public granaries, but dropped it in the face of a scathing onslaught from Edmund Burke, who was now in retirement on his Uxbridge farm.

In an economical light, I must observe that the construction of such granaries throughout the kingdom would be an expense beyond all calculation. The keeping them up would be at a great charge. The management and attendance would require an army of agents, store-keepers, clerks and servants. The capital to be employed in the purchase of grain would be enormous. The waste, decay and corruption would be a dreadful drawback to the whole dealing; and the dissatisfaction of the people at having decayed, tainted or corrupted corn sold to them, as must be the case, would be serious.

This climate (whatever others may be) is not favourable to granaries, where wheat is to be kept for any time. The best, and indeed the only good granary, is the rick yard of the farmer, where the corn is preserved in its own straw, sweet, clean, wholesome, free from vermin and free from insects, and comparatively at a trifle of expense. This and the barn enjoying many of the same advantages, have been the sole granaries of England from the foundation of its agriculture to this day. All this is done at the expense of the undertaker and at his sole risk. He contributes to government, he receives nothing from it but protection, and to this he has a claim.

The moment that government appears at market all the principles of market will be subverted. I don't know whether the farmer will suffer by it as long as there is a tolerable margin of competition, but I am sure that, in the first place, the trading government will speedily become a bankrupt, and the consumer in the end will suffer. If government makes all its purchases at once, it will instantly raise the market upon itself. If it makes them by degrees, it must follow the course of the market. If it follows the course of the market, it will produce no effect, and the consumer may as well buy as he wants. Therefore all the expense is incurred gratis.[1]

[1] Burke, *Collected Works*, ed. 1826, VII. 400–1.

However, the winter of 1794–5 was of extraordinary severity, and the price of wheat rose to 108s. 4d. in August 1795; 50s. in eight months. Faced with famine conditions, the Government had resort to *force majeure*. Neutral ships bound with corn for France were seized and brought to England, and their cargoes paid for with ample profit to the proprietors. "This was done", says Tooke, "because it was apprehended that our own merchants would be deterred from purchasing as freely as was desirable, by the great advance of prices, which had taken place in the North of Europe, in consequence of large purchases for account of the French Government."[1] But the scarcity continued into the winter of 1795–6, and more comprehensive measures were necessary. These were repeated in the second great scarcity of 1800–1; and the result was an elaborate code of war-time food control, which stopped short, however, of formal rationing. Corn imports were bountied: the consumption of the existing food supply was economised: alternative foodstuffs were canvassed: and every encouragement was given to enclosure and the increase of arable land.

The forms of wheat economy were numerous and varied. Hair powder, in which grain was used, was heavily taxed. Distillation of grain was prohibited in particular areas, the Government having an interest in lessening the stocks of colonial sugar which were piling up in London. It was forbidden to eat new bread; and in 1795 and 1800 self-denial was urged upon the people from bench and pulpit.

When, notwithstanding the recrudescence of war in May 1803, the measure that was to become law in 1804 was introduced into Parliament, the industrial North began to grumble. Liverpool was concerned with the threat to its American grain trade—the Liverpool that was to be represented later by Canning and Huskisson. Glasgow and its neighbours had been importing additional grain from America; and they feared that this would be impeded. But the apprehensions were unnecessary. For there was no further scarcity as acute as that of 1795–6 or 1800–1; and corn-law policy after 1804 was subordinated to the life-and-death struggle with Napoleon and his

History of Prices, 1. 182.

Continental System. During this period the grain trade was subjected to a system of licences by both belligerents, the effect of which, on prices and the terms of trade, is discussed in a later chapter. The trade was not suppressed and England was not starved into submission. Indeed, the response of British farming to the emergency was so superb that the country could have survived without the importation of a single quarter of foreign wheat. In this response Ireland, now a member of the United Kingdom, played a part.

When peace loomed in 1813 the champions of Ireland, with Sir Henry Parnell at their head, were the first to get busy. They procured the Corn Committee, which reported in the same year; and the result of their report was the act of 54 George III, c. 69 (1814), which allowed corn, grain, meal and flour to be exported at all times without payment of duty or receipt of bounty. In this oblique fashion the famous bounty passed away. To be sure, Ireland had no objection to receiving bounties, but the bounty on export was associated with restriction on export; and in freedom of export Ireland was greatly interested. For she exported much oats and a little wheat. The establishment of a free trade in corn between England and Ireland in 1806 had widened Ireland's market; and Irish corn merchants incidentally enjoyed a privilege which was denied to their English competitors. For Irish grain in England, being accounted foreign grain, might be re-exported without restriction. Therefore by shipment via England, Irish merchants could evade the Irish restrictions on export from Ireland and the English restrictions on export from England. During the Peninsular War the provisioning of troops and troop horses provided a new demand to which the general restrictions on export did not apply. But in 1813 the end of the Peninsular War was in sight, and free shipment via England was a privilege that might be withdrawn and in any case only of service for orders from the Continent of Europe. When, therefore, Ireland found that she was legally prevented from accepting attractive orders for direct shipment to Jamaica and the Brazils, she pressed for the abolition of all export restrictions. Parliament was more than agreeable. For with peace at home, English growers, too, cherished hopes of export;

and free export wi out a bounty was preferable to a restricted export and suspended bounty. In this form the agriculturists welcomed a freer trade; and two years later, in 1816, they tried to secure similarly the removal of the prohibition on the export of raw wool. But the Committee, to which the proposal was referred, declared against them. The manufacturers feared a shortage of supply and swelled with righteous indignation. The proposal, said Baring, a merchant and a Whig, came "with a very bad grace from the agriculturists, who had placed the country in an unnatural and artificial state by their Corn Laws". It was left to the Tory Huskisson to remove the prohibition in 1824.

Free export was only a part of the recommendations of the Committee of 1813. They were in name a Committee to enquire into the Corn Trade of the United Kingdom, though their concern was chiefly with Ireland. The witnesses they examined were all Irishmen or connected with Ireland. Ireland (these said) needed better organised markets, had benefited by the Royal and Grand Canals, had been unable to export directly to the Continent since 1804, had increased her output as the result of a free trade with England. But by the aid of the right question they were coaxed into saying that Ireland could supply any normal deficiency in the English output. This slender evidence the Committee embellished with Irish logic and the *histoire raisonnée* from which we have already quoted, in relation to the law of 1773 (above, pp. 32–3); and they proceeded to recommend that along with freedom of export a scale of duties of prohibitive height should be imposed on foreign imports of corn into the United Kingdom, as follows:

Wheat	s.	d.	s.	d.
If under, per qr.	105	2		
High duty			24	3
If at or above, per qr.	105	2		
But under ditto	135	2		
1st low duty			2	6
If at or above, per qr.	135	2		
2nd low duty			0	6

and for other grains proportionately.

The motives underlying this preposterous proposal are not easy to fathom. Possibly it was with the idea of elevating the demand for concessions to Ireland to the dignity of national and imperial statesmanship. They could not of course be accepted; and the House of Commons met them by demanding time for further discussion. The response of the country was not in doubt. Petitions flowed in from all quarters, merchants, traders, manufacturers, clergy, overseers of the poor and country gentlemen, "praying that the same may not pass into law".

Next year, 1814, the problem was examined more soberly from the British standpoint; but not less anxiously, for the very abundant harvest of 1813 had sent the price of all grains tumbling down. Parnell in Parliament lowered his tone. All that he desired was a reasonable protecting limit, say 84s. the quarter, and "if that was found too high, he was ready to concur in whatever the House might consider proper". But the House was being flooded by petitions from the great towns, from London, Liverpool, Glasgow and the rest; and so, declining immediate action, it referred the petitions to select committees of the Lords and Commons (1814), which sat and reported within the year. The witnesses this time were mainly British and in many cases they gave evidence before both—land agents, corn merchants, millers, farmers and an occasional landlord. Most weighty of all was Arthur Young, now an old and blind man, who communicated the details of the Board of Agriculture's Circular Letters, enquiring into the expense of raising wheat at different periods.[1] The result for a typical farm of 100 acres was

Year	£	s.	d.		£	s.	d.
1790	411	15	11¾: of which rent =		88	6	3¼
1803	547	10	11½: ,,	=	121	2	7¼
1813	771	16	4½: ,,	=	161	12	7¾

On the strength of this and other solid evidence the Committee of the Commons reported that if the admitted extension and improvement in the agriculture of the United Kingdom was to be

---

[1] *Committee (H. of C.) on Petitions relating to the Corn Laws of the United Kingdom* (1814). Evidence, p. 570.

sustained in the face of the admitted increase in expenses, 80s. per quarter (the figure suggested by most of the witnesses) was the lowest price which would afford an adequate remuneration to the grower.

Such a proposal, if carried and enforced, was calculated to raise rents, or at any rate to hold them to their war-time level; and it is open to anyone to suggest that it was inspired by the landlords. But landlords were in a minority among the witnesses, and the figures adduced served to show that the landlord's share was a diminishing one. Nor were hostile witnesses excluded. The Lords Committee advertised for evidence on behalf of the petitioners, but no one came forward except an egotistical gentleman of the name of Phillips, who declares that "according to my ideas, as having had a great deal of experience; it will at once render permanent that most terrible system of monopolizing the occupancy of land".[1] There were no railways in these days, and the industrial North had no representation in Parliament.

The last stage of the struggle opened on February 14, 1815, when Robinson,[2] Vice-President of the Board of Trade, gave notice of a new bill founded on a new set of resolutions and intimated that it was to be regarded as a Government measure. The first proposals issuing from the deliberations of 1814 had contained in one form or another, like Parnell's original plan, a graduated scale of import duties. The Government now turned its back on duties, and, following the lead of the Commons Committee, proposed a device which was without precedent in corn-law history: full freedom of import without any duty when the price was at or above 80s. the quarter, absolute prohibition when the price was below 80s. Baring, from the Opposition, suggested that the Government desired "to catch at a little popularity", "lest the idea of a duty upon corn should excite an outcry". Robinson denied this, as also a charge of favouritism to Ireland. "He was of opinion not only that our security would be greater, but even that the price of corn in the end might be

[1] *Lords Committee on the Growth, Commerce, and Consumption of Grain and Laws relating thereto* (1814). Evidence, p. 177.

[2] Robinson, F. J., Viscount Goderich, afterwards first Earl of Ripon, prime minister, 1827.

cheaper by home cultivation than by depending upon foreign countries."

In 1815, as in 1813 and 1814, petitions of protest poured in. Carlisle now declared that "any hope of success in restricting the importation of corn must arise from the people not being fairly represented—from the want of Parliamentary Reform". Westminster urged that

the system of prohibition is injudicious: and that wherever the produce of all the land which can be cultivated at a moderate expense is found insufficient for the support of a greatly increased manufacturing population, it is wiser to import, from countries where it can be grown at a low price, the additional quantity of corn required, which the spirit and industry of our merchants would at all times obtain in exchange for manufactures exported, than to diminish the national capital and increase the price of bread in attempting to force it from barren spots at home by an enormously expensive method of cultivation.

Manchester objected that the bill would raise the price of labour and handicap manufacturers in their competition with the foreigner; and Sir Robert Peel senior, in urging Manchester's case, hoped with the fervour of a Cobden or Bright that "ministers would convince the anxious multitude that they were alive to their vital and real interests".[1]

Such was the excitement in London that known supporters of the bill were maltreated by the populace on their way to the House. Mr Croker complained that he was "surrounded by a tumultuous mob who demanded his name and requested to know how he proposed to vote, and how he had voted on the corn bill". Mr Finlay "was assailed with sticks and his friend had his coat and waistcoat torn". Sir Frederick Flood "had been carried above a hundred yards on the shoulders of the mob just like mackerel from Billingsgate market, and he thought they meant to quarter him".[2] The debate was continued on a higher plane in the calmer atmosphere of the Lords. Lord Liverpool, the Tory premier, put the Government's case at its best. The great object was to prevent fluctuations. For this purpose it was necessary to secure a regular domestic supply from Great Britain, and also from Ireland, a new source of

---

[1] Hansard, xxx. 7.   [2] *Ibid*. xxx. 27–35.

supply since 1806. The object was not the protection of the English or Irish landlord, but the general interests of the Empire and the general interests of the great mass of consumers in the whole United Kingdom. It had been said at the end of the American war that our sun had set; but relying upon our own resources, we had been enabled to carry on successfully a twenty years' war and to cover ourselves with glory and renown.[1]

Lord Grenville, Pitt's old colleague, made a brilliant and crushing reply. If it was desired to keep agriculture on a level with manufacture, why not free the latter rather than fetter the former? Whatever the arguments of its supporters, the bill was unintelligible except as a device for keeping up the price of corn. Even they had to defend it as a measure for making food in the first instance dearer than it would be without the operation of the bill, in order at some future time to make it cheaper. To grow wheat on very bad lands was as sensible as trying to grow vines.[2] Grenville knew his *Wealth of Nations*.

The bill was carried on the third reading by a majority of 128 to 21, the minority availing themselves of the right of their House to enter a protest on the Journals. They opposed it because, *inter alia*, "Monopoly is the parent of scarcity, of dearness, and of uncertainty. To cut off any of the sources of supply can only tend to lessen its abundance; to close against ourselves the cheapest market for any commodity, must enhance the price at which we purchase it; and to confine the consumer of corn to the produce of his own country, is to refuse to ourselves the benefit of that provision which Providence itself has made for equalising to man the variations of season and climate". This from the dissenting Peers of 1815 is in the vein of Cobden and Bright thirty years later.

---

[1] Hansard, xxx. 181–5.   [2] *Ibid.* xxx. 193–9.

CHAPTER IV

DIGRESSION UPON THE CORN TRADE AROUND 1800

Article I

THE MILLER & THE BAKER

IN the spring of 1914, when I went to Laxton to see the only open-field village that remains in England, I found, framed on the wall of the smoking room in the Hop Pole, Ollerton (Notts), a broadside, which ran, in part:

To the Good people of Retford

This is the Time to stand Flast and True and see your Selves Righted (or be starved and pined to Death) For those Cruall Villions the Millers Bakers etc Flower Sellers rases Flowe under a Comebination to what price they please on purpose to make an Artificall Famine in a Land of plenty, so stand True and Let your Complaints be known to the High Bailiff and it is to be hope'd he will here you, and cause some Relieff to be made to keep the poor from being Famished.

EAST RETFORD, JULY 3, 1795

In that season of scarcity the millers and bakers were the object of general suspicion and odium both in the country and at the metropolis.

While consumers ate their own produce, no regulation of the trade in bread was necessary, for there was no trade to regulate. The structure of society was at this early time feudal; rights and duties centred round the lord. But with the growth of town life a consuming public appeared, separate and removed from the producers of food. It was considered impolitic to increase the distance between producers and consumers, and middlemen were therefore discouraged. When baking and milling appeared as independent steps in production, the status of those who exercised these functions was vigilantly controlled. In a matter so vital as the delivery of food, no autonomy, no rights against society were suffered. Bakers and millers were, in a literal sense, the agents of the public, working for the community.

The Assize of Bread crystallised this view of the baker's function. Fixing the amount of bread which he must sell for the price of a quarter of wheat, it regarded him virtually as a worker in receipt of a salary or public allowance, and thereby withdrawn both from profiteering and speculative loss.[1]

As a reporter to a House of Commons Committee put it in 1774:

If wheat be ever so dear, they are sure to be paid the market price of it in the price of the bread...as the Assize of Bread is liable to be altered whenever the price rises or falls threepence in a bushel; this circumstance renders it needless for them to employ large capitals, and secures them from being injured from the fluctuation of markets.[2]

But by 1774 the baker's position had been changed; and it was the miller who had changed it, "having stepped in between the growers of corn and the bakers". The same reporter states that:

The millers (who till within these late years had no other part, from time immemorial, in the manufacturing of Wheat into Bread, than the grinding of Wheat into Meal for the Bakers) are now for the most part become purchasers of wheat, and dressers of it into Flour for sale upon their own account.

The ultimate cause was the growth of the towns, led by the great and luxurious metropolis.

In 1815, as the result of a Committee,[3] which strongly condemned the manner of its working, the Assize of Bread was

---

[1] This was done in a Table which took as its constant the farthing loaf and varied the weight of the farthing-worth according to the price of wheat. In addition to his fixed allowance and a small profit, the baker might make what he could out of the bran. Different varieties of bread were specified: No. 1 Wastel to No. 7 (cf. the Canadian wheat grades of to-day). The figures for Nos. 2 to 7 had to be calculated from that for No. 1 Wastel; and since at high prices rival methods of calculation yielded different results, these were the subject of keen dispute in the late sixteenth century. After 1600 the old Assize Bread Table, as interpreted by John Powell, Clerk of the London Market, held the field till 1710, when it was replaced by the 8th of Queen Anne. See *Economic Journal Economic History*, January 1932, F. Nicholas, "The Assize of Bread in London during the sixteenth century".

[2] *Committee (H. of C.) on Methods practised in making Flour from Wheat*, 1774. App. H, Observations by Henry Pelham.

[3] *Committee (H. of C.) on Laws relating to the Manufacture, Sale and Assize of Bread*. Chairman, Frankland Lewis, 1815.

discontinued for London and its environs (55 George III, c. 99). The way had been prepared for this by previous legislation. By 8 Anne, c. 19 (1710), the Magistrates were authorised to have reference to the price of flour in fixing the Assize. By 31 George II, c. 29 (1758), it was explicitly stated that 20 peck loaves were to be made and sold from a sack of 280 lbs. of flour. In accordance with this direction "the Magistrates of the City of London proceeded to fix the price of Bread and from that time little reference has been had to the price of wheat".[1]

How did the change affect the public and the bakers? To answer this, mention must be made of one further act, confined to the metropolitan area, namely, 37 George III, c. 98 (1797). Hitherto the London magistrates had possessed, and for the protection of consumers had sometimes exercised, discretionary power in the matter of the allowance which they granted to cover the baker's costs and profits. In 1797 the discretionary allowance was replaced by a fixed allowance of so many shillings per sack of flour. The result, it was contended by a corn dealer in 1800, was to make flour dear. It

has opened a door to a class of speculators in the Market never known before; I mean the opulent Bakers; they, being large holders of Flour, come to Market prepared to buy flour at an advanced price, being certain that the Price of Bread must advance with the Price of Flour. Consequently they take advantage of their Stock on Hand, so as they must in the end be gainers. Before the Act, the Court having the Power of keeping down the Price of Bread notwithstanding the Price of Flour, Bakers did not dare to buy a sack of Flour in a rising Market, which it is now their Interest to do. For the same reason the Millers do not care what Price they give for their Wheat as they can dispose of it so readily to the Bakers.[2]

It may be objected that this was a panic judgment, uttered at a time of famine and before the results of the act of 1797 could be fairly appraised. But the contention was strenuously reiterated by the Bread Committee of 1815:

The peculiar operation of the Assize makes the price of bread exactly to depend upon and to vary with the returned prices of Flour

---

[1] *Committee of* 1815. *Report,* p. 6.
[2] *Committee (H. of C.) on the High Price of Provisions.* 7*th Report,* June 24, 1801. Evidence of W. Reynolds.

and by so doing prevents the Bakers (taking them as a trade collectively) from having any direct interest in the price at which they purchase Flour; whatever price they give for it per sack that price is to be returned to them for 80 Quartern loaves; if the price of Flour is reduced, a simultaneous and exactly corresponding decrease in the price of Bread prevents the Bakers from deriving the smallest advantage by it; but if it is raised, then a similar increase on the price of Bread prevents them from being exposed to the smallest loss.... It is to the operation of this principle which Your Committee attribute the indifference about the price as well as the anxiety about quality of Flour, for the best Flour will always make more Bread, as well as whiter Bread; and where the price by the Assize is uniform, the seller has no mode of seeking for better custom but offering a whiter Loaf than his neighbour.[1]

This quotation exhibits the alteration in legislative opinion since 1774. In 1774 the legislature would have approved the baker's indifference to fluctuations of price. But the liberalism of the next generation, sharpened by the memories of recent famine, saw in this security an offence against nature. The Committee of 1774 recognised the unreason of controlling the baker and withdrawing all check on the processes by which the flour, the baker's raw material, got its price. But this they desired to remedy by setting an assize on flour also.[2] The Committee of 1815, on the other hand, would have the baker assume the risks of competition in the faith that competition conduced to cheapness and cheapness to the public good.

When another Committee[3] sat a few years later (1821) to consider the removal of the last traces of medievalism, to wit the prescription of certain denominations of loaves or of weight, an ex-mayor of Leeds wrote urging "the most natural and best plan, namely competition". His advice was followed in the act of 1822, which applied to London only.[4] Penalties, indeed, were retained against adulteration; and bakers were ordered to keep legal weights and scales in their shops, and to weigh bread when required by their customers. But, "when by these means, facility has been afforded to the public to protect itself, it

---

[1] *Committee of 1815. Report*, p. 7.
[2] *Committee of 1774.* Resolution 3.
[3] *Committee (H. of C.) on Existing Regulations relative to the making and the sale of bread* (1821).
[4] 3 George IV, c. 106 (local).

appears conclusive that the Legislature can do no more to secure it against imposition".[1] (In 1836 by 6 and 7 William IV, c. 37, the facilities of this act were extended to the provinces.)

Pressed thus for a time (1774–1815) between free milling and regulated bread-selling, the London bakers lost their independence. They now attended neither the wheat market nor the flour market, being supplied by the millers or their agents, the flour factors, in whose debt they often were. They retained nothing of their ancient status, except that some were "full-priced" bakers, claiming to cater for the respectable public. The Committee of 1815 found that the sellers of flour

are eager to dispose of it at the high prices returned to the Lord Mayor; but that in order to do so, it seems they must be content to live on long and doubtful credits, and many of them have recourse to becoming proprietors of bake houses and carrying on the baking trade on their own account by means of journeymen, to obtaining leases of Bakers' houses, encouraging journeymen to set up for themselves, and to giving large sums for the goodwill of Bakers' houses.[2]

But others among them played a shrewder game. They sold their flour for ready money to a new class of cash-bakers, who were prepared to cut prices and sell for ready money below the Assize.

The excessive flour prices officially returned to the Cocket Office made undercutting easy. For these prices were inclusive of credit and based on sales of flour which was above the average quality; and sometimes they were not genuine prices, being higher than any actually paid. Thus, by the competition of baking millers on the one hand and that of low-class bakers on the other, the regular bakers suffered.

The Committee of 1815 expected that the baking trade, as the result of the removal of the Assize, would get into the hands of men of capital and that it would be carried on as a manufacturing concern on a large scale. But that expectation, according to evidence given some ten years later (1824), was not realised, for the baking trade was then upon the same level as before, as regards the number of bakers. The full-priced bakers were

[1] *Committee of* 1821, p. 5.
[2] *Committee of* 1815. *Report*, p. 8.

indeed trying to hold together and agree upon their prices; but, continues the witness,

I will be bound to say that...there are 500 different prices, some have one thing and some another; the trade is wholly in opposition ever since this business [*sc.* the abolition of the Assize]. I believe the full price bakers are not all of a price, and the cheap bakers are not all of a price; they are all dissatisfied.[1]

One feels rather sorry for the bakers! They had once been public servants with a status: they were now competitive establishments, with a trade to push. Where the same price is paid for the same thing at the same time, there a competitive market is. So runs the economist's definition. But it took time, even for bakers, to exhibit the competitive essence.

Meanwhile, in the provinces, consumers and bakers, as distinguished from corn growers and millers, had their troubles. London drew its supplies from the provinces, and in return gave them its fashions. It was for the rich Londoners that the millers first dressed the new and different sorts of flour which accorded with none of the traditional divisions. For London had to feed lords and ladies, their menials and other children of luxury.

The poor aped the gentility of their superiors, and the Londoners' passion for the whitest of white bread, whitened by the artifice of alum, set the fashion which has ruled up to this present day. Norwich, the metropolis of East Anglia, followed the example of London. Thus, in 1745 fine flour from Hertfordshire was retailed in Norwich, before which time a coarse household flour, inferior to meal, was the general bread used in the city and country.[2] But, though as producers the country districts profited by the metropolitan demand, as consumers they suffered. For a miller of Abingdon told the Committee of 1813 that it was the practice there to send the fine flour to London,

---

[1] *Committee (H. of C.) on Allowances granted to Bakers by 53 George III, c. 116, in those places where an Assize of Bread is set,* 1824. Evidence of Mr Turner, a baker, p. 6. This document informs us that in Oxford the Assize was set by the University: "The household bread is generally used by the inhabitants; the wheaten in the colleges, with the small bread".

[2] Brereton, 1825, *Practical Enquiry into the number...of agricultural labourers.*

keeping back the coarse thirds which were sold to the poor, as food for themselves or their pigs.[1]

The provincial bakers also were none too happy. Although the London bakers, as we have seen, thought themselves an unlucky body of men, the provincial bakers envied them; and during 1812–13 they were busy petitioning Parliament for a more adequate allowance on the principle of the fixed rate granted to London bakers in 1797. They showed how their expenses had mounted up since 1801 : yeast per gallon from 1s. 6d. to 3s., salt per cwt. from 15s. to 35s., wood per hundred of 6 score faggots from 20s. to 30s., candles per dozen pounds from 8s. to 13s., journeymen's wages (foremen) from 16s. to 24s., in all an increase of one-third to a half.[2] The county magistrates had power to increase the bread-makers' allowance, but declined. "They think they have not a right to give us more; and they think it is against the poor people."[3] The London allowance per sack of flour was several shillings more, but there was not, says the same witness, 3d. per sack of difference in baking costs. Rents were higher in London, but in Worcester "what makes it so high is that we find all our servants victuals and drink and lodging, which they do not in London".[4]

But this was not their only grievance. The provincial averages, they complained, were wrong, and the error told against the bakers.

A miller of Peterborough produced an assize of May 8, 1813, by which, on his calculation, the Peterborough bakers did not even get their expenses, let alone profit. What then was wrong with them?

First of all, the returns on which they were based were inaccurate. "It is made arbitrarily", says a Derby baker,[5] "by a person who has three guineas a year for making the returns; he returns the highest and the lowest and takes the midway between"—without regard to quantity sold. And of Lynn in Norfolk, we read, "The clerk takes the highest and lowest

---

[1] *Minutes of Evidence on the Country Bakers' Bill*, 1813, p. 7.
[2] *Committee (H. of C.) on Petitions of certain Country Bakers*, 1813. Evidence of a Worcester baker.
[3] *Ibid.*   [4] *Ibid.*
[5] *Minutes of Evidence on the Country Bakers' Bill*, 1813, p. 36.

prices and divides by two, regardless of quantity sold".[1] The days of weighting and of index numbers had not yet come.

Secondly—and this was a more serious defect—the returns were becoming irrelevant. In the country towns, in contrast with London, the magistrates went on setting the Assize by reference to the price of wheat, with side-glances at the price of flour. But by 1813 little wheat was coming into the local market, and few bakers were buying wheat. The millers or their agents bought straight from the farmers and sold flour to the bakers. London accepted the situation, basing the price of the loaf on that of flour, but the provincial magistrates muddled along on the old basis. Thus in Exeter, not one-quarter of the wheat sold went into the averages: for much more wheat and flour were sold by private contract than at public market.[2] The little wheat taken to market "was inferior wheat generally sold only to the poor people, and measured out in pecks and tubs". The London averages were at least relevant, being based on weekly returns from the actual buyers and sellers of flour. The provincial averages calculated the cost of the baker's raw material from sales of stuff which he never baked, on a market which he rarely visited.

On one occasion in Lynn (Norfolk) the allowances fell so low that the bakers, following the example of their London brethren, shut up shop. On another occasion the Bedford bakers, by way of protest, refused to sell to any but regular customers, and so were allowed a little more; and doubtless the same sort of thing occurred in many other towns. Most witnesses before the Committee of 1813 spoke mournfully of the condition of their trade. Thus at Bristol "the number of bakers is declining and baking is a losing trade". In Worcester "there are now 14 or 15 bakers. There were considerably more formerly, but numbers are falling". "No baker can pay his way if he has no other trade but that of baking to follow." The witness himself "was a maltster as well as other things," and so were many of his fellows".[3]

---

[1] *Minutes of Evidence on the Country Bakers' Bill,* 1813, p. 19.
[2] The same is recorded of Bath, Bristol and other towns. *Committee (H. of C.) on Petitions of certain Country Bakers,* 1813.
[3] *Committee (H. of C.) on Petitions of certain Country Bakers,* 1813. Evidence of Geo. Everet, Baker, of Worcester.

The general impression derived from this evidence is, not that bakers were suffering from an ordinary wave of depression, nor yet that they were being absorbed by large-scale enterprises, but rather that they were bearing the brunt of the popular indignation at the unparalleled food prices of 1813. It is noteworthy that in Manchester, where as many as half the families prepared their own bread, taking it to be baked for a fee at the public ovens, the bakers during the disturbed years of 1798–9 and 1813 were "not so obnoxious to the mob as the corn and flour dealers".[1] The Norwich bench, if out of date, was at any rate logical when in 1815 it wished to transfer the Assize from the bakers to the millers. They argued thus, "As little skill and no capital are required in the trade of baking, competition will prevent inordinate profit". But with the millers it was different, "as few situations are eligible for mills, and much science and great capital are necessary to carry on that trade. No competition exists to regulate the price of flour, but there is a monopoly destructive to the object of the Assize".[2] Their language was the language of a new century, their design—an Assize of Flour—was the design of 1774. In the result the same treatment was measured out to the provinces as to London, and in 1819 by 59 George III, c. 36, the Assize of Bread, which went back to the reign of Henry III, was abolished.

Article II

THE LONDON CORN MARKET

If we look only to the laws known as corn laws, which regulated the export and import of foreign grains, the eighteenth century seems to close in an atmosphere of regulation thicker and more aggravating than after or before. Certainly the trade in corn was freer in England in 1850 than it was in 1800, because in 1850 not only the home trade but also the foreign trade—the major department—was free. But the corn trade was freer in 1800 than in 1700. For in 1800 the home trade, representing nine-

---

[1] Committee (H. of C.) on Laws relating to the Manufacture, Sale and Assize of Bread, 1815. App. No. 8.

[2] MS. Minutes Quarter Sessions, Norwich, 1815, Easter. Quoted by S. and B. Webb, Economic Journal, June 1904 (vol. XIV), The Assize of Bread, p. 217.

tenths of the total trade, was altogether free, though the other tenth—the foreign trade—was rigidly regulated. The freedom of the inland trade in corn was slowly won. From medieval times, in particular from the fifth and sixth of Edward VI, c. 14 (1552), there were severe penalties against the statutory offences of forestalling, regrating and engrossing:

I.   Whatsoever person shall buy any merchandise, victual, etc. coming toward any Market or Fair, or coming toward any City, etc., or make any bargain for the having of the same, before it shall be in the Market, Fair, City, etc., or shall make any motion for the inhancing of the prices shall be deemed a Forestaller.

II. Whatsoever person shall regrate, obtain, etc., in any Fair or Market any Corn, etc., that shall be brought to be sold and do sell the same again in any Fair or Market within four miles thereof shall be accepted for a Regrator.

III. Whatsoever person shall engross or get into his hands, by buying, contracting or promise taking, other than by demise, grant or lease of land or tithe, any Corn growing in the fields or any other Corn, etc., to the intent to sell the same again shall be accepted an unlawful Ingrosser.

There is no mention of a time limit for re-sale; and III expressly excludes from illegality the holding of rents or tithes in kind, such as furnished the granary hoards of pre-Revolutionary France.

The offences arising in these three ways were not easy to distinguish. They had grown into confusion by historical accretion and changes in the middleman's function. The act of 1552 avowedly set out to clarify the existing law. In the original Assize of Bread of 51 Henry III the jurors were ordered to present *inter alios* "forestallers, that buy anything afore the due and accustomed Hour, or that pass out of the Town to meet such things that come to the Market, to the intent that they may sell the same in the town more dear unto Regrators".

Regrating was always a lawful function, provided it was properly exercised. (To regrate was to scrape again, just as to retail was to shred in small pieces.) The regrator was called corn-monger, -dealer, -badger, -blader. He bought to sell again to consumers and other retailers—not yet a wholesaler, but betwixt and between. He was encouraged to go out into the country for supplies; for this was an obvious service, whereas holding over a period of time was not. As the metropolitan market developed, the regrator changed into the urban meal-man or corn-chandler, who worked from the town outwards in competition with the country meal-man, working from the country inwards.

But the same metropolitan development produced the true wholesaler, the corn merchant who dealt in corn and perhaps in other things for the supply of London and for export to foreign countries. In the seventeenth century such a merchant, if native, was perforce welcome, because he was ousting the Dutch corn merchants, just as the goldsmith bankers ousted the Lombards. These merchants dealt in gross and might be big enough to engross the whole supply to their own profit—to contrive what we should call a corner. But engrossing was a statutory offence of old; and it had received the technical meaning of buying up the growing crops in the field, just as to-day Canadian and British buyers go through the Annapolis Valley in Nova Scotia buying apples on the tree, a practice distasteful to co-operating farmers. Therefore engrossing was a vague offence in principle, with a technical significance which by 1660 had ceased to be important. Indeed, forestalling, regrating and engrossing stood almost as a single general phrase for un-popular manipulation, in time or place, of the people's food. At this point came the relaxing act of 1662, an act passed for the encouragement of agricultural production and containing as a side-line an encouragement to the inland trade.

The statute of 15 Charles II, c. 7, s. 4 (1663), which Adam Smith eulogised—to exaggeration, as some think, for he says of it, "All the freedom which the trade of the inland corn dealer has ever yet enjoyed, was bestowed upon it by this statute" (*Wealth of Nations*, II. 34)—made it lawful for all and every person, when corn did not exceed a specified price, "to buy in open market, and to lay up and keep in granaries or houses and to sell again such corn", provided they were "not forestalling nor selling again the same in the same market within three months after the buying thereof". In 1772 by 12 George III, c. 7,

Parliament, zealously incited by Edmund Burke, repealed the ancient statutes saying in preamble that their enforcement "would bring great distress upon the inhabitants of many parts of this Kingdom and in particular upon those of the cities of London and Westminster"; and the corn law of 1791 repealed that part of the act of 1663 which related to the engrossing of corn.[1] Little more was heard of these offences till in the trial of The King v. Rusby (1800) it was held that, under certain circumstances, buying to sell again was an offence still liable to be punished by the Common Law with fine and imprisonment at least, if not with whipping and the pillory.[2] The decision, which excited much adverse criticism in the pamphlets of the day did not imperil the ordinary corn dealers, but only certain jobbers who were what we to-day should call professional bulls.[3] The result was not to abolish their practices, but to make them for a time more cautious.

[1] On this point Adam Smith observes, "The statute of the twelfth of the present King, which repeals almost all the other ancient laws against engrossers and forestallers, does not repeal the restrictions of this particular statute, which therefore still continues in force" (II. 34).

Mr Cannan's footnote is, "12 Geo. III, c. 71, repeals 5 and 6 Ed. VI, c. 14, but does not mention 15 Car. II, c. 7, which is purely permissive. If 15 Car. II, c. 7, remained of any force in this respect it must have been merely in consequence of the common law being unfavourable to forestalling".

But the Committee of the Council on Trade (1790), Report, p. 8, states that, in the matter of 15 Charles II, c. 7, "the laying it up in Granaries, except when the several Sorts of corn are below certain Prices therein mentioned, is the only law of this Description which will now be found in our Statute Book and ought certainly not to remain there any longer".

The position, therefore, between 1663 and 1791 was that, when corn did not exceed 48s. per qr., it was definitely lawful to engross it in granaries. But, inasmuch as 12 George III, when repealing the other statutes, did not repeal 15 Charles II, c. 7, the law by implication still forbade engrossing in granaries, when the price exceeded 48s. The annual averages for 1789 and 1790 were 52s. 9d. and 54s. 9d.; and it was, therefore, of practical importance to repeal in 1791 the statute of 1663. Mr Cannan's reference to the common law on forestalling (which was a different activity) raises another issue.

[2] See for an excellent account of the trial, Barnes, History of the English Corn Laws, pp. 81–3. Lord Kenyon from the bench denounced Adam Smith's dictum, that "the popular fear of engrossing and forestalling may be compared to the popular terrors and suspicion of witchcraft" (II. 35); and the jury gave the desired verdict. Excited by the decision the mob tore down Rusby's house. Rusby appealed the fine, and the court was divided, so that the sentence was never carried out. 7 and 8 Vict., c. 8 (1844), forbade prosecutions for forestalling, etc. under the common law.

[3] Committee (H. of C.) on the High Price of Provisions. 7th Report, June 24, 1801. Evidence of W. Reynolds, a corn dealer.

In 1795 and the lean years that followed there were murmurs among the populace—in Cambridge, for example, as we may read in the *Reminiscences* of Henry Gunning—expressive of a desire for vengeance on the middlemen; and in 1800 a Committee of the Lords examined the allegations that were floating about. They reported that "they had not been able to trace, in any one Instance, anything more than such suspicious and vague Reports as usually prevail in Times of Scarcity; and they are of opinion that what have been represented as deep schemes and fraudulent Practices to raise the market, have been only the common and usual proceedings of Dealers in all articles of commerce where there is a great demand and where great capitals and great activity are employed". And of the dealers in corn they reported that "persons engaged in this Branch of trade are highly useful and even necessary for the due and regular supply of the markets and may, therefore, be considered as rendering an important service to the Public at large".[1]

But the agitation had one good result. It induced the Commons Committee in the following year (1801) to take evidence from traders with a view to seeing whether defects of machinery were a cause of the high price of provisions. Their recommendations were not revolutionary, but these and the evidence on which they were based exhibit in fullness the structure of the trade in 1800.[2]

Forty to fifty years before 1800 the Corn Exchange had been transferred from Bear Quay to Mark Lane, a freehold property of eighty shares held by the factors and dealers in corn. The proprietors (i.e. the shareholders) allocated the stands and "although it is stated that the Possession of these stands is never transferred for a valuable consideration, as the lease

---

[1] *Committee (H. of L.) on the High Price of Provisions. 2nd Report.* Dec. 22, 1800.

[2] *Committee (H. of C.) on the High Price of Provisions. 7th Report,* June 24, 1801; respecting the Machinery of the Corn Trade. Their recommendations were:

    (a) A new and bigger Corn Exchange,

    (b) That factors should expose all their samples,

    (c) That factors should give bond not to deal on their own account,

    (d) "That the practice of purchasing Corn to sell it again, in the same or some subsequent market before Delivery and consequently before the payment becomes due on the first sale, ought to be discouraged".

would thereby be vacated; yet there seems reason to believe that in some instances large sums have been given for such an accommodation; without which it appears wholly impracticable for anyone to carry on the trade of a factor or dealer in corn to any material extent; though the Exchange is indeed considered as open to all who come to buy and sell; and there are instances of Persons attending the market at times who bring with them their samples in their pockets".[1]

Fourteen individuals, who were corn factors, held a controlling interest in the shares, and they took care, whenever any person applied to them for a stand, to prevent his obtaining one if he was likely to employ himself as a factor. But to the dealers, whose work was at this time not rival, but complementary, to theirs, they had no such objection. Hence the dealers were now almost as numerous as the factors. On the Exchange were sixty-four stands, occupied by some fifty people. Thirty of these were corn factors and twenty were dealers. Eight factors dealt for the Kentish people only and were known as "Kentish Hoymen".

Mark Lane was a general market for all the grains: wheat, barley, oats, etc., for home-grown grain and imported foreign grains. The foreign grain and most of the home grain reached London by sea. The amount brought down by river or by inland carriage bore a very small proportion to the total of London's consumption. The supplies from the home counties of Kent, Essex and Suffolk chiefly came from the growers direct, and were sold in "runs". One shipload would contain consignments from several growers to several factors; and the consignment on a particular ship from Farmer "A" to Factor "Z" was a "run". The supplies from the more distant parts of Essex and from Norfolk and elsewhere came chiefly from the corn merchants who had bought in the country from the farmers at the farms, or on the local markets. Among the several grains a greater part of the wheat came from farmers and a greater part of the barley and oats from merchants. Flour milled in the country and destined for London missed Mark Lane altogether, passing straight from the country miller to the town baker by the medium of flour

[1] H. of C. Report (7th) of 1801, p. 4.

factors. But barley, malted in the country perhaps by the farmers themselves, reached the London brewers through Mark Lane.

Very few farmers came up to Mark Lane to sell their own corn; 99 per cent. was, in the first instance, sold on commission by the factors. Through them the wheat passed to the millers or to shipping factors for reshipment. London millers bought direct for themselves and bought only for their own mills. Distant millers bought through factors. Cases sometimes occurred of wheat coming up to London and returning to the county from whence it came. "I have known", said a corn factor, "a run of wheat sold at the Corn Exchange, coming from the coast of Essex and bought to go back again into the same County for the supply of the Miller who could not obtain a sufficient quantity in his own neighbourhood."[1] Similarly, through the agency of the factors, the barley passed to the maltsters and the distillers; the malt to the brewers and the distillers; the oats to the dealers or "jobbers", as they had been called from old times. The dealer in oats was not a manufacturer, as the others were. He in turn would retail to the public, buy for stable keepers on commission, and perhaps keep horses for himself.

As a seller for his farmer clients the factor was in very much the same position as a modern stockbroker. In the home trade he took his regular commission per quarter and did his best for them. The seller's name was not disclosed except in case of a dispute, and the factor was usually given a free hand as to the price he should take. In the foreign trade there had been a recent change of practice. Here, on account of the extra risk and trouble caused by the outbreak of the French war (1793), factors now received, in addition to the commission per quarter, a percentage on the amount sold. Advices from importing merchants of consignments from abroad were usually accompanied by instructions to sell at specified prices. But whereas, according to the practice of the London Stock Exchange, the stockbrokers deal only with the stock-jobber—buying from him or selling to him according to the client's orders—the corn factor was primarily a seller only and dealt with trade consumers, the millers or their agents. One witness before the Committee

[1] *H. of C. Report* (7th) *of* 1801. Evidence of J. Stonard.

of 1801, Nathaniel Brockwood, who was at once a corn factor and buyer for the London Flour Company, was careful to state that he kept his two businesses rigidly separate. "It is the duty of the Factor", said another, "at all Times to do as well as he can for his Correspondents; it is the interest of the buyer or the miller to buy as cheap as he can. These two operations, the one or the other, will generally give the market its fair value."[1]

It was complained in these days of rising prices that the factors, selling on sample, exposed only a selection of their samples, so that the buyers had no index of the quantities they represented. What would be the result—this same witness was asked—of compelling factors to mark on the samples the quantity to which they related? He replied, "Great fluctuations would be continually taking place, because it is not infrequent that corn particularly from abroad, as also from the Coast, particularly the Norfolk Coast, is kept back by contrary winds and from the Foreign Countries by frost, etc.; in consequence of large Fleets arriving greater quantities of Corn are for sale on the same Day, the Buyers are timid, and the Corn feels a great depression".

The answer is obscure. Does it mean, "Where ignorance is bliss, 'tis folly to be wise"? More probably the witness, whose principals were at once factors and dealers, desired to imply that the correction of irregularities of quantity was being better performed by the machinery for equalising prices already at work behind the scenes.

To understand this machinery we must analyse the functions of the dealer. A comparatively new personage in the trade of wheat, the dealer was an established institution in that of oats; and this for two reasons. In the first place, the dealer in oats corresponded to the miller and was as indispensable as he, but, as the miller in addition to buying the wheat made it into flour, he was called a miller. The buyer of oats contributed no change of form to the product, and so he called himself a dealer in oats. In the second place, a great amount of oats was imported from abroad. Between 1697 and 1765 oats comprised more than two-thirds of British imports of grain, and over the whole period

[1] Evidence of the Clerk of Messrs Wilson (Corn Factors and Corn Merchants).

from 1697 to 1801 the oats imported into Great Britain were twelvefold those exported: whereas for the other cereals there were in the aggregate big balances of exports.[1] Most of the oats came from Ireland; for until 1806 Ireland was, for the purposes of the grain trade, a foreign country. Parnell's Corn Committee in 1813 made much of the increase in the food supplies derived from Ireland. But the increases were still mainly in oats,[2] much of which was purchased by Government for the service of troop horses in the Peninsular War (cf. above, pp. 3 and 38).

The growth of this import trade stimulated a class of traders who were objectionable to the old-fashioned dealers, and by common consent called "jobbers". "I mean by jobbers", said Mr R. Snell, a *dealer* in oats, "people who stand between the consumers of this metropolis and the factors, those who buy up the Oats and before the arrival of the fair Buyer or Consumer place them in the Hands of the Factor to sell again the same day on the same market....There is a term at Market when we ask for a sample of Oats, wishing to know whether they are on Board ship or in granary, and why we ask is we suppose all oats in granary to belong to those Jobbers and all People who know the true character of Jobbers will not buy of them."

With the growing importations of wheat towards the end of the eighteenth century, parallel changes occurred in the wheat trade. The dealer dealing in wheat on his own account made his appearance. Dealers, we are told in 1801, "occur largely in the importing line"; dealing on independent account in British corn "was not usual but may happen". Several of the witnesses to the Committee styled themselves dealers. It was a respectable profession. There was doubt, however, about the advisability of factors becoming dealers on their own account, a practice which was becoming common, though it is spoken of in 1801 as "a recent thing". The factors, it was admitted, "do at times import on their own account"; and the factors contended it was for the

[1] Skene Keith, *The Farmers' Magazine*, Aug. 2, 1802 (III. 277).
[2] Corn exported from Ireland (barrels):

	1801	1813
Wheat	168,397	334,886
Twenty-three other kinds, i.e. mainly oats	494,421	1,058,325

Quoted from Murray, *Commercial Relations between England and Ireland*, App. B, p. 441.

benefit of the country. The Committee thought differently, and recommended that they should be placed "on the footing of Brokers in other Trades carried on within the City of London". It was felt that the factor ought not to employ the confidential knowledge he had of the home trade for foreign dealing on his own account, since he then might have an interest in conflict with that of his clients.

But what of the jobbers? All the witnesses complained of their existence and indeed displayed an inside knowledge of their functions, but nobody admitted to being one or specified any jobber by name. A member of the Committee, giving evidence, said, "I cannot say that any persons make it their chief business". Who then are they, asked the Committee?—"Persons connected in one way or another with the corn trade, and having property and credit and considering the Prices will go still higher, may make purchases with a view to sell again." Men of property and credit! Respectable men did it, but it was not done! What then was "it"? In its most refined form it was buying to sell again without handling the produce; with an eye to profit on the rise of price in the interval. It was, as we should put it to-day, the operation of "bulls" buying for a rise. A witness describes it thus: "A person coming to the Corn Market on Friday and finding many Country Buyers, concludes the Market will rise on Monday; he purchases a quantity of Wheat, 400 or 500 qrs., with a view to selling the same on Monday, and the interval between his buying and selling requires no capital to carry that practice on". The factors, said the dealers, look up to the jobbers because a sale to them means a second sale later. The dealers, said the factors, are the parents of the jobbers! The decision in the trial, The King v. Rusby (noted above), scared the jobbers for a time; and the Committee of 1801, relying on the fact that buyers of corn were allowed a month's credit by the custom of the trade, suggested that re-sales within the month should be prohibited with a view to forcing jobbers to take delivery of the stuff and pay for it. But neither the judicial decision nor the suggestion (for a suggestion it remained) offered any real solution of the problem. What the country was suffering from was a prolonged scarcity, with prices mounting ever upwards.

Traders themselves recognised that speculation was inevitable; but in the last few years the movement of prices had been all one way. Jobbers rarely had to re-sell on a falling market. They seemed to be growing fat on the necessity of the people. As a very level-headed member of the Committee put it, "In times of plenty speculators tend to keep the market more on a level; in times of scarcity they have it in their power to influence the market too much".

Could any device have reduced their influence to its proper proportions? There was only one device, and that device, from the immaturity of speculative organisation, was precluded. For these Friday to Monday incursionists were embryo dealers in futures. Their service to the country could have been increased and their profits curtailed only by the appearance of that other set of animals which we call "bears". For then the contest would have been equal. Bulls would have worried and won from bears, and bears would have clipped the tails of bulls. But the bear, the animal who sells what he hasn't and covers his sale at a later date, could not appear so long as wheat was sold in the old way by sample or pitch. America was the first country to grade its wheat, and from America, a generation or two later, the bears came to the port of Liverpool.

Article III

TAKING THE AVERAGES

Although after 1800 the setting of the Assize of Bread gradually fell into disuse, the official prices of corn were still needed for the delicate task of regulating the bounties and duties established by the corn laws. Hence in the general corn laws, or in special acts supplementary to them, there was a section relating to the returns of prices from the different markets and the determination of the averages on the basis of these. The returns were made by agents of the Government, called Inspectors of Corn, to the Receiver of Corn Returns at headquarters; and we find that, as one corn law follows another, the paragraphs relating to their functions increase in bulk with the efforts to secure accuracy and prevent fraud. Up to 1820 the Inspectors outside London were underpaid, receiving only 5s. for each return, but with the appointment of William Jacob to the Comptrollership of Corn Returns in 1822, a post which he held for twenty years, many defects of administration were removed.

By the act of 1791 (31 George III, c. 30), which continued the trend of previous regulations,[1] the returns were taken from those parts of England more immediately accessible to the sea, denominated the Twelve Maritime Districts. These districts were independent of each other, the foreign trade in corn being governed in each by its own district price, so that the ports might be open in one district and closed in another. Scotland also was divided into four districts; the foreign corn trade of each being governed in the like manner. The inconveniences of provincialism were most clearly exposed in the years immediately following 1770, when England was now an exporting, now an importing country. It used to happen that bounties were given on corn leaving for a foreign country from one district at the very time that foreign corn was being imported into a neighbouring district at the low duty rate. Therefore, in the next general corn law (44 George III, c. 109, 1804) a change was made. It was decided to regulate the entire foreign corn trade of England by one internal price, and the aggregate average price of the twelve maritime districts was taken as the basic or regulating price; it was also enacted in the corn law of 1804 that the entire trade of Scotland should be governed by the aggregate average of the four Scotch districts.

But the change did not suit Scotland. For when the price of wheat rose sharply in 1805, the rise was not duly reflected in the returns from the remote districts. The general average worked out at 62s. 11d., a penny under the low duty point, and thus left foreign wheat still liable to a prohibitively high duty at a time when wheat stood at 80s. in the markets of Glasgow, Paisley and Greenock. Although the manufacturing population were now

---

[1] After 1685 there were numerous attempts to improve the method of determining the official price of corn—in 1732, 1766, 1770, 1773, 1774. In 1781 (21 George III, c. 50) an Inspector of the Returns of Corn was appointed to make an average of each kind of grain and publish weekly prices in the *London Gazette*. In 1789 (29 George III, c. 58) the scope of the act, which had been confined to London, Essex and Kent, was extended to the Maritime Counties.

within sight of famine, it was, nevertheless, impossible to relieve them by duty-free imports from America. Petitions poured into Parliament. It was prayed that Scotland should come under the English averages, which were always higher, and the prayer was granted (45 George III, c. 86, 1805). The adoption of a single average for Great Britain removed the last obstacle to the freedom of internal trade. The regulation permitting grain to pass at all times without hindrance from one part of the country to another gave to the inhabitants of the less productive counties a more regular and plentiful supply. It also assisted the producer, assuring, for example, a constant market to the growers of Norfolk barley: which they had not possessed hitherto. As matters had stood in 1804, "the [sc. Scottish] ports might be shut against the importation of grain from England by the returns made during the first plentiful year that might occur".[1]

Up to 1806 Ireland was accounted a foreign country in relation to its trade in corn with Great Britain. After 1806, when the trade in corn between the two countries was made entirely free, the foreign trade of Ireland was regulated by the English averages. Thus Great Britain and Ireland, which had been a United Kingdom since 1800, arrived at a single ruling price. Henceforth the English averages were the sole object of attention; and on the appearance of agricultural distress in 1820 a Committee[2] sat to enquire into their operation. The general average, they reported, was ascertained thus:

The total quantity of corn sold in each town is cast up, and the total of money for which the same was sold; and then dividing the money by the quarters, the result gives the average price of that town; these average prices of each town being thus found are added together, and being again divided by the number of towns, give the average of such district; and the averages of the districts thus found are added together, and being divided by 12, give the aggregate average of the whole twelve districts; and the combined aggregate average price of the six weeks preceding the 15th May, August, November and

<hr />

[1] *Committee (H. of C.) appointed to consider the petitions relating to the Corn Law of 1804* (1805, III). Evidence of Wm. Macdonald, M.P., p. 15.

[2] *Committee (H. of C.) on Petitions complaining of Agricultural Distress*. They "were instructed...to confine their inquiries to the mode of ascertaining, returning and calculating the average prices of corn, etc." The Report was issued July 1820.

February determines the opening and shutting of these ports at those periods respectively.[1]

But to regulate the course of trade for a whole three months by averages taken from the six weeks preceding the beginning of the period was found to be inadequate for the purpose of the inelastic corn law of 1815, 55 George III, c. 26 (free entry to foreign wheat at prices below 80s. a quarter, absolute prohibition at prices at or above 80s.). A provision was therefore inserted in this law to the effect that

if after the opening of the ports to the importation of foreign corn, etc., the price of any such corn, etc. should in the first six weeks following such opening fall below the prices at which foreign corn is allowed to be imported, the ports shall be shut against the importation of that sort of foreign corn, from any place from the Eyder [Denmark] to the Bidassoa [on the Franco-Spanish boundary]—[i.e. from the Near European ports]—for the last six weeks of that quarter, or until a new average shall be made up and published.[2]

The Committee of 1820 found serious defects both in the making of the returns and the calculation of the averages. As the law compelled returns from factors only, these were only complete in London, where most of the corn was sold on commission, but in the provinces, where it was usual for the growers and importers to sell direct to millers and merchants, the bulk of the sales did not enter into the returns. In Liverpool, especially, the returns were ludicrously inadequate. It was the practice for buyers of corn resident in Manchester, Warrington and other considerable towns to make their purchases in Liverpool, but because they did not live there they were not asked for any returns. Furthermore, Liverpool and district consumed a great deal of Irish corn, which, not being British, was not returnable. The corn, though good of its kind, was inferior to English; and therefore the Liverpool average represented the average not of what was bought and consumed there, but of a high-priced fraction of English-grown corn. In other towns there was just sheer neglect. "It often occurs, particularly in Manchester, Macclesfield and Stockport, that returns are made to

---

[1] *Committee of* 1820. *Report*, p. 8.
[2] *Ibid.* p. 5. This provision was in actual operation between September 1818 and November 1818.

the Receiver of 'None Sold'." In Bristol, "although there are about forty factors and dealers in corn, yet not more than six or seven...ever make any returns".[1] Now, if there had been no inducement to falsify the returns it is possible that these random samples would have deviated but little from the true average. But there were such inducements. "Millers and bakers, when concerned in making the return, may have an interest in making the price (particularly in towns where an Assize of Bread is set) appear high. Merchants and factors of foreign corn may have the same inducement to open the ports and warehouses. Farmers have a pride in the quality of their growth of corn as proved by the sale, and often give large measure, or make up deficiency of weight by additional quantity."[2] A notorious case of manipulation was quoted from Liverpool. On a recent occasion returns had been made to the following effect: "2,300 qrs. of British wheat at 50s. per qr.", while the true average of the market had been from 68s. to 70s. "The parties by whom these returns were made were understood to be considerable holders of British corn, and were induced to resort to this mode of reducing the general averages to promote the purposes of their speculations and to render more improbable the ports being opened for the importation of foreign grain."[3] Inasmuch as each maritime district, like each State in the American Senate, counted equally, regardless of its numerical importance, in the determination of the general average, manipulation was most likely to be tried in the sparsest districts; and accordingly the Committee, while urging an all-round increase of vigilance, proposed to remedy this particular defect by lumping together the returns from all the towns, some 150 in all. They hoped for safety in numbers! The act of 1 and 2 George IV, c. 87 (1821), gave effect to this. The total of the prices of each sort of corn, divided by the total of the quantities of each sort, gave the average which was to be published in the *London Gazette*, and which was to "regulate the importation of foreign corn, meal and flour for consumption, and the taking the same out of warehouse for the purpose of being so consumed, until

---

[1] *Committee of* 1820. *Report*, p. 6.   [2] *Ibid.* p. 6.
[3] *Ibid.* Evidence of John Gladstone, Esq., p. 54.

new average prices shall, under 55 George III, or this act, be made up and notified to the officers of customs ".

On the occasion of a temporary act (7 and 8 George IV, c. 57), passed in July 1827 to permit the entering of warehoused corn for home consumption at certain duties, a further improvement was made (7 and 8 George IV, c. 58). It was an inevitable weakness of the averages that, while used to regulate the future course of trade, they themselves were based on past prices; and this was a serious weakness in a commodity so fluctuating as wheat. The averages might be registering starvation while traders were dealing in plenty. Some check on this had been provided in 1815 for the protection of home growers from Near European shipments by the conditional revision of the averages at the end of six weeks. Otherwise they held for a period of three months. By the 1827 act the averages were revised weekly on the following ingenious plan. The receiver of corn returns got out the average of each week, added that of the preceding five weeks, and then divided by six to get the aggregate average regulating the payment of duties. The principle is the same as that which was employed in the calculation of tithes. The method was retained in the two subsequent corn laws of 1828 and 1842, which embodied one further change. Up to 1828 no returns were taken from the inland districts. They were collected there for statistical purposes but were not used for the corn averages. In the list of 1828, Leicester, Birmingham, Nottingham and Derby occur for the first time. Peel's list of 1842 was obviously intended to include *all* towns of any importance, but not even in this last act was there any town of Scotland or Ireland.

The story of the averages, although of itself, like the history of Poor Law Settlement, intolerably dull, yet throws sinister half-lights on a policy of agriculture which won applause for promise more often than for performance. If the repeal of the corn laws did nothing else, at any rate it abolished a profession from which the country derived no benefit and which in 1846 was said to be very popular along the coast of Norfolk—the profession of "working the averages". Riggers of the market or rum-runners, bootleggers or workers of the averages, they are all part of the human tribe whose absolution was pronounced in advance in paragraph "thirdly" of Article 4 of Part II of chapter II of the Fifth Book of *The Wealth of Nations*. For what is a smuggler? "A person who, no doubt highly blameable for violating the laws of his country, is frequently incapable of violating those of natural justice, and would have been, in every respect, an excellent citizen, had not the laws of his country made that a crime which nature never meant to be so."[1]

Article IV

SALE BY MEASURE OR SALE BY WEIGHT

A commodity like corn may be sold by measure or by weight. In order to be able to publish official prices of corn, Parliament in times past found it necessary to select one of the bushels in use as the legal or official (but not compulsory) bushel. The one selected was the Winchester bushel. Others were known as customary bushels. The Winchester bushel was the smallest in common use and held eight gallons. Sale by measure was the method in general use at the end of the eighteenth century. Sale by weight, in a complicated form to be hereafter explained, is the method which was used during the latter part of the nineteenth century down to a recent day.

In the eighteenth century, as in previous centuries, the bushel varied in capacity in different parts of the country. When, therefore, the magistrates were called upon to fix the price of bread with reference to that of wheat, they had first of all to find out what a bushel in their locality signified. If it was a customary bushel it had to be reduced to the Winchester bushel, and the magistrates had recourse to tables in which the necessary calculations were made.[2]

Arthur Young complained that "magistrates are very embarrassed to fix the Assize of Bread...from the variety of customary measures, for they are confined to the average price of corn and the Winchester bushel; hence the Assize where large customary

---

[1] *Wealth of Nations*, II. 381.
[2] One such table is reproduced at the end of Charles Smith's *Tracts on the Corn Trade and Corn Laws, Observations...in setting the Assize of Bread*, p. 14.

bushels obtain is necessarily favourable to the baker....This is an evil of very serious magnitude".[1]

The conversion tables, we may suppose, were not always used, particularly in country districts; and in any case, if several measures were in use in the same locality, the magistrates could not find out how many sales were made with each. This point was enlarged upon by Charles Dundas, a correspondent to the Scarcity Committee of 1795–6.[2] "The uncertain practice of selling corn in the country market by measures of various sizes", he wrote, "is an evident fraud upon the consumers of Bread and an advantage to none but the jobbers in corn; who from practice are as well acquainted with the size of every farmer's bushel as with his face. As the measure varies almost every ten miles, the difference is a great encouragement to corn-dealers."[3] Hence, table or no table, the averages were falsified. For suppose in a place where the nine-gallon measure was customary a ten-gallon measure was offered by a farmer. The dealers, observing this, would bid it up, but the clerk would return it as a sale at the customary measure of nine gallons; thus making the market price of wheat by the customary measure too high.

Young and his correspondent were but acting in accordance with the universal maxim, *Where prices rise blame the middleman*, and so they blamed the bakers and dealers, just as a later age would have blamed the railway companies. The errors of which both complained favoured the baker by bringing the officia averages too high. But there were other errors in the Assize, errors in the opposite direction, such as reference to the prices of coarse wheat, when the baker was only buying fine flour. Peradventure Providence cancelled error by error! As for the people who were supposed to be the sufferers, they abetted the dealers in their supposed double-dealing. The Winchester bushel was a small one, and the people hated it because it was small. They loved their own because it was their own and because

---

[1] *Annals of Agriculture*, vol. XIV (1790).

[2] It sat for two sessions and reported on the High Price of Provisions and the High Price of Corn respectively. The Committee of 1800–1 issued all its Reports under the title of High Price of Provisions.

[3] *Committee (H. of C.) on the High Price of Provisions. 3rd Report*, App. No. 3. Letter from Charles Dundas of Barton Court near Newbury.

it was big. The bigger it was the better they loved it, for they thought thereby to get cheaper measure, brimful and running over. On popular unreason reform, as so often happens, stumbled.

By 5 George IV, c. 74 (1820), the Winchester bushel was, for official purposes, statistics and the calculation of the corn averages, replaced by the Imperial bushel, a slightly bigger bushel.[1] But the new measure was not made compulsory, and in this position it remained for a century—until the Corn Sales Act of 1921, which came into force on Jan. 1, 1923, made the hundredweight of 112 pounds the only recognised unit of measurement for the sale not only of cereals but also of meal, beans, potatoes and agricultural seeds. "How it was that steps to this end had not been taken years before will always be a mystery," says Mr J. A. Venn in his *Foundations of Agricultural Economics*, p. 253. Some part of the mystery may perhaps be dispelled by an examination of the evidence contained in various Parliamentary Papers between 1790 and 1900.

The reformers of 1800, dissatisfied with what they had, thought they knew exactly what they wanted, namely, sale by weight. They appealed to the example of Ireland, where all forms of grain were sold in barrels by weight. The practice was of long standing and had been made compulsory by legislation in 1705 and 1733. In Ireland, of all places, the land of contrariness, there was uniformity of measure! From those days to these there was no further legislation for Ireland, which thus retained a monopoly of uniformity.

In 1770 an anonymous pamphleteer wrote: "It is hard to say why this method has not been introduced; for if it was general, every person might be then his own factor. Possibly this very reason is the obstacle, as it is in the interest of some people that the Corn trade should continue to be a mystery".[2] The Scarcity Committee of 1795–6 recommended that corn should henceforth be bought and sold by weight, the standard Winchester bushel to be converted into sixty pounds avoirdu-

[1] Winchester bushel = 35·24 litres.
  Imperial   „   = 36·35 „
Cf. Tooke and Newmarch, *History of Prices*, VI. 353.
[2] *Considerations on the Exportation of Corn* (Anon.), p. 69.

pois, and other grains proportionately; and that weights and balances should be kept in cities and market towns at the charge of the county.[1] In 1800 a well-known writer of the time,[2] when drafting a new corn bill for the consideration of the House of Commons, suggested that in the rates of bounties and import duties a small preference should be given to corn sold by weight. This he thought would introduce the practice without any friction and oust rival methods. In one part of England, indeed, sale by weight was already practised, namely, in Liverpool and district. Liverpool got it from Ireland, as it got so many things— harvesters, potatoes, dockers and slums. By 1801 it had spread from Liverpool through Cheshire, Staffordshire and Shropshire.[3] But doubts of its legality were entertained. "I believe", said John Gladstone, Esq., father of the statesman, to a Committee of 1820,

the opinions of His Majesty's Attorney and Solicitor-General were taken, and I understood that they were disposed to think that the law as it now stands permits the sale of corn by weight, but the trade in Liverpool are by no means satisfied with those opinions and feel great dread of persecution and anxiety that all apprehensions may be removed by a legislative enactment; could the system of selling corn throughout the kingdom be simplified, so as one rule, whether weight or measure, was adopted, a great benefit would be obtained.[4]

There the matter rested until 1834, when, with agriculture again in sore straits, a large and representative Committee, including among others the celebrated statistician and corn factor Thomas Tooke, was appointed "to enquire into the present Practices of Selling Corn throughout the United King-

---

[1] *Committee (H. of C.) appointed to take into consideration the present High Price of Corn*, 1795–6. *5th Report*. They were acting on the advice of their correspondent, Charles Dundas, from whom quotation has already been made. He wrote: "Salt was originally sold by measure, it is now sold by weight (fifty-six pounds to the bushel); the Act which regulated this in one instant equalised all the salt measures in the Kingdom; the same effect would follow a similar proceeding in the sale of corn by which the assize on flour might be justly set and the relation between the articles of corn, flour and bread clearly ascertained and fairly regulated".

[2] Skene Keith, "A General View of the Corn Trade and Corn Laws of Great Britain", *The Farmers' Magazine*, Aug. 1802 (III. 277).

[3] *Committee (H. of C.) on the High Price of Provisions*, 1801. *7th Report*. Evidence of W. Reynolds, a corn-dealer.

[4] *Committee (H. of C.) on Petitions complaining of Agricultural Distress*, 1820. Evidence of John Gladstone, Esq., a Member of the House, p. 55.

dom, with a view to the better regulation thereof ". A map appended to the Report of this Committee shows that sale by weight now extended from Whitby in the north-east to Gloucester in the south-west throughout the area comprising the growing industrial counties of Lancaster, York, Nottingham, Derby, Stafford, Worcester and Warwick. Now this Committee met in a reforming spirit, and we expect them to declare for the reformer's nostrum, sale by weight, but they do not, and their reasons discover the very real difficulties involved in this apparently simple change.

For what determines at any time the value of corn? The state of supply in relation to the state of demand. But states are silent and impersonal; and value is a subjective thing, the product of the clash of individual opinions. In order that buyers and sellers may form a correct opinion of their respective strengths, they must bargain in uniform terms and be able to consult the results of similar bargains concluded by others. It is here that the importance of a good standard comes in. The standard of sale bears to the value of corn the relation which methods of remuneration bear to the value of labour—with this limitation, that the ear of wheat will not, if inaccurately remunerated, shrink in sorrow or burst with indignation. A good standard must be uniform and tell as much as possible.

Now in the sale of corn, argued the Committee of 1834, three things are wanted to be known—quantity, quality and condition. Quality signifies the inherent properties of the corn; condition, its accidental state. The standard can tell nothing about condition. Corn loses condition if badly stored or carried; but if the sample exposed represents fairly the condition of the bulk, be it good or bad, then no inaccuracy is created and no injustice is done. If not, then it is both desirable and just that the bargain should be repudiated or altered. But in the matter of quality the position is different. For a good standard can tell both quantity and quality. Sale by weight gives quantity only. Sale by measure again gives quality only; but sale by measure combined with a description of the actual weight of corn per measure gives both quantity and quality. For the heavier the corn (i.e. the greater the number of pounds which a given measure of it weighs) the better in general will be its quality.

With this in mind and having regard to the fact that sale by measure was in general use in the wheat-growing districts of England and universal throughout the Continent, the Committee of 1834 proposed a bill to secure the following points: (i) that all corn should be sold by the Imperial measure; (ii) that the weight per measure of corn sold should be returned to the Inspectors who kept the official records; (iii) that a memorandum of the quantity sold with the weight per measure should be given by the seller to the buyer; (iv) that, for the special case of Ireland, all shipments from Irish ports should be made in measure with the weight per measure, or in weight (as the custom already was), with the weight per measure. Committees propose and farmers dispose! The bill was never carried.

Pass now over a period of fifty years to a date when British agriculture was again in distress and British growers were well-nigh drowned under the deluge of American wheat. In 1891–3 another Committee on Corn Sales took evidence and made another set of recommendations, which once again were not carried out.

This Committee found that the home trade had evolved for itself a standard which combined quantity and quality, but combined them in a characteristically British fashion—that is to say, with numerous local diversities. The Committee of 1834 had observed the beginnings of this practice and strongly discountenanced it for that reason. In 1891 the great majority of home-grown wheat was sold by "weighed measure", and was so sold until recently. Sales were made by a reference to a measure of capacity such as the bushel or quarter, but the seller guaranteed that the measure would weigh up to a given number of pounds. If the measure of wheat offered for sale weighed up to this or more than this number of pounds, well and good—the buyer made no objection. If it weighed less, the buyer could demand a reduction in the price or even return the corn on the farmer's hands. This practice, which seems to the farmer's disadvantage, had a reason behind it. Wheat, which is lighter than the standard by 3 per cent., may for that reason lose as much as 5 per cent. in value.

This measure of a given number of pounds, this ideal or standard measure, varied in different localities according to the weight of the wheat which is typical of the locality, and as even neighbouring districts vary considerably with regard to fertility, diversities arose at very short distances from each other. The result was a grotesque complexity. To begin with, not all districts which had the "weighed measure" reckoned by the same measure. Whereas most parts of the country reckoned by the statutory bushel, Cumberland used the Carlisle bushel, which was three times the size of the ordinary one. The Eastern Counties reckoned by the coomb of four bushels, the Midlands by the bag, parts of Lancashire by the windle, Lincolnshire by the sack, Newcastle by the boll, Flint by the hobbet. Then each of these measures was weighed up to the standard measure of the locality, to the bushel of 60 or 62 or 63 or 64 pounds, to the coomb of 18 stone, the windle of 220 pounds, the boll of 27 stone, the hobbet of 168 pounds, and so on. Finally, though the most usual standard among traders was the bushel of 63 pounds, the standard employed in the official statistics in accordance with the Corn Returns Act of 1882 was the bushel of 60 pounds. Could confusion be worse confounded? And what did it all avail? It availed the farmer nothing save to gratify his fondness for tradition; and it gave the buyer a check on quality at the cost of persistent complexity and occasional friction. The problem, therefore, before the Committee of 1891 was: how get rid of the hybrid?—by reference to the Imperial bushel in the way that the Committee of 1834 proposed, or by reference to weight, leaving the check on quality to be independently provided? Inasmuch as the "weighed measure" was ultimately a standard of weight rather than of measure, they declared for weight and recommended:

(1) that the sale of all cereals and the products thereof should in future be conducted in Great Britain, as in Ireland, by a reference to the hundredweight of 112 Imperial pounds, and that no other weight or measure of capacity be referred to in any sale;

(2) that in every case where conversion of weighed measure takes place, the weights laid down in...the Corn Returns Act...should always be published in the Returns of Corn Sold in the *London Gazette*, and a statement made to the effect that the prices quoted in

the *Gazette* are the prices for the quarter of eight bushels of such statutory weights.[1]

But nothing happened. Successful as the spirit of the nineteenth century was in drawing a steam-roller over the life of the agricultural labourer and flattening it into a moribund dullness, it failed comically before the marketing peculiarities of the farmer, his master. There was, however, one ground for consolation. In 1891 the farmers were not standing between the country and uniformity, for in the meantime Liverpool had moved on to a weight of its own, different from any used hitherto. Liverpool was now selling by "centals". Mark Lane disliked the innovation and scented an Americanism, but the ex-chairman of the Liverpool Corn Exchange[2] declared that this was untrue. Only California bought and sold by the cental; the rest of America by the bushel of sixty pounds.[3] The cental was adopted in 1858, when the regulation of the weights used in the sale of grain was being agitated in Parliament, and since then it had been carried by merchants in their dealings with millers (not with farmers) over a large part of the country. It "extends up to Carlisle in the north, down the Welsh coast as far as Cardiff; to Oxford in the midlands, to Leicester towards the eastern coast, and to Hull on the far eastern coast; so that the millers and dealers in grain over this enormous area—half England—are entirely familiar with the cental, and yet men talk as if it were an unknown weight".[4] Liverpool's dignity was outraged.

The convenience of the cental of 100 pounds, which is employed in these areas at the present day, is that it is more convenient for calculation than the hundredweight of 112 pounds. One sack—and it is in sacks that the grain is sold from Liverpool —contains 250 pounds, or two and a half centals. "But you

---

[1] *Report*, issued May 15, 1893, p. 7.

[2] *Committee* (*H. of C.*) *on Corn Sales*, 1893. Evidence of Mr H. C. Woodward, Qs. 505, 599.

[3] In 1858, i.e. ten years after the gold rush, California began to ship flour and wheat to the European market around Cape Horn. In the 'eighties wheat was superseded as an export crop by citrus fruits, the bulk of which are marketed on the American continent.

[4] *Committee* (*H. of C.*) *on Corn Sales*, 1893. Evidence of Mr H. C. Woodward, Q. 522.

told us", Mr Woodward was asked, "that you buy wheat 60 pounds to the bushel; does that mean that every bushel must weigh 60 pounds?" "No, it is scarcely this; the bushel has practically nothing to do with it; you simply shovel so much wheat into the sack and then weigh the sack, and when you have weighed the sack you lose sight of the bushel altogether."[1] Did Liverpool then of all places pay no attention to quality? No; for the quality had already been checked and determined by the elaborate system of grading which was conducted in America. England led the way with the grading of metals in the eighteenth century, America extended the grading system independently to the great agricultural staples; and it was a pure coincidence that at the time Liverpool was introducing the cental, Chicago was building grain elevators and grading grain.

Therefore we must, in conclusion, ask a question which we have hitherto suppressed, namely—How was a big market like Liverpool able to sell by weight before the days of grading?[2] The answer seems to be that Liverpool did not altogether do so. The grain was weighed in sacks containing so many bushels, so that any serious deviation from the normal weight per bushel could be detected. This means that Liverpool was in effect using a "weighed measure". But how did Ireland or any other place ever get on with sale by weight only? The answer seems to be that Ireland was mainly a producer of oats and that in this ruder cereal variation is less important. In England malting

---

[1] *Committee (H. of C.) on Corn Sales*, 1893. Evidence of Mr H. C. Woodward, Q. 553.

[2] Mr S. Dumbell, in a memorandum upon this article, observes here: "Before the coming of grading in a highly organised market dealings are only made possible by the use of samples, whether on a basis of sale by weight or by measure. The weight of a sack of given capacity would indicate the natural weight of the grain, but only the sample would tell its colour and dryness. The weight of the sack would roughly determine the quality, but in the hand of the expert the sample would give, with sufficient accuracy, both quality and condition" (*Economic Journal*, March 1925, p. 144).

I take leave to emphasise this. Whether grain is sold by weight, measure or "weighed measure", it must be supported by sufficient guarantee or by sample. In Canada, under the elaborate provisions of the Canada Grain Act, the wheat receives its final grading in terminal elevators equipped with Automatic Samplers; and on the certificates then issued Liverpool trades. But formerly (and to-day in the wheat of countries possessing less assured machinery) samples were employed. Mr Dumbell quotes authority for the use of samples in all corn sold at Liverpool in 1821.

barley, which often sells at a higher price than wheat, has hitherto been sold by measure alone; for weight was of no consequence, or rather it was a drawback, the best barley being thin-skinned and light. But grinding barley, which is frequently cheaper than oats, is sold by weight, since the question of quality does not enter in.

There is generally a reason for the way in which things are done, even though there are transcending reasons for doing them differently; and a mystery ceases to be mysterious when we pry into its historical evolution.

CHAPTER V

1815 ON TRIAL

WE resume now the story of the corn laws at the point where the bill of 1815 became law.

The average price of wheat in 1814 was 74s. 4d. But peace and a decent harvest in 1815 brought it down in January 1816 to 52s. 10d., the lowest since July 1804; and agriculture gave evidence of distress. The Chancellor of the Exchequer attributed the fall to the delay of the legislature in passing the corn bill; and it is, indeed, possible that speculation upon its terms was responsible in part for the heavy imports of 1814 (850,000 qrs.). But the debate of 1816 on agricultural distress went further afield. Squire Western's Resolutions (it was he who had introduced the corn law of 1804) complained of the insufficiency of demand, of excessive taxation as compared with other countries, of excessive taxation as compared with other occupations and notably of the burden of tithes and poor rates.[1] The Resolutions were printed for further consideration. For the time being the agriculturists found some relief in the operation of the new law: for, the price being now under 80s. a quarter, importation was prohibited. During the next seven years, 1815–22, the ports were alternately open and closed, according as the price of wheat, computed from the averages, was over or under 80s. the quarter. No revenue was derived from import duties, foreign grain either entering free or being shut out altogether. It was a rigid, inelastic law. From 74s. in the midsummer of 1816 the price of wheat rose irregularly to 112s. 8d. in June 1817; and then fell irregularly to an average of 39s. in the last quarter of 1822.[2] The fluctuations of price were attended by irregularity of import which, reacting on the home supplies, made the three-monthly average still more irregular. The ports were now open and now closed:

---

[1] Hansard, XXXIII. 1086.
[2] Cf. Table in Tooke, I. 390.

1815   –Nov. 1816 closed.
Nov. 1816–Nov. 1817 open.
Nov. 1817–Feb. 1818 closed.
Feb. 1818–Sept. 1818 open.
Sept. 1818–Nov. 1818 closed (for imports from near ports).
Nov. 1818–Feb. 1819 open.
Feb. 1819–1822   closed.

The law conformed tardily and clumsily to the requirements of
the market. Thus the harvest of 1816 was short, but prices
having to remain over 80s. for three months, the ports were not
opened till November 1816. This aggravated distress in the
industrial districts. The harvest of 1818 was good, but by accident or contrivance the November return of the averages was
80s. 2d. Therefore from November 1818 to February 1819 importers rushed in wheat, swelling an abundance to which the
expectation of an 80s. price had given birth. The law of 1815
recoiled on the head of its authors.

As late as 1820, however, Huskisson, who was one of them,
was ready to defend it. It had saved from destruction the
capital of farmers who occupied inferior soils: it had continued
the policy of encouraging the growth of corn in Ireland: it had
relieved us from a dependence on other countries which might
involve us in revolution and the subversion of the State. It had
therefore "answered the purposes for which it was intended".[1]
In 1825 he surveyed its shortcomings:

He had always understood that the great *desideratum* in this
important question was, to provide for a steadiness of price, and to
guard against excessive fluctuations in it from the vicissitudes of
trade. How did the present law provide for these ends? By
limiting the markets from which we drew our supplies—by destroy-
ing the vent which we should otherwise have for our produce,
whenever we were blessed with a superabundant harvest—and by
exposing us to an alternate fluctuation of high and low prices.[2]

In 1828, two months only before his resignation, virtually over
corn-law policy, his language was that of warm denunciation:

He lamented, from the bottom of his soul, the mass of evil and
miseries and destruction of capital which that law, in the course of its
twelve years' operation, had produced. And he did believe that he
could make it distinctly appear, if the moment were a proper one, that

[1] *Speeches*, II. 47.   [2] *Ibid*. II. 395.

the effect of the bill, as far as regarded the agriculturists themselves, had been to keep the prices of produce lower, for those twelve years, than they would have been, even if the trade in corn had been entirely open.[1]

But the pages of Hansard tell only half of the tale. In the early 1820's in the Committee Rooms of the Commons and among the pamphleteering public the activity was great. In 1821 the petitions of distress were referred to a Select Committee. T. S. Gooch was chairman, and Huskisson drafted the report. Huskisson was ever a learner, and this time his teachers were the witnesses before the Committee, and in particular the corn merchants, Thomas Tooke, David Hodgson, a partner in the Liverpool house of Cropper, Benson and Co., which since 1815 had been issuing crop surveys, and also William Jacob, a merchant (and incidentally the father of the Senior Wrangler of 1816), appointed Comptroller of Corn Returns in 1822—he it was who reported to the Government in 1825 and 1827 on the conditions of agriculture in Northern Europe, and at the instance of Huskisson made *An historical Inquiry into the Production and Consumption of the Precious Metals* (1831). To the precision of the experts Huskisson added his own genius for historical retrospect and cautious change. In his Report he recalled the period between 1773 and 1815, when owing to the moderation of the law and the suspension of its provisions during the French wars, the trade in corn was "practically free". (Here we have yet another version of 1773.) In this period agriculture prospered, and the question now was "whether the only solid foundation of the flourishing state of Agriculture is not laid in abstaining as much as possible from interference, either by protection or prohibition, with the application of capital in any branch of industry". The admission of corn by fits and starts raised freights and depressed the exchanges. Greater protection was impossible, because "protection cannot be carried further than monopoly". The Report therefore advocates a return, with safeguards, necessitated by the sensitive nature of the corn market, to a comparatively free trade, such as prevailed before 1815; and, suddenly switching from agriculture, concludes with a homily on the sanctity of the return to cash payments.

[1] *Speeches*, III. 257.

This was a change of face, as repulsive to the Tories as Peel's sudden conversion to Catholic Emancipation in 1829. Huskisson was accused of having mystified his coadjutors, and in 1822 a second Committee was appointed, which fully concurred in the defects of the present system and made proposals for disposing of the large stock of corn accumulated in bond. These were the basis of the abortive corn law of 1822 (3 George IV, c. 60).

Huskisson had desired to use the existing congestion as a means of returning to a permanently open trade in corn; whereas the act of 1822 opened the ports to new wheat only when the home price should have reached 80s. and *closed them again* when it should fall below 70s. As the former figure was never reached, the act never came into effect except for the section relating to colonial corn. The discussion preceding this law evoked a proposal from Ricardo for a fixed duty on corn, which he elaborated in his *Protection to Agriculture* (1822); and though he died in 1823, his proposal occupied reformers for many years.[1] From 1823 to 1827 the corn-law question was in abeyance. Huskisson was promulgating his great commercial reforms, which, when accomplished, took away from the land-lords the *tu quoque* they had so often employed against merchants and manufacturers. The people were absorbed, under the inspiration of Owen, as never before or since, in searching speculation upon the fundamentals of society. For these were the birth years of Co-operation and Socialism. However, without raising the general principle, it was expedient for Canning and Huskisson to do something for the corn merchants of Liverpool (their constituents past and present), where corn lay rotting in

---

[1] Ricardo argues that the depression of agriculture in 1821 was due to the lower prices caused by abundant home crops and Irish imports. But the fall had been aggravated by the operation of the corn laws, which made the price of corn in average years greatly to exceed the price in other countries, and in proportion as it was raised liable to a greater fall. To obviate this enormous evil, the undue protection to agriculture should be gradually withdrawn. A fixed duty, beginning at 20s., should be lowered by annual reductions of 1s. to 10s.: which would represent a liberal allowance for the extra taxes paid by farmers, as compared with those paid by the other classes of producers in the country.

Those, however, who find in this tract an argument for the return to agricultural protection to-day may be reminded that, if pressed with Ricardian logic, it would prescribe the extra taxation of agricultural produce, to offset the immunity from local rates.

bond. In 1824 permission was given to grind it for re-export
(5 George IV, c. 70). In 1825 a limited quantity of old warehoused grain was admitted into the general consumption of the
country on payment of a substantial duty (6 George IV, c. 65).
These were trifles, but even so they alarmed the agriculturists
and Huskisson had to soothe them in language that is laughably
sententious. He protested in 1824 that the agriculturists need
not be alarmed. Nothing would escape on to the home market,
except a little bran. Nay, rather, they ought to rejoice.

The tubs, hoops, etc. in which flour came from Dantzic were
formed in that country, and gave employment to a vast number
of industrious mechanics. If we allowed foreign grain to be ground in
this country, and afterwards exported from it, the tubs which contained it must be formed of staves taken from the demesnes of English
gentlemen and brought into shape by the industry of their tenantry.[1]

Home-made tubs carried the day, and the bill was allowed to
pass.

In 1827, when Canning was premier, Huskisson made a final
effort for a general settlement. There was no talk yet of total
repeal; the choice lay between a fixed duty and a sliding scale.
The fixed duty avoided reference to those slippery things "the
averages", and it had the approval of Ricardo. But the ground
on which Ricardo had based his *Protection to Agriculture*, the
special disabilities of agriculture, ruled it out for a Tory
Government. For such protection was grounded on quicksand.
If the farmer's poor rate or the tax on farm horses was diminished, so would his claim to protection, and all the while he
would be a lame dog, whining for special treatment. Huskisson,
therefore, chose a sliding scale, which was in accordance with
corn law precedent and seemed to meet the worst feature in the
law of 1815, its rigidity. A gradual scale would help to restore
smoothness to the course of trade. But a scale assumed a pivot
point at which reasonable protection was afforded and from
which, as prices rose, the duty would gently descend. The
agriculturists declared that Huskisson's pivot point of 60s., with
the duty of 20s. set against it, was inadequate and threw out the
bill on a technical point. (A clause, which had formed a part of

---

[1] *Speeches*, II. 280.

every corn law since 1773, permitted warehousing without duty;
and to guard against abuses of this the Duke of Wellington
introduced an amendment, which in effect would have permitted a single individual to veto the importation of grain.) In
its place a one-year act confined to bonded corn was hurried
through (7 and 8 George IV, c. 57). In handling the general
bill Huskisson had fallen foul of the Duke of Wellington. He
re-drafted the Duke's amendment in a way which the Duke
accepted but misunderstood. The Duke's point was that having
pointed out what he considered to be a permanent evil Huskisson
had no business to provide only a temporary safeguard. But
they were at cross-purposes fundamentally. "My object", said
Huskisson, at the close of the long explanation which he made
to the House on June 18, 1827, "is to restore the corn law to
what it was in 1773."[1] That was the object of his Report of
1821. But it was not the object of the Duke and his friends.
They, without regard to the course of trade, were bent on
consolidating the fortress which they had taken over from a
generation of war. Relations, therefore, were already strained
when Huskisson accepted office under Wellington in 1828; and
he was out of office when the law of 1828, sometimes known
as the "Duke of Wellington's Sliding Scale", was passed
(9 George IV, c. 60).

This law was in force until 1842, when it was replaced by
Peel's sliding scale (5 and 6 Victoria, c. 14), which held the
field till 1846, the year of general corn-law repeal. The sliding
scale was not a revolutionary device like the prohibition of
1815; for the corn laws before 1815 had been developing in
this direction. Thus, in the act of 1804, there were six distinct
stages:

At or above 66s.	2nd low duty	$7\frac{1}{2}d.$[2]
63s. to under 66s.	1st ,, ,,	3s. $1\frac{1}{2}d.$
Under 63s.	High duty	30s. $3\frac{3}{4}d.$
Over 54s.	Export prohibited.	
Over 48s. to 54s.	Export without bounty.	
At or under 48s.	Export with bounty.	

The stages would have been increased to nine if a proposal to

---

[1] *Speeches*, III. 174.
[2] As augmented, see above, p. 31.

grade the bounty, emanating, Dr Skene Smith tells us, from himself,[1] had been adopted:

Under 45s. Bounty of 1s. 6d.
Under 42s.   ,,   3s.
Under 39s.   ,,   4s. 6d.
Under 36s.   ,,   6s.

To the mind of Parliament at that time, 54s. to 63s. was the range representing equilibrium. In the sliding scales of the later laws the range was contracted to a point, known as the pivot. At prices below the pivot the duty rose till it reached a prohibitive height. It was an argument addressed to the foreigner *ad terrorem*. At prices above the pivot, the duty declined till it reached zero in accordance with the traditional regard for the consumer on the advent of scarcity. The precise point that would register equilibrium was a matter of fancy. In 1814 Parnell suggested 85s.: in 1815 Parliament took 80s., at the same time converting the pivot into a peg. Huskisson in 1827 suggested 60s. or 62s. The act of 1828 took 66s. Peel in 1842 avoided the specification of a pivot by ranging the duties in a single descending scale from 18s. downwards to zero. But in his introductory speech he suggested that 56s., the average of the last ten years, was a fair remunerating price. "I do not believe, that it is for the interest of the agriculturist that it should be higher."[2]

The duty set opposite the pivot was the protection to which the farmer was considered to be entitled in normal conditions. In 1815 no amount of duty was thought equal to the task of repressing the foreign deluge; and so below 80s. there was prohibition. In 1828 (as in Huskisson's one-year act of 1827) the duty opposite the pivot was 20s. 8d. Peel had no pivot, but the duty opposite the "fair remunerating price" was 15s.

The sliding scale of 1828 was Huskisson's sliding scale spoiled. But even Huskisson's scale would have failed to satisfy. For just as the law of 1815 deluded the farmer into the belief that he was secured in a price of 80s., so those of 1827 and 1828 encouraged the belief that he was safe for 62s. or 66s. But the law did not protect him against himself and the bounty of nature. Superior production, abetted by favourable weather,

---

[1] *The Farmers' Magazine*, August 1802 (III. 294).
[2] Hansard, 3rd S. LX. 226. (See Appendix, p. 176.)

reduced prices again and again to an unremunerative level between 1815 and 1842. In returning to a scale of duties the legislature went only half-way towards ancient practice. The eighteenth century had a remedy for surplus, the export bounty. The logical complement to a sliding scale on imports was a graduated bounty on exports, but this no statesman after the war dared to propose. It would have seemed unholy even to the Duke of Wellington; and a bounty on production, regardless of its destination, would have beggared the Treasury.

Furthermore, the machinery of the sliding scale involved irregularity in the flow of imports. At a time of impending scarcity it was to the public interest that the inflow of foreign corn should begin at once. But the sliding scale turned the interest of the merchants to the opposite. For since the duty declined as the price rose, the rise in the home prices offered to the importer not only a higher price when it reached our market, but also easier terms of entry when it passed the customs. The importer, therefore, withheld his corn until the duty was nominal, and this meant holding it until scarcity and suffering were acute.

This defect was inseparable from any sliding scale, but that of 1828 was so contrived as to magnify it. For in order to combine a greater measure of protection with an equal concern for a hungry public, the point of free import was left at 72s. a quarter as Huskisson had proposed, but the pivot point of "reasonable" protection was raised by 4s. to 66s.; and therefore instead of even drops of 2s. per 1s. of higher price, as Huskisson intended (20s. 8d. at 62s., 18s. 8d. at 63s. to 1s. at 72s.), there were big jumps at the lower end of the scale:

Price	Duty	
s.	s.	d.
66–67	20	8[1]
67–68	18	8
68–69	16	8
69–70	13	8
70–71	10	8 ⎫
71–72	6	8 ⎬ 4s. drops
72–73	2	8 ⎭
At or over 73	1	0

[1] The odd 8d. appears to be due to the adoption of the rather larger Imperial bushel in 1825.

After 70s. the duty had to gallop in order to be at 1s., when the price was 73s. This played into the hands of speculators, who now had a big and palpable interest in withholding sales, since if prices rose by a few shillings many shillings of duty might be avoided. The extent of this speculative profit was worked out in detail by Mr D. Salomons[1] in a pamphlet which was widely read.

For the same reason there was an additional inducement to hold British wheat for a rise. For speculators calculated that foreign wheat would be held back until it could come in free. A handsome profit was assured, provided that Parliament did not suspend the law.[2]

Between 1828 and 1841 the rival merits of a sliding scale and a fixed duty (no one suggested a reversion to prohibition) were canvassed with academic vigour. Some farmers favoured the fixed duty as the one device which had not been tried. The Radicals supported it unanimously. Lord John Russell committed the Whigs to it in 1841, on the eve of losing office, and J. R. McCulloch published a powerful pamphlet in its support. He showed how the corn laws disturbed the export of manufactures and the money market:

Under ordinary circumstances, an increase of imports is always accompanied by a corresponding increase of exports; but to bring this about, the increase must neither be sudden nor excessive; for, if so, the chances are a thousand to one that this foreign demand for our products will not increase to an equal extent. Corn is the principal means which the Poles have of paying for English goods; and, as we frequently shut it wholly out, their imports from England are unavoidably below even the average amount of their exports, so that when we have an extraordinary demand for corn, the greater part of the excess must be paid for in bullion; and instead of bringing benefit by its occurrence our commercial and manufacturing interests are deeply injured....

Most fortunately we did not require to import any foreign corn in 1835 and 1836; but no one either in the Bank of England or out of it acquainted with the circumstances can have the smallest doubt that had it been necessary to make the same payments for foreign corn we had to make in 1830 and 1831, and in 1838 and 1839, the Bank must

---

[1] *Reflections on the Operation of the present Scale of Duty, etc.*, 1840.

[2] Cf. *Commons Committee on Agriculture*, 1836. Evidence of Mr Ruding, Corn Factor, Qs. 170–82.

have stopped payment.... The severe pressure on the money market in 1839 mainly originated in the same circumstances.[1]

But McCulloch was as little helpful to Peel as Ricardo to Huskisson. He offered the duty as a sop to farmers' disabilities and "not because we think it is required to protect agriculture or that it will be of any material service to agriculturists". The sop, moreover, was insecure. For the corn merchants examined by the Agricultural Committees of 1833 and 1836 were agreed that a duty of 15s., 10s. or even 5s. per quarter would lead to popular disturbances in dear seasons and have to be dropped. This, too, was Peel's view in 1842; and furthermore there was a constitutional objection to a suspension of the law by the executive. Peel, therefore, made one last effort to improve the corn laws in accordance with the ancient tradition of protection in seasons of plenty and free import in seasons of scarcity. As a sliding scale, Peel's corn law of 1842 was perfect; for as the duties throughout were very much lower, they declined no faster than the price rose—a shilling fall of duty for a shilling rise of price—and at the point where free import approached there was a halt in the scale instead of a sudden jump. But the real merit of Peel's scale was that it concealed in ancient clothing a considerable reduction of protection all along the line.

Meanwhile, the Anti-Corn Law League had been founded and declined to listen either to sliding scale or fixed duty. Fiscal melioration was translated by the efforts of the League into a nation-wide campaign for the overthrow of a social injustice. They regarded the corn laws as Gladstone regarded corrupt charities: "it is better to remove an iniquity than to tax it".[2] Total repeal was the cry that had won the anti-slavery fight in 1833, and it was to win again now.

[1] *Statements, illustrative of the Policy and Probable Consequences of the proposed repeal of the Corn Laws; and the imposition in their stead of a moderate fixed duty on foreign corn when entered for consumption* (Edinburgh, 1841), p. 10. I venture to add Professor Foxwell's note in the copy in the Goldsmiths' Library: "Wise and moderate advice by the best informed and most level-headed economist of his day: unfortunately the question was referred to the mob and the hustings. The country paid dearly for this blunder".

[2] Cf. F. W. Hirst, *Gladstone as financier and economist*, p. 288.

CHAPTER VI

THE LEAGUE AND REPEAL[1]

THE Anti-Corn Law League originated in a dispute concerning the apportionment of housing accommodation in a very desirable residence called Old England. The family had been away for a long time, warring with Bonaparte on the Continent, and while abroad they had drawn freely on the old place for provisions, clothing, money and men. When they came back they expected to find things as they had left them, but the moment they entered the house they noticed differences. Bales of cotton littered the floor, and charts depicting the exports of British manufactures since 1800 covered wall space that had been sacred to the fox's brush. The library table was soiled by ink. Cicero and Bolingbroke lay flat on their backs in a corner of the bookshelf, and standing upright were huge folios marked "Ledger", "Cash Account", "Profit and Loss". From this sad scene they were hurriedly called away, and entering my lady's boudoir, found her prostrate over a dissenter's hymnal.

Clearly there must be domestic re-arrangements. But why could not the parties settle it quietly among themselves? Why must the poor at the park gates be dragged in? Why must a League be created, to educate the people in statistics and make them glow with a sense of their wrongs? The reason is this. The new-comers believed that they were fighting for a national cause intimately affecting those very poor. The old occupants stood for the England that had been, they for the England that was and was coming to be. The issue, as it happened, was fought out over the propriety of certain statutes affecting the importation of foreign corn, known as the Corn Laws. The intruders demanded total repeal, the old occupants scented a conspiracy to eject them from their home, and so a great campaign was waged over the length and breadth of the country. No such tumult attended the last days of the navigation laws.

Manchester sent two Radicals to the Reformed Parliament of

---

[1] The reader is reminded that this chapter appears in substance in the author's *Life and Labour in the Nineteenth Century* (now out of print).

1832, of whom one was C. E. Poulett Thomson, later Lord Sydenham and Governor-General of Canada; but for six years the corn law question hung fire. Attempts to re-open it in 1833 and 1836 were pronounced inopportune by the Whigs in power. The country was enjoying industrial prosperity, and Lancashire had its share of the good times. But in 1837 the trade boom began to crack, and in March 1838, Charles Villiers, the Member for Wolverhampton and a disciple of Bentham, made the first of his annual motions for an enquiry into the corn laws. The House, however, would not give him a hearing, and the Government left the question an open one. Lord Melbourne declared that the Government would take no decided part till it was certain that the mass of the people wanted it. The challenge was promptly taken up with a fury which bewildered this easy-going champion of *laissez-faire*.

In September 1838 a certain Dr (later Sir John) Bowring happened to be passing through Manchester on his return from a commercial mission on the Continent. He was a much-travelled man, with leanings to poetry, and is the author of the hymn, "In the Cross of Christ I glory". Invited by some Manchester free-traders to address them, he opened with a reference to the desolation produced by the recent war between Turkey and Egypt and to the advantages that would be gained by a more general recognition of the principles of peace, and then proceeded to discuss the corn laws:

When I went into Normandy and Brittany, what said the Normans and Bretons? "Why," said they, "admit our corn and then we'll see whether anybody can prevent the importation of your manufactures into France." (Cheers.) "We are millions," said they, "willing to clothe ourselves in the garments you send us, and you have millions of hungry mouths to take our corn." The same language is held by every nation in trade....I have heard it said, and it seems to have had some influence upon the labouring people, that the introduction of foreign corn is the inevitable way to lower wages. I say that, if there be any certain means of raising wages, it is by the admission of foreign corn. (Cheers.) What are the two countries that have had the wisdom to avoid Corn Law legislation? They are Holland and Switzerland; in which wages are higher than in any country in Europe! (Hear, hear!) And that is invariably the case.[1]

[1] A. Prentice, *History of the Anti-Corn Law League* (1853), 1. 65–7. Prentice headed the invitation to Dr Bowring.

Now wages in Lancashire were then falling.

After the address, one of the audience proposed the formation of an Anti-Corn Law Association in Manchester, and a provisional Committee met shortly afterwards to give effect to the idea. Manchester succeeded where London two years previously had failed. October was spent in forming a powerful Committee and collecting subscriptions; and on Thursday, October 25, 1838, Mr Paulton delivered his first Anti-Corn Law Lecture to an enthusiastic Manchester audience. When the Manchester Chamber of Commerce held its meeting on December 13, the excitement was such that it had to be adjourned until December 20, when an amendment drafted by Richard Cobden in favour of complete Free Trade was carried. Mr Thomson, their member —said Cobden—while representing the free-traders of Manchester, had attempted less than Huskisson had done while representing the monopoly interests of the old borough of Liverpool.

By the middle of January 1839, the organisation of the League had been settled, and subscriptions were coming in. Other towns held meetings and sent delegates to a dinner given by the Manchester Association. On January 28, 1839, the Manchester Anti-Corn Law Association was officially launched. A few days later, in the elections to the Manchester Chamber of Commerce, the successful candidates were free-traders, and most of them were members of the newly formed Association.

Shortly after the opening of Parliament delegates from different Anti-Corn Law Associations met in London at Brown's Hotel, Palace Yard, and on February 18, 1839, Charles Villiers moved in the House that the petitions against the corn laws which had been entrusted to him should be referred to a Committee of the whole House. But the motion was negatived without a division.

Before leaving for the North the delegates recommended that the different Associations should be formed into a League, with federal headquarters at Manchester, and that a League circular should be issued. Both recommendations were carried out forthwith; and on Tuesday, April 16, 1839, the first number of the *Anti-Corn Law Circular*[1] was published at Manchester.

The League was now becoming important. The agricultural interest paid it the compliment of forming local associations in defence of the corn laws and finally (1844) in London a central "Agricultural Protection Society". The Conservative press without more ado burst into vituperation. The *Morning Herald* denounced the members of the League as "many of them unprincipled schemers, while of those members who may claim credit for honesty of purpose, there are few of whom it may not be alleged that they are at best conceited socialists".

In May 1839, one of the League's lecturers ventured into the stronghold of Cambridge University; and No. 4 of the *Anti-Corn Law Circular* gives a report of the meeting in the theatre at Cambridge:

When Mr Smith appeared on the stage, he was met by applause from the townspeople and hooting and hissing from the gownsmen. Having commenced, his voice was immediately drowned amid shouts and the blowing of a guard's horn....

Mr Smith: I trust there will be no disturbance. I am anxious for peace. I am a stranger and in physical force you are a hundred and fifty on one.

Gownsmen: Ha! ha! Down with the Chartists.

Citizens: Put them out! Put them out!

Gownsmen: Damn you, come on! Will you fight? Curse the rascals, &c.

Mr Smith: Gentlemen, I implore you not to irritate the people.

Gownsmen: Three cheers for the Corn Laws. Huzza, huzza! While to the cries of the people, "Put them out", &c., they answered, "Damn your eyes—three cheers for Sir Robert Peel, huzza, huzza!" Here the gownsmen exhibited their bludgeons and put themselves in attitude for a battle. The townsmen rose from the pit, climbed into the boxes, amid the most fearful blows, and a regular battle was the result. Hats, gowns, surtouts and coats flew in all directions...and the issue was the complete overthrow of the gownsmen, and their

[1] The Journal was published under three titles:

I. *The Anti-Corn Law Circular*, No. 1 to No. 57, Vol. II, April 16, 1839–April 8, 1841. (Published in Manchester.)

II. *The Anti-Bread Tax Circular*, No. 58, Vol. III to No. 140, Vol. IV, April 21, 1841–Sept. 26, 1843. (Published in Manchester, larger size.)

III. *The League*, No. 1 to end. Sept. 30, 1843–1846. (Published in London, at the League's Office, 67, Fleet Street.)

expulsion from the theatre, amid deafening shouts of victory and three cheers for Mr Smith.

The *Circular* alluded to the incident in its leading article:

The labours of the Council of the Anti-Corn Law League were this morning interrupted by the arrival of Mr Shearman from Cambridge bearing a large blue sack, the contents of which upon being emptied upon the table, proved to be the remains of University caps and gowns (the former very much broken and the latter torn), together with the fragments of divers benches and chairs, which were gathered up by him after the riot in the theatre at Cambridge. As many of our plodding members have yet to learn how the members of our learned Corporations dress, we invite all who are anxious in matters of academic costume to inspect the contents of our blue bag. But still more do we invite those parents and guardians who may think of sending their youth to Cambridge, to inspect these evidences of the kind of discipline their minds are likely to undergo at that University.[1]

The *Cambridge Chronicle* gave the other side.

It was determined to thwart the fellows in their intentions. And the friends of good government and the upholders of the religious institutions of the country, having mustered in great strength, the lecturer had hardly commenced the opening of his budget, ere he was interrupted by the intelligence that his notions did not exactly correspond with those of his audience.[2]

Before the delegates revisited London the League secured official representation in Parliament and an official meeting-place in Manchester. When Poulett Thomson left for Canada in September 1839, R. H. Greg, an active member of the League, was elected in his place; and shortly afterwards the Free Trade Hall was built in St Peter's Fields on a site owned by Cobden. The purses of the manufacturers and the industry "of 100 men for 11 days"[2] avenged the massacre of Peterloo. This temporary pavilion was subsequently replaced by the present Free Trade Hall.

Villiers' third annual motion (1840) was dropped on adjournment, and the Whig Government continued lukewarm. Lord John Russell temporised, while Melbourne was sceptical about manufacturing distress and said that repeal was impracticable.

---

[1] *Anti-Corn Law Circular*, No. 4.
[2] Prentice, *op. cit.* I. 142.

But the League worked on for itself. Their delegates, back again in London, examined agricultural labourers from Bucks, Somerset, and other counties, with a view to proving that wages did not rise with the price of food. Lecture tours were arranged in the Provinces, and an Anti-Corn Law *Almanac* was circulated. The Report of Joseph Hume's Import Duties' Committee (1840) was a bull point for the League, notwithstanding Peel's insistence in December 1841 that he had not read a particle of it.[1] For henceforward the repealers were able to cite the evidence of experts, like MacGregor, Porter and J. Deacon Hume, in favour of complete Free Trade. The estimated burden of the protective duties, as set forth in the Report, made first-class fighting material, which was reprinted and constantly quoted. However, the party leaders were too busy struggling for the Treasury to pay much attention to the Customs House. At the last moment, namely on May 7, 1841, Lord John Russell declared for a fixed duty of 8*s*.,[2] but the death-bed repentance availed nothing, and on May 27, 1841, Peel carried a vote of "no confidence" by a majority of one.

At the ensuing General Election Cobden was returned for Stockport.

With the Tories in office under Peel, the tone of the controversy became more bitter. The League's *Journal* screamed and opened its columns to poetry. The Tories were insolent to the point of folly. In the debate on the Abolition of the Corn Laws (1843) Sir Edward Knatchbull said: "There are pecuniary liabilities created by family settlements, liabilities created under a system of protection, which could not be met if that Protection was removed. Did hon. Gentlemen mean to say that a sweeping measure of the Corn Laws was to make no provision for these liabilities?"[3] The League caused the country to ring with the name of "Dowry Knatchbull". If Peel's supporters (the young Disraeli among them) found some of his measures hard to digest, the League gave itself no such trouble. It labelled them all "poison" and spat. The new Income Tax was an imposition on

---

[1] C. S. Parker, *Sir Robert Peel*, II. 309. Peel to Goulburn, Dec. 18, 1841.
[2] Cf. Spencer Walpole, *Life of Lord John Russell*, I. 369.
[3] Hansard, 3rd S. LXIX. 225.

the middle classes and introduced in order to perpetuate monopolies.[1] The new sliding scale, by a trick of the averages, would increase the degree of protection at the crucial point.[2] The reduction of the timber duties was a great sacrifice of revenue "wholly without necessity *at the present time*. People do not want houses *now*. There are 30,000 empty dwellings within 30 miles of Manchester and a like proportion of unemployed mills, manufactories and workshops".[3]

This is the language of hysteria, but there was cause enough for it. In the summer of 1842 the cloud of industrial depression settled heavily over the North. The air was charged with human electricity. Amid the solemn hush which preceded the storm of August 1842 (the month of the Chartist risings and the General Turn Out), the manufacturers, assembled at Palace Yard, told London the tale of Lancashire's anguish. The Duke of Sussex, on behalf of the Queen, received them favourably. Sir James Graham, the Home Secretary, disgusted them by a statistical survey of mills recently erected, but Peel was visibly impressed and accepted a pamphlet: *How does cheap bread produce high wages?* At this moment of the League's history its members were citizens first and Leaguers second. At other periods of the long struggle they were trying to raise the country to their own high pitch by all the artifices that their shrewd minds could devise—by the passion of their speech and the satire of their pens, by prayers and statistics, by defiance and gibe, by thunderous iteration of their damning monotone—monopoly, landlords' monopoly. But now one great cry of national despair, unorganised, illiterate, with no statistics and with curses for prayers, monotonous only because the pitch was too high for the human ear to catch distinctions, made the League's agitation paltry by the side of its simple passion. The red-hot orators of the League were transformed into pale policemen. The delegates left London for the North, to keep there the peace of Her Majesty whom Peel and Graham served. "They wished for

---

[1] *Anti-Bread Tax Circular*, No. 84. No. 86 quotes from the *Liverpool Journal*: "We fully agree with the League in thinking everything bad of the Income Tax.... It is the very wickedest and most vexatious of taxes which the ingenuity of man ever conceived".

[2] *Anti-Bread Tax Circular*, No. 89.   [3] *Ibid*. No. 87.

peace—they wished for no violence," said John Bright on July 14, 1842, "they would not have the Corn Laws or any other law removed by the shedding of one drop of blood."

By the summer of 1843 the tension in the North had eased and trade showed signs of revival. On July 25, 1843, John Bright was elected member for Durham, to sit beside his friend Richard Cobden, with whom he had made a compact two years before not to rest till the corn laws were repealed. But the year 1843 was a trying one for the League. Peel operated behind the screen of general tariff revision. The Canada corn bill gave them a little scope, and they thanked Lord Stanley for his "back door to the corn growing regions of the United States".[1] But Parliament was more concerned about factory legislation; and the leading members of the League, being manufacturers and Nonconformists, cut a poor figure. In criticism of the educational clauses in the Factory Bill, the journal of the League wrote:

Sir James Graham's plan may stuff the brains of the poor, but it will grind their faces and empty their stomachs. Where was the very peculiar need of this interference? Why pick out the factory poor? They are not worse taught than the agricultural poor. We would join heart and soul to aid an efficient plan of education; but no one can be blind to the animus of this peculiar feeling for the factory districts. ...The whole thing is a masked battery against the march of the League.[2]

However, the heads of the League were resourceful men. They announced "new steps" (inter alia, the circularising of 300,000 electors[3]), and collected £100,000 to put them into effect. "They were not going to waste more time in petitioning Parliament, they would memorialise the Queen and appeal to the whole country." When Cobden made this announcement in Covent Garden Theatre, the audience, we are told, "almost in one mass, rose and burst into a series of the most enthusiastic cheers, which lasted for several minutes, accompanied by waving of hats and handkerchiefs and other tokens of satisfaction".[4]

The appeal to the country took the form of a rural campaign. Hitherto, said the Circular, we have been thinking mainly of

---

[1] The League, No. 72.   [2] Anti-Bread Tax Circular, No. 122.
[3] September 28, 1843. Cobden, Speeches, I. 73.
[4] Ibid. Cobden, Speeches, I. 65.

the towns, now we appeal to the farmers: "A free trade in corn can alone save the farmers".[1] Led by Cobden and Bright, they deluged the countryside with a rain of oratory and tracts. Cobden carried meetings in the strongholds of protection: in Essex, where the squires in vain "mounted their horses and posted up and down the country":[2] in Buckinghamshire at the very gates of Stowe, whose ducal lord was derided for distributing prizes to servants who brought up their families without recourse to the parish.[3] Honest Hodge found tracts in his village inn and learned to spell the big word "MONOPOLY". And even the farmers were persuaded. The League, to be sure, had its rebuffs, but the good harvest of 1842 and consequent low price of wheat, which dissipated the zeal of the towns for instant repeal, disgusted the farmers with Peel's new law, and in meeting after meeting votes were carried against the corn laws. There can be no greater testimony to the persuasive power of the League than this.

In 1844 the pace slackened. Parliament was preoccupied with other things, railways, banking, and factory reform. More dangerous still, the *Times*, the spokesman of the Whigs, called for a rally around the fixed duty. The League was not to be caught: "a fixed duty is a fixed injustice". But certainly a new cry was wanted, and Cobden, taking a leaf out of Tadpole's[4] book, declared for registration. News went round that good free-traders were to qualify as county voters by purchasing 40s. freeholds. "The registration movement", wrote Bright to his sister-in-law, "is creating a great sensation, and in truth I regard it as the ulterior measure of our contest. We shall make short work of some of the monopolist county seats at another election."[5]

In 1845 the tide turned, and when Parliament, after a six months' struggle, dispersed for the summer holidays, the ship of the League was running on the flood. Disraeli averred that

---

[1] *Anti-Bread Tax Circular*, No. 120.
[2] *The League*, No. 2, October 1843.
[3] *Ibid*. No. 10. Article on "Taming the Duke (of Buckingham)".
[4] Taper and Tadpole are the two "politicians" in Disraeli's novel, *Coningsby*.
[5] G. M. Trevelyan, *Life of John Bright*, p. 123.

the League succeeded by a fluke just at the moment when the country was becoming heartily sick of it.[1] But the League knew full well that the country was behind it and listened with glee to the ferment which it was at last creating in Parliament. Its journal[2] reviews the Parliamentary proceedings of 1845. The session began with the retirement of "keep-your-station" Knatchbull from the Conservative Cabinet. On the day before the Queen's speech, the Duke of Buckingham declared that the Cabinet would maintain the existing level of protection; Peel denied that the Government was under any such pledge. Cobden moved for a Committee of Enquiry: "Give me this Committee and I will undertake to explode the whole delusion of agricultural protection". Sidney Herbert, for the Government,[3] besought the landed interest not to come whining for protection. Mr Miles, goaded on by the Rump Parliament of No. 17, Bond Street (the headquarters of the Protection Society), bewailed the low price of corn and cattle. Low wages throughout the manufacturing districts, retorted Graham,[4] was what depressed the price of meat. Reduced to desperation, the country gentlemen plunged their hands into grease and lard.[5] The Customs' Act, pursuant to the new budget, had placed lard and grease on the free list. Mr Branston complained that, if grease were admitted, butter would slip in under the name of grease. Mr Ward called grease protection "the policy of an area sneak". Colonel Windham, the Conservative free lance, who did not "like" Free Trade, now rounded on his own friends. "In 1841 the manufacturing members of Parliament were like Jacks-in-the-box, continually jumping up and down in their places... and he was now sorry to see his agricultural friends following their example."[6] How Peel must have smiled! Not all the pricks of this session came from Disraeli's pointed tongue! My Lords of Buckingham and Richmond received an occasional chastisement.

The hold of the League on the British farmer was clinched by a final move. On February 27, 1845, Bright asked for, and was

---

[1] Trevelyan, *op. cit.* p. 129. Cf. Disraeli, *Life of Lord George Bentinck*, p. 9.
[2] *The League*, No. 99. [3] Hansard, 3rd S. LXXVIII. 818.
[4] *Ibid*. 995. [5] *Ibid*. 1161 sqq.
[6] *Ibid*. 1182.

granted, a Select Committee to enquire into the operation of the Game Laws. The day before, Lord Ashley had written to Peel:

I have made up my mind to vote for Mr Bright's motion if it be fairly and decently introduced. This I much regret, because I had hoped that the subject might be handled by some respectable country gentleman; and I have no satisfaction in following a person who is almost unfitted by his manners for educated society, and of whom I never heard it proved that he was either honest or humane.

But the abuses of the Game Laws are so frightful, and so repugnant to public feeling, that I cannot undertake to refuse, so far as a single vote can go, the prayer that the whole evil be examined, stated, and, if possible, removed.[1]

The Committee rejected the draft report written by Bright, who recommended the complete abolition of the Game Code. The time, he argued, was especially appropriate, since the cultivators of the soil were now about to be subjected to a free competition with the foreign grower. It was an ironical situation. John Bright proposes to relieve the special burdens of agriculture, in order that the agriculturist may be able to sustain a free trade in corn. Lord George Bentinck, as chairman, behaved throughout with scrupulous fairness. But what shall we say of the League?

Cobden, as he was never weary of informing an agricultural audience, was the son of a farmer. Near his house in Heyshott in Sussex were some allotments, one of which was cultivated by a labourer named William Elcomb. Elcomb stated to the Committee that the rabbits ate up all his turnips. They made "50 or 60 holes in which you could bury your fist".[2] "That", he added unfortunately, "is what the gentleman told."[3] The League was always thorough in its methods.

Meantime, between the first and last session of the Game Laws Committee the corn laws had fallen. For in October 1845 the failure of the Irish potato crop compelled Peel to open the Irish ports to wheat and to purchase American maize for the famine-stricken population of Ireland. In the state of public feeling the remission of duties for Ireland meant their remission for England;

---

[1] Parker, *op. cit.* III. 179–80.
[2] *Commons' Committee on the Operation of the Game Laws* (1845), Part I, Q. 16370.   [3] *Ibid.* Q. 16371.

and once remitted, Peel was convinced they could not be re-imposed. Therefore, in November 1845 he asked his Cabinet to consider repeal. Failing to carry the Cabinet with him he resigned, but Lord John Russell, who had declared for free trade in corn on November 22, 1845,[1] was unable to form a government; and (December 20) Peel came back to carry repeal, supported by the leading members of his former Cabinet with the exception of Lord Stanley. The bill was introduced forth-with, and in the face of a running fire from Disraeli and Lord Bentinck, the leaders of the Tory revolt, it reached the Statute Book on June 26, 1846. The act specified that from the date of its passing to February 1, 1849, small duties varying with the home price should be paid on imported grains and that on and after February 1, 1849, there should be a uniform registration duty of 1s. per quarter. The registration duty lasted till 1869. Robert Lowe, when repealing it, remarked, "It is no more difficult to register the arrival of corn without levying a duty of 1s. per quarter on it than it is to roast a pig without burning down the house". But these were incidents of the winding up. The year of decision was 1846, just as 1847 was the victory year of factory reform.

In surrendering office on June 29, 1846, Peel made his apology for the step which his party condemned as "the great betrayal":

The name which ought to be, and will be, associated with the success of these measures, is the name of one who, acting, I believe, from pure and disinterested motives, has, with untiring energy, made appeals to our reason, and has enforced those appeals with an elo-quence the more to be admired, because it was unaffected and un-adorned: the name which ought to be chiefly associated with the success of these measures is the name of Richard Cobden.

Finally of himself he said:

I shall leave a name execrated by every monopolist who, from less honourable motives, clamours for protection because it is conducive to his own individual benefit; but it may be that I shall leave a name sometimes remembered with expressions of goodwill in the abodes of those whose lot it is to labour, and to earn their daily bread by the

---

[1] "Edinburgh Letter to the Electors of the City of London" (*Sir Robert Peel's Memoirs*, II, 175-9): published in the *Times*, Nov. 27.

sweat of their brow, when they shall recruit their exhausted strength with abundant and untaxed food, the sweeter because it is no longer leavened by a sense of injustice.[1]

And Thomas Carlyle agreed. "Here has a great veracity been done in Parliament, considerably our greatest for many years past".[2] Once again a strong Tory had saved the country from its Toryism.

Who, or what, was really responsible for the repeal of the corn laws? The Duke of Wellington swore it was rotten potatoes. "Rotten potatoes have done it all; they put Peel in his d—d fright."[3] Mr Croker declared that Peel's conversion was "nothing but the result of *fright* at the League".[4] Rather, let us say that it was Time in his fullness, celebrating the majority of an infant registered in the Wealth of Nations, and tended in his boyhood by two most estimable nurses, William Huskisson and Sir Robert Peel.

Where dispossessed villagers, starving knitters and wild-eyed Chartists failed, the Anti-Corn Law League succeeded. What was its strength, that it could impose its will upon the Government?

The Anti-Corn Law League was strong in the personality of its leaders. In arguments and persuasive power Richard Cobden was easily first; his greatest accomplishment being the gradual conversion of Peel. ("You must answer this, for I cannot," said Peel to Sidney Herbert in the House after Cobden's speech of March 13, 1845.) After Cobden came John Bright, after Bright the Rev. W. J. Fox. The rest also spoke. Before the crowded audiences in Covent Garden Theatre or the Manchester Free Trade Hall Cobden would lead off with what he loved to call "one short statistical statement".[5] From statistics he passed to an exposure of the latest landlords' fallacy, and then he closed

---

[1] Hansard, 3rd S. LXXXVII. 1054–5. Speech on Resignation, June 29, 1846.
[2] Parker, *op. cit.* III. 378. Carlyle to Peel, June 19, 1846.
[3] C. C. F. Greville, *The Greville Memoirs*, 2nd part, II. 351.
[4] Croker to Duke of Wellington, April 5, 1846. *Croker Correspondence*, III. 65.
[5] Cobden, *Speeches*, I. 66.

on a moral note, with a reference perhaps to the purity of the League's cause or the bribery and corruption which disgraced the League's opponents. Bright followed, to do "a little prize fighting".[1] But Bright's armoury was the Holy Bible. When the corn laws are repealed, "we shall see no more ragged men and women and children parading our streets,...but we shall have the people happy, 'every man sitting under his own vine and fig tree'".[2] Fox lacked the genius of Cobden and Bright, but he was grandiloquent and high-principled. "Our strength is in the principles we hold."[3] "Our principles are not only the dictates of nature but they are the morality of nations."[4]

The League was strong in the nature of its purpose. Its purpose was single and clear—the total and unconditional repeal of the corn laws. To the half measures of the Whigs it turned a deaf ear. The Complete Suffrage Movement, which divided the Chartists in 1842, was the work of a corn law repealer, Joseph Sturge, but Joseph Sturge was the first to remonstrate with the Editor of the *Anti-Bread Tax Circular*, when he dared to suggest that a fixed duty was better than a sliding scale.[5] Chartism was a welter of vague desire frothing behind a political document; the Anti-Corn Law League a palpably peaceful cause exuding sentimental earnestness.

Furthermore, the League's purpose was negative. There was no need for its spokesmen to understand the intricacies of agriculture. They left that to others. Their task was to thwart the wickedness of landlords and to rescue the country from the bondage of monopoly. Negative causes are often exhilarating, and the narrow platform of the Anti-Corn Law League assuaged a combination of desires. It offered to those who would tread it the satisfaction of their business instincts, the chastisement of their social superiors, the applause of the working man, and the undoubted blessing of Heaven.

The League was strong in the quality of its opponents. If the country gentlemen had been craven, there would have been no

---

[1] Trevelyan, *op. cit.*, p. 97.
[2] Speech reported in *Anti-Bread Tax Circular*, No. 116.
[3] Covent Garden Theatre, Feb. 15, 1844. Fox, *Collected Works*, IV. 69.
[4] Free Trade Hall, March 6, 1845. Fox, *Collected Works*, IV. 200.
[5] *Anti-Bread Tax Circular*, No. 73.

controversy at all, but being sensitive folk, who, according to their lights, did their duty by their property and dependants, they took up the challenge and fought a good case on weak ground.

The League can hardly be regarded as an exponent of class warfare, for they welcomed the adhesion of landlords to their cause. They sang the praises of free-trade Peers like Earl Fitzwilliam, Earl Spencer, the Earl of Durham, and Lord Kinnaird; and when their lordships presided at Anti-Corn Law Meetings, they were received with deference and applause. The voting in the House of Commons on the second and third readings of the Repeal Bill has recently been analysed according to occupation. It shows, as we should expect, that the merchant and manufacturers were in strong support. The railway interest, however, was protectionist. "They belonged to the soil, preferring, when need arose, to act as the advocates of its cause rather than to accept the rôle of guardians of any other industry."[1] Landowners, of course, were strongly represented on railway directorates. In the United States, by contrast, in the Granger movement of the 'seventies, the agricultural West was in sharp conflict with the railroading East. There pioneer farmers sought to curb the entrenched monopoly of Eastern finance. But in England in 1840 the boot of monopoly was on the other foot.

In controversy the landlords usually got the worst of it. The League twitted them for the backwardness of their methods. "We have a right", said the League's journal virtuously, "to demand that the same degree of science, industry, capital and enterprise, so far as they are available, should be applied to land which have been so successfully devoted to manufactures."[2] Only the landlords themselves knew the thousands they had sunk in drainage (and "nitrate o'soder"), but when Cobden, on a railway journey from Stafford to Manchester, espied some watery tracts, he entered it in his notebook as material for his next big speech. "Three-quarters of the finest fields left to undisturbed

---

[1] *Economica*, April 1929, p. 60. J. A. Thomas, *The Repeal of the Corn Laws*, 1846.

[2] *Anti-Corn Law Circular*, No. 9.

dominion of rushes, not a shilling spent in draining...hedge-rows of every imaginable shape except a straight one."[1] Indeed, according to the League, it was their prodding which kept the landlords up to the mark. "We", said Cobden, "are the great agricultural improvers of this country."[2] So the League had the argument both ways. If swamps were undrained, the fault was the landlords'. If land was improved, the credit lay with the League. If the country gentlemen modestly referred to the achievements of progressive landlords, the League retorted with the example of Scotland, whose landlords were free-traders and more progressive and gave long leases to boot. If the agriculturists protested that they suffered under special burdens, the manufacturers declared that they suffered under worse, for they suffered under the crushing burden of the corn laws.

The country gentlemen were persuaded that the object of corn law repeal was cheap bread and low wages; and their accusation was not unnatural. When repeal was first argued in Parliament by Villiers, his central argument was that the legislature had burdened manufactures with an immense weight of taxation, the direct tendency of which was to offer a premium on the consumption of foreign products and to induce British capitalists to seek an investment for their money in other countries.[3] Now, how could the corn laws be said to add an immense weight of taxation to the manufacturers, except by increasing their labour costs, and how would the repeal of the corn laws lighten this burden, except by reducing those labour costs? A reduction of labour costs is not the same thing as a reduction of wages, but the country gentlemen could hardly be blamed for connecting the two. And the scandalous conditions of employment in factories and mines, into which a Royal Commission was then enquiring, made the employers of labour an easy target.

"We tell the people", said a reverend pamphleteer, "that if corn

[1] Covent Garden, Sept. 28, 1843. Cobden, *Speeches*, I. 70.
[2] Manchester, Oct. 19, 1843. Cobden, *Speeches*, I. 104.
[3] Hansard, 3rd S. XLI. 909, March 15, 1838.
Cf. also: "In France, in Switzerland and various other countries the manufactures were now successfully competing with England in consequence of the cheapness of food and of production, and would in a short time completely exclude us from the Continental markets" (*ibid*. 919).

declines 50 per cent., their wages will decline in exactly the same proportion. So that the millowners, the perpetrators of white slavery in our factories, the advocates of the grinding New Poor Law, the greatest enemies of the real liberty of the subject, will be the only gainers."[1]

When the League started its propaganda, it saw the danger of Villiers's line of argument. Again and again the orators of the League repudiated the notion that they wished to reduce wages. Thus Cobden:

If the members of the Anti-Corn Law League, who are manufacturers, want a repeal of the Corn Laws with the idea that to cheapen food would enable them to reduce wages they are the most blind, and apparently the most besotted class of men that ever existed; for, if one may trust all experience, the effect of a free trade in corn must inevitably raise the money rate of wages in the North of England, at the same time that it will give the working classes their enjoyments, comforts and the necessaries of life at a cheaper rate than they have hitherto had them....I say, from the facts I have told you, that the effect of the repeal of the Corn Laws, if it be to cheapen the price of food, will be to lighten distress and to give a demand for labour by extending our foreign trade. If it reduce the price of bread, looking to all past experience, the effect in Lancashire, Yorkshire, and all the manufacturing districts, must be to raise the money rate of wages.[2]

The League contended that the persistence of this charge was due to the mistaken idea of agriculturists, that in industry wages followed the price of food. They answered Ricardo out of Adam Smith: "Wages of labour do not in Great Britain fluctuate with the price of provisions. These vary everywhere from year to year, frequently from month to month. But in many places the money price of labour remains uniformly the same sometimes for half a century together".[3] Then they went on to show by statistics that the labourers' comforts had been greatest when the price of corn was lowest, and that "every extreme rise in the price of food during the last 50 years had been attended with riots and bloodshed".[4] They accused the corn laws, not only of

[1] Rev. S. Isaacson, M.A., *The Duties of the Electors at the Present Crisis* (1841), p. 5.
[2] Covent Garden, July 3, 1844. Cobden, *Speeches*, I. 200–2.
[3] *Wealth of Nations*, I. 76.
[4] *Anti-Corn Law Circular*, No. 5.

raising the price of food, but also of producing an unnatural clash of interest between agriculture and manufacture.

I challenge anyone to point out an instance ever since these Corn Laws were introduced, wherein the agriculturalists and the manufacturers have had simultaneous prosperity. Now, I ask, is this a natural state of things? Is this alternation of distress—this intermittent fever, now attacking the one great portion of the body politic, and then the other...is this a natural state of things?...No; there is an unnatural cause for this unnatural state of things, and that unnatural cause is the law which interferes with the wisdom of the Divine Providence and substitutes the law of wicked men for the law of nature.[1]

The agricultural and manufacturing interests Cobden compared to the two buckets in a draw-well, the one going down empty as the other comes up full. "In proportion as there is a revival of manufactures, consequent upon moderate prices in food, we hear the cry of manufacturing distress."

The moral appeal reinforced an economic appeal to which Peel's Government itself subscribed. Gladstone, justifying Peel's revision of the tariff, argued in 1895: "Though we cannot in every particular case assume an immediate trade outwards when we trade inwards, yet it is manifest that upon the whole such is the law which must govern our commercial transactions".[2] Quite so, said Cobden; and every cargo of corn which comes from abroad will benefit the working man in two ways: there will be the corn for him to eat, and the corn will be paid for by manufactures which increase the demand for his labour.[3]

The charge which should really be levelled at the manufacturers is their exaggeration of the effects of the corn laws. It never seemed to occur to them that they had it in their own power, whether there were corn laws or whether there were not, to raise wages and improve the conditions of employment. They were not selfish, so much as enthralled; intensely practical in business, in their economic philosophy they were superstitious to the last degree. They cowered before bogies of Population and Foreign Competition; and had they but known it, they were

[1] Covent Garden, Sept. 28, 1843. Cobden, *Speeches*, I. 68.
[2] Quoted in F. W. Hirst, *Gladstone as Financier*, p. 77.
[3] Cf. Covent Garden, Jan. 15, 1845. Cobden, *Speeches*, I. 252-3.

suffering from the same malady as that which infected their arch-enemies, the Protectionists.

Cobden lived to see one great prophecy falsified (a Free Trade Europe), and a second apparently justified. His second prophecy concerned the effect of corn law repeal on agricultural prosperity. "I have never been", he said in 1843, "one who believed that the repeal of the Corn Laws would throw an acre of land out of cultivation."[1] He was right—for a time. The twenty years which followed the repeal of the corn laws were the golden age of English agriculture: and why? Just because that bounty of the New World, that "vast super-abundance", which the League promised would flow in, if import was free, from the granaries of the United States, did not flow in for another twenty years. The circumstances of the harvests and the outbreak of war, first in Russia and then in the United States, helped to delay the deluge, but in the late 'seventies it descended. By this time, however, Cobden was in his grave, and the Anti-Corn Law League a memory; and the English farmer, with his landlord behind him, had to stand the shock, or make way for the hardy Scot. If England had possessed, as Cobden and Bright desired, a strong peasant proprietary, would the story have been the same, or would the country have saved its peasants from ruin by returning to that protection which Cobden and Bright destroyed?

Let us leave the controversy in the environment of the day.

In those days railways were new, and they were a boon to the League. The snorting monsters, whom the landlords were trying to keep away from their grounds, carried the lecturers on their tours, and the Manchester merchants to and from the Metropolis. To them time was money. Few of the delegates could have gone so frequently to London, if they had been limited to a post-chaise or the stage-coach. The cheap press, too, was a new thing; and the League was able to foster, in the columns of provincial newspapers, a strong free-trade opinion. Not less important was the introduction of a cheap post. The League used the post for the exchange of correspondence among its own members and for the showering of Anti-Corn Law literature on the towns and

[1] Manchester, Oct. 19, 1843. Cobden, *Speeches*, I. 103.

villages of England. When the penny post came in 1839, the League's correspondence increased a hundred-fold.

In pictorial appeal later generations have left the League far behind. Big loaves and little loaves, manacled Chinamen and starving widows directed our judgment at the General Election of 1906, when Free Trade again (and was it for the last time?) swept the country. Besides these the League's cartoons and placards are paltry things. Thackeray drew for the *Anti-Corn Law Circular* of July 23, 1839 its one decent cartoon.[1] But the League had allies which we are more shy of claiming. They had God and the Bible. Corn, Church and Constitution were the three C's dear to the Tory heart; and the League dealt in the same coin. Its journal never wearied of recalling the Conference of 645 Christian Ministers (of whom only two were members of the Established Church), which met at Manchester, August 17–20, 1841. "Our duty", they announced, "as ministers of religion is plain. On scriptural grounds we are called upon to denounce all human restrictions upon the supply of food to the people, and to employ all appropriate means to place the fatherly provision of God within reach of his suffering and famishing children."[2]

And having religion on their side, the Anti-Corn Law League availed itself of the ornaments of religion. It issued an *Anti-Corn Law Almanac*; and in July, 1842, it held at the Theatre Royal in Manchester a National Anti-Corn Law Bazaar. "Women's zeal", says the historian of the League, "was enlisted in the cause of benevolence, and thousands of fair fingers were instantly set at work."[3] The receipts amounted to nearly £10,000. On Stall 16 lay a memorial from the women of Manchester, containing 75,800 female signatures. Stall 10 was more attractive still, for on it were Anti-Corn Law pincushions. Take your pick! Here is one showing a Sheaf of Corn with the motto "Let me come free"; or perhaps you would prefer a Windmill which says, "Freely give and freely I will grind".

---

[1] Reproduced in Trevelyan's *Life of John Bright*, p. 56. A Russian and a Pole, bringing corn for a family of starving English weavers, are repulsed by the myrmidons of the Landlord State—soldier, policeman and beadle.

[2] *Anti-Bread Tax Circular*, No. 70.

[3] Prentice, *op. cit.* I. 206.

The *Quarterly Review*, commenting on the presence of ladies at the Bazaar, said, "it has ever been a frequent device of revolutionary agitators to bring women forward as a screen and safeguard to their own operations".[1] But with Chartists to worry them and the whole country in an excited mood, the Government had no time to prosecute the promoters of an Anti-Corn Law Bazaar.

*   *   *   *

Recent research exalts the statesmanship of Peel in the crisis of 1845–6. A. A. W. Ramsay, *Sir Robert Peel* (1928), epitomises Peel's achievement in terms which he himself would have desired—"the greatest effort ever made to raise collectively the standard of life of the whole lower class" (p. 329). D. G. Barnes, *History of the English Corn Laws* (1930), works up to the conclusion that "the repeal of the Corn Laws, without the active support of Peel, was impossible *at this time*" (p. 269). Between them they shatter the verdict of Rosebery that although the policy of repeal was right, Peel was not the man to do it. Finally, G. Kitson Clark, in *Peel and the Conservative Party, 1832–41* (1929), depicts the rise to power of a scrupulously honest man, who, in opposition or in office, will put the welfare of the nation, as he judges it, before the advantage of his party or himself.

Mr Kitson Clark strikes a true note when he says that Peel thought statistically. This is abundantly clear in the two speeches, printed in full (with précis) in the Appendix, pp. 156 sqq. In the first he is still upholding the Corn Laws, in the second he has abandoned them. The speeches lack the crispness and the imperial flare of Huskisson, but they reveal a statesman who is devoting the resources of a strong will and a logical mind to the final solution of a grave domestic problem.

[1] *Quarterly Review*, Dec. 1842, vol. LXXI. p. 261.

CHAPTER VII

THE EFFECT OF THE CORN LAWS ON THE PRICE OF CORN, 1815–1846

IN the period from 1815 to 1846 the corn laws had a material influence on prices; but how far, if at all, they raised prices it is impossible, even approximately, to determine. Several of the witnesses before the Import Duties Committee of 1840—whose report is nothing more than a manifesto in favour of Free Trade—attempted the task, but arrived at their conclusions by making assumptions which were unwarranted. Thus Mr Bowring said:

> Supposing that of every sort of corn the consumption of this country is 45 millions of quarters; I do not speak of wheat only, but corn generally; upon that, if (*sic*) the rise of price be 5*s*. per quarter, it is clear that the Corn Laws impose an indirect taxation of more than 11 millions sterling upon the community.[1]

And again, Mr Smith, President of the Manchester Chamber of Commerce:

> Assuming that the consumption of grain of all kinds in this country be 60 millions of quarters per annum (Mr McCulloch, I think, estimated it at 52 millions of quarters many years ago); supposing (*sic*) that the effect of the Corn Laws be to raise the price of grain in this country 10*s*. a quarter higher than it would otherwise be, and supposing that the consumption of all other agricultural produce together be equal to the consumption of grain, then you have a consumption equal to 120 millions of grain, which at 10*s*. a quarter would amount to 60 millions of money.[2]

If we confine these two estimates to cereals (for this is what Mr Bowring meant by "corn generally" and Mr Smith by "grain of all kinds"), Mr Smith's figure must be halved, Mr Bowring's remaining at £11 millions and Mr Smith's becoming £30 millions. But these were estimates for a single year; and the orators of the Anti-Corn Law League, multiplying by 25, so as to cover the whole period between 1815 and 1840, arrived at a

---

[1] *Commons' Committee on Import Duties*, 1840. Q. 692.
[2] *Ibid*. Q. 2153.

total which paralysed the imagination and elicited appropriate rage.

If there had been a regular duty on grain, and if all sorts of grain had been at all times largely imported from abroad, this method of calculation would have been on the right lines. But neither of these conditions was fulfilled.

Under the law of 1815 no duty was paid at all, and it is impossible to calculate the indirect effects of a non-existent tax. The calculation was no easier with the sliding scale introduced by the act of 1828; for most of the corn was held up until the duty was nominal. In 1838, for example, out of 1·7 million quarters of imported wheat, 1·2 were entered at the duty of 1s.[1] It is even possible that the violent fluctuations which these laws occasioned may have caused the total of wheat sold in a particular year to fetch in the aggregate a lower price than it would have fetched had there been no restraints on importation. In this case the loss of value would be an index of the burden on the nation and would be comparable with the kind of loss which might occur if organised speculation in the world's wheat markets was repressed by law. Furthermore, even if we suppose the amount of protection afforded by the corn laws fairly translated into a fixed duty of 5s. or 10s. or 15s., it is not allowable to argue that English prices must have been this much higher than they would have been under Free Trade. For in the period between 1815 and 1846 there were years in which, from the abundance of the home harvest, the country practically fed itself at prices which would not have allowed of profitable importations of any magnitude. There were years, too, in which, through the failure of the Continental harvests, there was almost no wheat available for shipment to England, and in which the little that did come in would have commanded the same high price, Free Trade or no Free Trade.

These estimates, however, were a fair party retort. For British growers perpetually assumed that in normal times, if deprived of a protective duty of something like 20s. a quarter, they would be smothered beneath a deluge of foreign wheat. It was, therefore, natural for their opponents to reply: " In normal

[1] Cf. Peel's speech, Feb. 9, 1842. (Appendix, p. 174.)

times, when you have this protection, the price of your wheat is *pro tanto* higher". If the growers protested, "But in point of quantity England nearly feeds itself, not deriving, even in short years, more than one-twelfth of its supply from abroad", the Free Traders could, and did, in their turn retort, "This independence is nevertheless purchased at a price, and unnecessarily purchased, when the bounty of foreign lands might be made to flow to Britain in exchange for British goods. You talk of insurance against famine, but do you realise the vastness of the premium?"

What we really want for an impartial estimate of the influence of the corn laws on prices is some notion of the range of foreign resources which England actually commanded, and of the degree in which they were capable of extension had there been no restrictions on trade. To understand the position in 1815, we must go back for a moment to the beginning of the century.

Early in 1800 a corn merchant communicated to Parliament[1] the following information concerning the possibility of foreign supplies from the preceding harvest:

The supply will be moderate; the crops in general abroad have not been very productive; and in some parts, where we usually look for supplies, the exportation has lately been prohibited—I mean the Prussian provinces bordering on the Elbe. Our principal source of supply may be looked for this year from the Baltic, and chiefly from Poland; for the produce of the harvest in the Prussian provinces bordering on the Baltic has been unusually bad, and the quality very light and inferior. A considerable quantity may be looked for from Poland, if there is no obstruction to its passage to the shipping ports. ...The King of Prussia has already prohibited the export of all other grain but wheat; and it is apprehended that prohibition may be extended to wheat, particularly in the event of a further advance in the prices in Great Britain, which might create an alarm in those countries. Some quantity of wheat may also be expected from Russia....The exportation of corn is strictly prohibited from Holland, Flanders and France....The produce of the crop in America last year exceeds that of any year for the last seven years, but is far short of what has been the produce preceding that period; the reason is the devastation caused by the Hessian fly, which has discouraged the growth of wheat.

During the war the restraints on import did not come from

---

[1] To the Commons' Committee on the Assize and Making of Bread, which reported Feb. 10, 1800.

the side of England.[1] In the worst years the British Government
went out of its way to bring in foreign food. In 1795 all neutral
ships bound with corn for France were seized and their cargoes
purchased; while Government agents bought corn in the Baltic
ports. Between September 1795 and September 1796 a bounty,
varying from 10s. to 20s. per quarter, was offered on imported
foreign wheat.[2] In 1800 the bounty was repeated in a different
form. Importers were guaranteed the difference between the
average price of English wheat in the second week after importation and a price of 90s. (extended in 1801 to 100s.). But inasmuch as the price continuously exceeded 100s. in 1800 and 1801,
the measures, while lending confidence to importers, cost the
Government nothing. Between 1803 and 1813 importers of
foreign grain had to furnish themselves with licences which
were issued by the Privy Council. These were either general
licences, which covered corn as well as other things, or special
licences (issued only from 1809 onwards) for corn only. Objection was raised to them by Francis Horner in 1808. Nobody,
he complained, knew on what principles they were issued; the
fees paid for them amounted to a tax on imports; it was a serious
breach of the Constitution that the Executive should thus take
upon itself the levying of taxes.[3] But the licences cost very little,

[1] For further detail see W. F. Galpin, *The Grain Supply of England
during the Napoleonic Period* (1925).

[2] The bounty on every full quarter of wheat was:

20s. from Mediterranean ports	up to	400,000 qrs.
20s. ,, the British Colonies or the U.S.A.	,, 500,000 ,,
15s. ,, other parts of Europe	,, 500,000 ,,
10s. ,, any of the above regions for quantities exceeding the several amounts.		

The wheat and wheat flour imported 1794–1814 was:

Years	Quarters	Years	Quarters
1794	327,902	1805	920,834
1795	313,793	1806	310,342
1796	879,200	1807	404,946
1797	461,767	1808	84,889
1798	396,721	1809	455,987
1799	463,185	1810	1,567,126
1800	1,264,520	1811	336,131
1801	1,424,765	1812	290,710
1802	647,663	1813	559,000
1803	373,725	1814	852,567
1804	461,140		

[3] Hansard, 1st S. x. 183.

their design being to keep the trade in neutral as well as British ships under the control of the Admiralty. However, they played havoc with the navigation laws which were so dear to administrative England, and by specifically legalising importation from France, an enemy country, created anomalous situations in international law. On the balance, they were easily defensible, as a necessary concession to the exigencies of war.

Napoleon, on the other hand, tried to starve England by withholding Continental supplies. This phase reached its height in 1808. Then he reversed his policy and tried to drain England of its bullion by encouraging exports of corn and prohibiting imports of British manufactures. He was moved to this piece of mercantilism by the bursting granaries of France. He permitted the export under licences, which, unlike the English licences, cost a substantial sum, and were reckoned in 1813 to add 10s. to the cost of importing a quarter of wheat.[1] But the design failed. By a smuggling trade at high profits, English exporters penetrated the barriers of the Continental System and maintained the balance of trade. In Poland, whence most of the corn was derived, a great trade in British goods sprang up, warehouses were established and roads were improved. Goods, intended originally for consumption in the southern parts of Europe, were transferred to the Baltic, and the mode of packing was altered to allow of conveyance into the interior in the small carts of the country.[2] Free-traders in later years recalled these feats of British industry when they wished to show the improbability of a total cessation of imported food, even in the event of war.

Peace came in 1815. But the Continental countries which were the theatre of war took longer to recover from their prostration than the island kingdom which furnished the money for it. France for a time dropped out as an exporter. Between 1815 and 1828 England derived its foreign supplies (which were only a fraction of the total home consumption) either from America, whence it was shipped chiefly in the form of flour, or from the Baltic countries, the latter being the main source and Danzig

[1] *Lords' Committee on Corn*, 1814, p. 112.
[2] *Ibid*. Evidence of Isaac Solly, p. 77.

the main port of shipment. Both in America and the Baltic countries the conditions of supply were peculiar.

More than half of America [*sc*. the U.S.A.] is cultivated by slaves, that is an expensive mode of cultivation; the other part, which does not yield more corn, if so much as suffices for its own consumption, is cultivated by a free peasantry; they raise other productions, though not corn, cheaper than the slaves; it is a singular circumstance that almost all the corn which comes to this country from America is the produce of countries cultivated by slaves.[1]

In the Baltic countries, too, the conditions of production were very different from those prevailing in England. Whereas in Great Britain one-half of the inhabitants were providers of food and brought to market one-half of their produce, in the Baltic countries the cultivators consumed nine-tenths of their produce on the farms and brought only the remaining one-tenth to market for consumption at home or export abroad. Moreover, Napoleon's industrial and military operations had produced an abnormal position. The production in Europe of colonial wares, such as sugar, indigo and tobacco, of which Napoleon was deprived by England's command of the sea, caused a diversion of good land from ordinary agriculture and a consequent scarcity of agricultural produce, which was met by the ploughing up of very poor lands. Hence when peace came in 1815, there were a large number of petty accumulations in the hands of growers, and the land temporarily diverted to colonial produce was restored to the production of grain. The position presaged a severe drop in prices. But agriculture being still in the main *Natur-Wirthschaft* (the poorer classes living on potatoes and the more prosperous on rye bread), the declension could not reveal itself in the commoner items of agricultural enterprise. It was therefore concentrated on wheat, which the nobles of Poland and Russia grew as a speculative surplus to be sold for what it would fetch on the best foreign market. This, hitherto, had been England. In 1814, for example, England was computed to consume two-thirds of the total corn exports of Poland and to warehouse for a time a part of the remainder; and in return, as

[1] *Commons' Committee on the Distressed State of Agriculture*, 1821. Evidence of Wm. Jacob.

we have seen, English manufacturers had the biggest share in the import trade into Poland.[1]

The price of wheat in Danzig was regulated by, and moved in sympathy with, the price on Mark Lane. A rise of price, sufficient to open the English ports, was followed by an immediate flow from the Baltic ports of wheat which had been waiting patiently for its only good market. Sufficiently prolonged, low prices in England, instead of being met by a disposal of the produce elsewhere, might quite likely force the Polish nobility to revert to the production of staples such as rye and to retire from foreign production. The position for the moment seems to have been that rare one in which a tax imposed by the importing country would have been paid mainly by the foreigner, enriching the British Treasury without burden to British consumers.

But to British growers this was small comfort. The Pole's dependence on England was to them his chief offence. It is possible that a faint recognition of the Continental situation may have induced the legislators of 1815 to be content with nothing less than a prohibition till scarcity was really acute. But prohibition, instead of lessening the evil, heightened its psychological influence. From 1815 right down to 1828 the thought of the Polish corn piled up in bond and ever piling was a nightmare to the British farmer. Forth it would pour, at the first opportunity, heedless of the price it fetched. From the behaviour of the bonded corn under abnormal conditions it was erroneously inferred that there was a limitless supply growing in Poland which would be offered at the same low price were the trade in corn free. As a contemporary writer observed: "It is this accumulation, not the supply which would regularly reach us were no prohibition in existence, that depresses the agricultural interests".[2]

It is characteristic of a seasonal commodity like wheat, when it is also a staple of subsistence, that it exhibits in the market a high degree of inelasticity. That is to say, a small excess in the supply of corn, compared with the average rate of consumption,

---

[1] *Commons' Committee on Corn*, 1814. Evidence of Isaac Solly, p. 84.
[2] William Jacob, *Second Report*, 1828, p. 127.

is apt to cause a fall in price very much beyond the ratio of the excess. When the small excess comes from a distance, and when its terrors by unfortunate legislation are bulked, its effect is greater still. There was sufficient truth in the farmer's diagnosis to blind him to his greater errors. Nothing could have alleviated his apprehensions short of a pilgrimage to Poland and a prolonged sojourn when he got there.

William Jacob, Comptroller of Corn Returns, made two such investigations, in 1825 and 1827, on behalf of the Government, visiting, among others, the celebrated German economist von Thünen at his estate in Mecklenburg. In his second report (1828) he expressed the opinion that the extensibility of the foreign supply either immediately or in the calculable future was very small. "At the present time, had the harvest of 1827 required it, it is doubtful if ten days' consumption of wheat could have been drawn from the whole Continent, even at 100 per cent. advance on the prices of that period."[1] As to the future, he was of opinion that the technique of production, the fertility of the soil and the accumulations of capital in Continental Europe were such that "if a great portion of our necessary supply should be wanted from foreign countries, there is no probability that it could be furnished without such an advance of price as would be enormously heavy".[2]

Estimates [he went on] have been presented to the public, founded on the supposition that twenty millions (£) might be saved to the public annually by the importation of ten million quarters of corn at forty shillings a quarter less than our English price, which sum has been represented to be extorted from the pockets of the community to gratify the luxury of the landed proprietors and the greedy selfishness of the farmers; though the authors of such estimates must have known, or must have been woefully ignorant if they did not know, that the demand of one-twentieth part of what they reckon upon could not be extracted from the whole Continent without raising the price there as high as, or even higher than, the average price in England.[3]

From 1828 to 1846 England continued to depend on the Continent of Europe for the greatest part of its foreign supplies.

[1] *Second Report* (1828) *presented to the Lords of the Committee of H.M.'s Privy Council for Trade, respecting the Agriculture and the Trade in Corn in some of the Continental States of Northern Europe*, p. 131.
[2] *Ibid.* p. 98.   [3] *Ibid.* p. 129.

During the eleven years 1828 to 1838 the total annual importations of wheat and wheat flour were considerably under one million quarters, and of that quantity more than three-fourths was derived from Germany and the north of Europe. During the four years 1839 to 1842 the importations rose to 2·5 million quarters annually, and a considerable part of these imports were, for the first time, obtained from France, Italy, Canada and the United States. During the three years 1843, 1844 and 1845 the imports again fell to little more than one million quarters, and three-fourths of this import were from Germany and Prussia. In 1846 the corn laws were repealed. During the nine years 1846 to 1854 the annual imports rose to the very big figure of nearly five million quarters, and a very considerable part of that supply was derived from France, Italy, Turkey, Egypt and Syria, Canada and the United States.

Is it possible to infer from this that, if repeal had come in 1828 when the Duke of Wellington's sliding scale was adopted, or in 1838 when the agitation of the Anti-Corn Law League began, the big expansion of imports which followed after 1846 would have followed after either of these earlier dates? Once again the materials for an exact answer are not available. The case for such a view is that the prospects of a steady foreign trade with England would have materially stimulated the recovery of Continental agriculture and materially hastened the expansion of America. But each country, it must be remembered, had its own independent development, in which the course of its internal affairs played much the most important part.

Thus it is hard to believe that the American policy of land settlement or the financial chaos which prostrated it in 1837 would have been altered or alleviated by freedom of trade with England. It was the progress of settlement under a rather more liberal land policy and the return to healthy finance which enabled America in the late 'forties to appear as a serious factor in the international market for wheat. Our final judgment, therefore, is this: corn law repeal in 1828 would have been an act of faith, hazardous in the light of precedent, but justified by events. Almost as much wheat would have been grown from British soils, and prices would have been considerably steadier at a slightly lower level. The repeal of 1846 removed obstructions just when their retention would have caused them for the first time in corn law history to raise materially the price of English bread.

The course of prices between 1846 and 1855 forms an interesting comment on this judgment. By repeal the manufacturers got what they wanted, a greater flow of imports and a steadier foreign market for their own goods. But what they held out to the public, and what the agriculturists feared, was a material reduction in the price of food, and this did not occur. The quinquennial average of wheat prices (per quarter) in England was as follows:

			£	s.	d.
1841–5	...	...	2	14	9
1846–50	...	...	2	11	10
1851–5	...	...	2	16	0

Whereupon the advocates of Protection declared that the predictions of Cobdenites were falsified and the arguments for repeal were lies. Certainly their predictions were falsified, but none the less their case was good. For prices would have been still higher and still more abrupt in their fluctuations if the corn laws had continued in force after 1846. This general proposition can be established in detail. From 1847 to 1852 the home harvests were very bad, but abroad (including France) they were good. Wheat therefore was imported in large quantities and checked the home rise. Tooke and Newmarch estimate that in September 1848, when the price advanced to 56s. 10d., it would certainly have reached 73s. under the operations of the old law, and that similar situations would have occurred in subsequent years to the great privation and peril of the country.[1]

The harvests of 1853 and 1855 were bad; that of 1854 was very good. But prices rose the whole time. The reasons why between 1853 and 1855 prices were higher than in the years immediately preceding were, first, because in 1854 and 1855, unlike 1847 to 1852, the foreign harvest, particularly in France, was bad, so that no cheap foreign wheat was available; and, secondly, because, even when we had a good harvest in 1854,

---

[1] *History of Prices*, v. 57.

the shortage abroad was so great that British wheat was actually exported to realise the high prices there obtainable. The higher level was maintained and intensified in 1855 by the outbreak of the Crimean war, which obstructed some of the usual sources of supply, especially Russia, and raised freight charges from those sources which remained open.

All that repeal could do, it did. In those years when the home supply was scarce and the foreign supply good, free imports kept down home prices and steadied them by assuring constant access to the widest available market. When both home and foreign supplies were deficient, and when in addition there was war, prices inevitably rose. Free trade in wheat does not create cheap bread; it merely prevents an artificial rise in the price of the raw material of bread.

It is one of the ironies of history that during the half-century in which British agriculturists lived in terror of a bogey the bogey did not exist. British farming surmounted the repeal of the corn laws on a scale of ascending prices. The more immediate causes of this ascent we have indicated. Remoter influences were the general rise of prices due to the discovery of Californian gold in the 'fifties, and a growing industrial population at home, unaccompanied by any great expansion of population in America, which, in the 'sixties, was prostrated by civil war. Then in the 'seventies the bogey came from a quarter to which men had hardly been trained to look. McCulloch in 1841, with the classical economist's sure instinct for the short run, wrote:

It is needless to take up the reader's time by entering into any lengthened details with respect to the corn trade of the United States. It is abundantly certain that we need not look to that quarter for any considerable supplies. American flour, though decidedly inferior to British wheat, is seldom under 40s. a quarter in New York, and is frequently much higher. Latterly the culture of wheat has been decreasing in the United States, and a material decrease has taken place in the exports of flour. Indeed, everybody acquainted with matters knows that, within the last half-dozen years, considerable quantities of flour have been shipped from Dantzic to other European ports for America.[1]

[1] *Statements Illustrative of the Policy and Probable Consequences of the Proposed Repeal of the Corn Laws* (1841), p. 8.

But from America in the 'seventies the bogey descended. Its feet were ships of steel, its arms railroads stretching over the prairies, and in its belly was Chicago wheat.[1]

[1] Attention is drawn to the remarkable correlation between the import of corn from Turkey, Syria and Egypt and the export of cotton goods to these parts in the decade 1846–55.

The corn imports rose from a trifle in 1841–5 to an average of 205,000 qrs. in 1846–50, and of 669,000 qrs. in 1851–5 (Tooke, *History of Prices*, VI, 453).

Dr A. Redford, in *Some Problems of the Manchester Merchant after the Napoleonic War* (Manchester Statistical Society, December 1930), gives the expansion of cotton exports. "It was not until 1839 that England obtained favourable trading concessions from Turkey: thereafter a brisk trade developed in the export of plain cotton goods to the Levant, and by 1855 the Sultan's dominions were taking far more Manchester piece-goods than all the European countries put together": and again (quoting the Chairman of the Manchester Chamber of Commerce in 1856), "As to cottons in Alexandria we have no rivals and mainly by reason of the increase of our grain trade...there has been a large increase in our exports of cotton to that place. In 1843 we exported to the value of £141,000: in 1851 £519,000: in 1854 £1,000,000".

This supports strongly the contention of the Manchester School that corn law repeal would stimulate the export of British manufactures.

CHAPTER VIII

HUSKISSON AND IMPERIAL STATESMANSHIP

As Minister of Woods and Forests, William Huskisson was a member of the Committee which prompted and of the Government which passed the protectionist corn law of 1815. In 1830, two years after losing office, he was killed by an engine at the opening of the Liverpool and Manchester Railway; and forthwith Ebenezer Elliott, the corn law rhymer, burst into lamentation:

> Oh Huskisson! oh Huskisson!
> Oh Huskisson in vain our friend!
> Why hast thou left thy work undone?
> Of good begun is this the end?
> Thou shoulds't have lived, if they remain
> Who fetter'd us and hated thee;
> Oh Huskisson, our friend in vain!
> Where now are hope and liberty?
> Thou shoulds't have lived, if with thee dies
> The poor man's hope of better days:
> Time stops, to weep, but yet shall rise
> The sun whose beams shall write thy praise.
> Thy widow weeps—but what is she
> And what her paltry common woe?
> Worlds weep—and *millions* fast for thee;
> Our hope is gone! why didst thou go?
> Pleased hell awhile suspends his breath,
> Then shouts in joy and laughs in hate,
> And plague, and famine, call on death,
> Their jubilee to celebrate,
> A *shadow* bids improvement stand,
> While faster flow a nation's tears.
> Oh dead man! with thy pallid hand
> Thou rollest back the tide of years.

No such voice was raised in mourning for Peel when in 1850 he was thrown from his horse on Constitution Hill.[1] Yet he had

---

[1] The horse, I am credibly informed, was sold to him by the grandfather of the Librarian of Cambridge University.

lost place and power by removing those very laws which
Huskisson had helped to stiffen. Was there then in Huskisson's
career a sudden conversion? No, for such would have been
foreign to his nature. But when conditions change, policy should
change; and there can be no greater change than that from a long
war to a long peace. Huskisson was at once an imperialist and a
democrat, foremost an imperialist while the flush of battle
lingered around, foremost a democrat in the chilly morrow of the
peace. It was to the democrat of 1830 that Ebenezer Elliott
addressed his elegy.

Into three years of reform, 1823 to 1825, Huskisson crowded
a life's work. He overhauled the navigation laws and the tariff,
replacing discrimination and prohibition by reciprocity and
moderation. Then in 1827 he was again caught up in the controversy which had beaten him in 1821 and 1822; and again he
failed. But throughout, both where he succeeded and where he
failed, he had a steadfast vision of empire. In the navigation
laws he reserved inter-imperial trade; in his tariff revisions he
created, or maintained, imperial preference over a wide range of
commodities; and in the corn laws he not only secured and
maintained the colonial preference in the corn-law schedules,
but also secured an important modification for Canada in 1825,
which was the precedent for further special consideration in
1843.

In the isolation of war the fostering of an imperial food supply
could be considered without affectation to combine the ends of
imperialism and democracy. With Australia, New Zealand and
South Africa still in their mother's womb, with the East and
West Indies specialised to tropical cultures, the territory of
British North America was the only source of an imperial food
supply for the now United Kingdom of Great Britain and
Ireland. Eastern Canada entered into English economic history
when the export of its staples, timber and wheat, began. The
claim of the British North American colonies to favourable
treatment was enhanced by the fact that a new stock was added
to their area by the influx of United Empire Loyalists after
1783. Of Ontario's wheat England had no urgent need, but the
closing of the Baltic by Napoleon's blockade compelled the

merchants of Glasgow and Liverpool to look for an alternative source of supply in the Maritime Provinces and the St Lawrence. From 1815 to 1820 colonial timber was admitted free, while a heavy rate was imposed on Baltic timber at the expense of British users; for Baltic timber was cheaper to lay down in England and for many purposes better. In 1821, in order to reduce this handicap without undue sacrifice of revenue, the duty on Baltic timber was lowered by 10s. and a duty of the same amount was imposed on colonial timber. But Huskisson in his revisions of 1823–5, while reducing the rates on most raw materials to a nominal figure, deliberately held his hand with timber despite requests to the contrary.

With regard to the timber trade he was surprised that the honourable gentleman who had the other night presented a strong petition to the House in favour of the duty on Cape wines on the ground of their being the production of one of our own colonies, should now argue, in fact, against the protection afforded to the timber trade of Canada. Why! he must recollect that Canadian timber, considering that it grew in one of our own colonies and was transported in our own ships, was a most valuable trade to Great Britain....In conclusion, he begged to repeat, that he could not accede to the suggestions of the honourable member for Montrose; inasmuch as no trade was more flourishing at present than the rival trade (as with respect to Canada it might be called) of Baltic timber.[1]

One notes his conviction that home and colonial interests could be reconciled. It was only after his time that the lowering of the tariff on timber and other things narrowed the margin within which effective preference was possible.

Huskisson did not institute the corn preference. In the act of 1791, as already noted, British North America was associated with Ireland in a preference on the English market. In that of 1804 the preferential margin of 2s. per quarter was increased to 10s. In June 1813 Parnell's Committee recommended that corn grown in British North America should be allowed in, whatever the price might be, without payment of duty. In 1814 this generous proposition was dropped, but the margin of 10s. was retained in the new resolutions submitted by Parnell in that

---

[1] *Speeches*, II. 362.

year. Whereupon Huskisson rose to deliver, on May 5, 1814, his first corn law oration, and concluded thus:

He had only one more word to offer. It related to the Colonies. It was proposed to lay a smaller duty on corn imported from the Colonies, than on that imported from foreign countries; but the difference, he would contend, was not sufficiently great; and, therefore, he would propose to make the duty on corn imported from the Colonies, half the amount of that imposed on foreign corn. This would tend to promote the growth of it in our own settlements.[1]

The amendment moved by Mr Huskisson was agreed to.

However, the proposals of 1814 did not become law. The act of 1815, which took their place, made 80s. the free duty point for foreign wheat; and 67s. that for colonial wheat. The rigidity of prohibition, however, offset the gain of 3s. in the margin (13s. instead of 10s.).

The corn law of 1822 only came into operation as regards the colonies. By this act the duties payable on wheat from the British colonies or plantations in North America were as follows:

Whenever the average price of British wheat was	Duty	Additional for the first 3 months
Under 67s. per quarter	12s.	5s.
At or above 67s. but under 71s.	5s.	5s.
At or above 71s.	1s.	—

In this act, as in the one-year act of 1827, Wellington's act of 1828 and Peel's act of 1842, there were preferences for the wheat, rye, barley, oats and grains of the colonies. In 1827 it was necessary to adopt the preference to the framework of a sliding scale: in 1828 the scale of duties ranged from 5s. to 6d. as against the foreign scale of 20s. 8d. to 1s. In 1842 Peel lowered slightly the pivot point at which the declension from the 5s. duty began, but inasmuch as he reduced the foreign pivot point more, the amount of preference was in effect diminished. These preferences the legislature granted without demur, but in 1825 under Huskisson, and again in 1843 when Lord Stanley was Colonial Secretary, special acts were passed relating to Canada, which brought the colonial preference into controversy. For it was feared that by these acts the now important supplies of the United States would find their way illegally into England.

[1] *Speeches*, I. 295.

In 1790, when the Committee of the Council on Trade drew attention to the possibility of North America supplying the threatened deficiency of Europe, they were thinking chiefly of the revolted colonies. In 1805 the question arose of giving American produce (owing to its distance from England) a period of grace in the calculation of the rate of duty. Samuel Scott, a corn merchant examined by the Corn Committee of 1805, was asked "If this extension were limited to the British Colonies in America, could it have any pernicious effect on the agriculture of Great Britain". He replied: "I think not, because the supply received from the British Colonies is seldom of much importance and the quality not generally suited to the British Market". Parnell's Committee in 1813 was equally conservative: "Your Committee cannot comprehend the policy of encouraging the importation of corn into these countries, as attempted by the existing laws, from our North American possessions, while the natural market for it is clearly in our West India islands".[1] They were, of course, dressing the case for Ireland. But in 1825 Huskisson contended that the periodic closing of the ports was a matter of legitimate grievance to Canadians. Canada, he argued, was so distant from Great Britain that the regulation of entry by reference to the averages involved Canadian shippers in risk and disappointment; after they had shipped their wheat the ports might be closed or the rate of duty raised under a new average.

The measure which I have to propose in respect to Canada appears to me to be no more than an act of common justice to that Colony. It is simply this: to admit at all times the corn of that country into our consumption, upon the payment of a fixed and moderate duty. When it is considered that corn is the staple of that Colony, I cannot conceive a greater act of injustice than to have declared to a part of our own Empire, as much entitled to protection as any other part of it, that against that staple the markets of this country were closed. How are the Canadians to pay for the supplies which they draw from this country? Is it fitting, that, when they make their remittances in this staple, they should do so without being able to know whether it can be received here? Whether it is to remain in warehouse, unavailable and unproductive, and at a ruinous expense for five or six years,

---

[1] *Committee of* 1813. *Report*, p. 3.

depending for its admission into our market upon the fraction of a half-penny, according to the average price in our markets for a few preceding weeks; that average, influenced by the conflicting tricks and artifices of the home grower and the home dealer, the result of which cannot be known in Canada for many months afterwards? When this subject is considered by the British agriculturist it is impossible that he can view the indulgence which I propose with jealousy or apprehension. That indulgence is, to allow the free import of Canadian wheat, at all times, upon the payment of a duty of 5s. a quarter. In addition to the protection of that duty, the British grower will have that of the freight from Quebec to England, which is not less than from 12s. to 15s. more.

The greatest quantity of wheat which Canada can now supply, may, I understand, be estimated at not more than 50,000 quarters, but even if the importation were double that quantity, and were it to increase more rapidly than I consider probable, such an addition is not likely to keep pace with the growing demand of our population; and whether so or not, I should still maintain that the principle of the measure is one to which no fair or impartial man can possibly refuse his assent.[1]

This noble plea occurs at the conclusion of his great "Exposition of the Colonial Policy of the Country"; and he submitted it as part of a general plan of commercial liberation, whose purpose was to bind the colonies into "one great Empire". But the landed interest was sensitive about corn; and after amendment in the Upper House the concession was limited to two years, 1825–7 (6 George IV, c. 64). However in 1827 and 1828 the principle was retained in the laws of those years, but applied to foreign as well as to colonial grain. Through Canada Huskisson worked towards greater freedom. After Huskisson's death the cause of imperial preference fell into disrepute. Especially after 1833, when the emancipation of the negroes in the British West Indies upset the economy of those islands, appeals on behalf of the colonies were usually appeals for the relief of distress. And the corn preferences continued, less because the new generation had a lively faith in them than because they were of old establishment and to touch them might disturb the general fabric of the corn laws. Nevertheless, when Peel came into office, one final gesture of imperialism was made. In 1843 it fell to Lord Stanley, as Colonial Secretary, to place on the statute book 6 and

---

[1] *Speeches*, II. 325–6.

7 Victoria, c. 29. By this act, in consideration of a duty of 3s. per quarter having been imposed by the legislature of Canada (i.e. of Upper and Lower Canada, recently united into one province) on wheat imported into that province from other places than the United Kingdom or British possessions, the duty on wheat and wheat flour, the produce of Canada, imported into the United Kingdom after October 10, 1843, and during the continuance of the duty of 3s. in Canada, was to be at all times 1s. per quarter on wheat (with an equivalent duty on Canadian flour).

The position before 1842 had been that American wheat was being exported to Canada free of duty and after conversion into flour was being shipped to England as colonial produce at colonial rates. To secure the admission into England of *bona fide* colonial wheat and flour at the normal rate of 1s. a quarter, Canada in 1842[1] placed on American wheat a duty equivalent to that which it would have to pay when re-exported to England as colonial flour; and Stanley's bill was the British Government's rather reluctant share in the completion of the scheme. They felt that their hand had been forced, and, as they feared, the bill aroused a lively opposition. Some members protested that it should have originated with the Imperial Parliament rather than with Canada. Stanley himself had been anxious to allow free admission of colonial wheat in the general act of 1842. But (he says) "I was overruled; the duty on colonial corn was fixed at from 5s. to 1s. Then followed the Canada Corn Bill".[2] Thus the mother country stood by an arrangement with which it was in lukewarm accord.

Not so the country gentlemen. "Canada won't collect the duty", said one. "I shall vote against the Canada Corn Bill", said another, "because that also is a Free Trade measure and that is not what I like." And the obstruction persisted into the session of 1844 when an endeavour was made by a private member to have the privilege extended to other colonies. Stanley protested that "when last year he warned the Colonies

---

[1] Canadian Statutes, c. 31.
[2] *Correspondence and Diaries of J. W. Croker*, III. 114. Letter of June 20, 1847.

not to expect a relaxation of that law he did not think that the
House would for a slight, almost an inappreciable, advantage to
the Colonies, disturb a general system of laws of infinite importance, infinite delicacy, and watched with the deepest interest
by the people of this country ".[1]

But the proposer was not the sort of man to accept a rebuff.
He was William Hutt, member for Gateshead, a commissioner
for the foundation of South Australia and a prominent member
of the New Zealand Company. On February 6, 1844, Governor
Grey of Adelaide wrote to him, "You could not fix upon a gift
more beneficial and just than the permitting of the wheat of
this country, not only to have the same favour shewn to it, as is
shewn to the wheat of Canada, but to allow it to be imported
duty free". The colonial press, public meetings, the legislative
councils, and individuals of influence appealed strongly to the
mother country. And Hutt constituted himself their spokesman
in the British Parliament in 1844 and again in 1845.

The problem (he urged) should be considered from the
Australian standpoint, and not merely as it affected domestic
protection. Indeed, liberality to Australia would repay itself;
for a prosperous agriculture in Australia would lead to a demand
for British manufactures in exchange, and at the same time
constitute a real fund for the encouragement of emigration.
Adverting again to Canada, he observed

There is no use disguising the matter. It is impossible to prevent
smuggling along that extended line of frontier which divides the
States from Canada, utterly impossible. In the course of this year
you will see corn and flour, the produce of the United States, come
into our market at nominal duties. As American corn finds its way
into the British market, the demand for agricultural labour in the
Republic will be proportionately increased; and the tide of emigration,
which under an enlightened system of colonial policy would flow
towards our Australian settlements, will be directed to the United
States. Will you persevere in a course of legislation, the inevitable
consequences of which will be to accelerate the progress of the
United States and retard the progress of the British Empire?...
Oh! the incurable perversity of human folly! When shall we begin to
make as rational use of the mighty means which Providence has
placed within our reach? When we shall have a Colonial Minister

[1] Hansard, 3rd S. LXXIII. 1573.

worthy of the name, a Statesman sagacious and capable enough to turn the direction of our overflowing capital and redundant labour towards the dependencies of the British Crown, and to raise up, as he may raise up in rapid progression, new Anglo-Saxon nations in Southern Africa, Australia and New Zealand....I ask the House to concede to them the right of importing their grain into this country free....To the Colonies it opens out a new avenue to prosperity and power, to this country it offers extension to commerce, a stimulus to manufactures, and relief to the suffering rural population; and while its tendency will be to spread British colonisation over the most distant regions of the globe, it will also unite and knit together the various dominions of our widespread Empire in the bonds of mutual interest and mutual goodwill.[1]

The Government's reply was feeble in the extreme. For the country gentlemen now lived in terror of anything that savoured of concession to the diabolical Anti-Corn Law League. The Vice-president of the Board of Trade argued: it won't do the colonies any good, because they can't stand the charges of sending wheat here. Then, shifting his ground, he said, "Although the alteration would have no material effect on prices in this country, the House should recollect how sensitive the agriculturists were with regard to any measure calculated to effect an alteration in the price of corn".[2] Peel was equally feeble; and this gave the Opposition their chance.

Does he [said Viscount Howick], resist the motion because so much corn will come in that it affords a just subject of alarm to his agricultural friends? If that is the ground on which he objects to it, it follows that it would be of great advantage to the Colonies. Or, on the other hand, does the Right Honourable Gentleman refuse it because it is so small a boon that it is immaterial to the Colonies? If he does, then I want to know what becomes of the apprehensions of his agricultural friends.[3]

Others of the Opposition supported Hutt because, whatever its imperial implication, it was a step in the direction of Free Trade for the consumers of food. But when the vote was taken the motion was rejected by 147 to 93. This debate was on May 8, 1845, and was the end of the matter; for from July onwards the country was absorbed with the more urgent problems of

[1] Hansard, 3rd S. LXXX. 301.   [2] Hansard, 3rd S. LXXX. 307.
[3] Hansard, 3rd S. LXXX. 335.

Irish Famine and Total Repeal. Let us, therefore in conclusion, address ourselves to a problem of historical interpretation.

What was the effect on Canada of (a) the preferential legislation of 1842–3, and (b) the repeal of the corn laws in 1846 (whereby, apart from the shilling registration duty which the colonies did not pay, the corn preference disappeared)?[1] We may distinguish (1) the effect on opinion, from (2) the effect on the course of affairs.

Of (a) (1) we can speak with confidence. The preference was not a new departure, but the extension of a policy to which Huskisson had given comprehensive aid; and since it was the outcome of joint legislation by the Canadian and Imperial Parliaments, it symbolised the liberal loyalty that was dear alike to Huskisson and Durham. As such, Canadian opinion stoutly supported it. It encouraged Canada to go forward with the policy of canal building and river improvement (the Beauharnois and enlarged Welland Canals were opened in 1845); and it accorded with the policy of reconciliation which distinguished the Governor-Generalship of Lord Sydenham. Inasmuch as the Imperial Government had agreed in 1841 to guarantee the interest on a large loan for public works in Canada, it could not be indifferent to the progress of Canadian trade and revenue.

Of (b) (1) we can also speak with confidence. For although Francis Hincks, the Inspector-General of Canadian Finance, saw as early as 1841 that complete Free Trade would eventually triumph in England, Canadians generally, not without reason, did not see so far. The crisis of repeal took Canada by surprise, as it took many in England itself. In 1842 it still looked as though, if any breach were made in the sacred citadel of the corn laws, it would not go further than the moderate fixed duty of the Radical programme; and this would be enough to allow Canada all she wanted in preference. Repeal administered a profound psychological shock, the intensity of which may be

[1] The repealing act of 9 and 10 Victoria, c. 22, imposed a temporary scale of low duties on "corn imported from any foreign country", i.e. not being the produce of and imported from any British possession outside of Europe. This was to last for three years. In 1849 under the same act these duties were replaced by a uniform duty of 1s. per quarter, which lasted till 1869. The latter was reimposed as a revenue duty in April 1902 and repealed in July 1903.

measured by the extraordinary episode of 1849. In the words of Adam Shortt:

The loss of the Canadian preference in British food supplies coincided with other political and economic troubles precipitated by the Lafontaine-Baldwin Government in Canada, and produced, in 1849, a severe and complex crisis centring in Montreal....The commercial and financial interests, in despair of both the economic and political future of Canada as a separate country, organised and advocated, albeit in very moderate and reasonable terms, with expressions of the friendliest sentiments towards Great Britain, a proposal for the annexation of Canada to the United States.[1]

It was a momentary despair only, but it is evidence of reaction to something which was altogether out of the common; for Montreal was the stronghold of shrewd and patriotic Scottish Protestants.

(a) (2) and (b) (2) are, of course, more complex. For each is a question of the influence of a piece of overseas legislation on the general stream of Canadian history, with its own factors of geography, technology, economic opportunity and racial drive operating all the while. It is, however, safe to say that the legislation of 1842–3 encouraged wheat-growing and the milling of flour from domestic wheat, and also, while the navigation laws lasted, the use of Canadian waterways and harbours. The preference was not great enough to distort development. The two staple exports of continental Canada were lumber and grain, and lumber had long enjoyed a heavy preference. Grain thus was put on a more equal footing. At this time wheat and wheat flour from North America were but a small part of the total British imports of these commodities, and the total imports were but a small part of the home consumption. The percentage of imports derived from Canada varied with the harvests, at home and abroad, and the comparative progress of settlement in Canada and the United States.

Percentage imports of Wheat and Wheat Flour into Great Britain

From	1836–40	1841–6	1846–50	1851–5
B.N.A.	2·2	10·5	5·4	2·2
U.S.A.	6·5	4·6	19·9	22·6

[1] *Cambridge History of the British Empire*, VI (Canada), 382.

Thus under the Canada Corn Act the Canadian proportion grew, but after 1846 it fell, and continued to fall as the United States entered upon that long period of easy supremacy which terminated only with the opening of the Canadian West about 1900.

Adam Shortt states the causal relation thus: "This [i.e. preferential] arrangement gave an immense stimulus to the Canadian milling industry, especially in the neighbourhood of Montreal, and greatly promoted Canadian shipments *via* the St Lawrence".[1]

In a well-informed article in the *Cambridge Historical Journal* of 1928 Mr D. L. Burn appears to cast doubt on a verdict of this sort. He says, "The orthodox view that the Canadian corn-exporting trade was encouraged by the English grant of increased preference in 1843, and in the midst of consequent expansion was injured by the repeal of the Corn Laws in 1846, and later revived in some measure by the compensating repeal of the Navigation Laws in 1849, was the view normally held by Canadian writers in 1850"; and he seeks to show that this interpretation "is in the main a legend".[2]

The dispute is not unlike that between Cunningham and Unwin over the economic policy of Edward III, in which, as I think, Cunningham surrendered too much. For when we isolate economic policy for purposes of study, we adopt one of those conventions by which alone history can be written. Severely considered, the economic policy of all ages from Edward III to Gladstone is hardly more than the glimmering of intention through the manifold distractions of reality—witness, not least, the debt policy of Gladstone. Events bend and mar policy, as often as policy guides or moderates events. Mr Burn, after a display of documentary evidence, writes, "It is clear that the Act of 1843 did not work in isolation as a stimulant of expansion in the corn trade":[3] but surely one might venture this much *a priori*.

More significant is the next stage of his argument. In 1849 the navigation laws were abolished and in 1849 the United

---

[1] *Cambridge History of the British Empire*, VI (Canada), 382.
[2] *Cambridge Historical Journal*, II. No. 3, p. 252, D. L. Burn, "Canada and the Repeal of the Corn Laws".
[3] *Ibid.* p. 256.

States permitted the bonding of Canadian produce for re-export. As Adam Shortt notes for the period of 1840–67 as a whole, the result was that much Canadian produce passed through New York, which offered a greater variety of tonnage and the probability of inward cargoes. Access to a better port of shipment helped the Canadian grower in his difficult competition with the new Middle-West. The opening of the St Lawrence to foreign ships did not bring the increase of grain shipments that was expected at the time. Mr Burn dovetails with his account of the corn trade an account of the timber trade, and finds that the latter benefited substantially from the incoming of foreign shipping in quest of timber cargoes. The interaction of the two trades is most ably set forth.

On this evidence, however,—so it would seem—Mr Burn takes Lord Elgin to task for asserting in 1848 that the free navigation of the St Lawrence and reciprocity with the United States were essential to Canadian recovery. But I confess that I am unable to see much myth in Lord Elgin's view or where Mr Burn explodes the myth. In particular, I find unconvincing such a sentence as, "the business of exporters and millers expanded more after the lapse of the Act of 1843 than during its lifetime" (*op. cit.* p. 266). Its lifetime was only three years; and it is impossible to measure the value of the policy which it expressed by the increase of production and milling equipment within those three years. The quinquennial average of corn rose after corn-law repeal for two successive periods. Are we then to argue that the repeal did nothing to lower the price of corn? It has been so argued, of course; but it is customary to pronounce the argument fallacious.

In judging policy we must raise our eyes a few inches from the ground. The Canada to which Lord Elgin came was a young restless democracy, with sores to heal and slowly learning to tread the narrow path of responsible government within the Empire. Elgin realised the importance of psychology at such a season. He demanded for Canada freedom of navigation, that is to say, freedom to exploit the element which was the very marrow of her life: and in addition a measure of reciprocity, which would call in a new neighbour to redress the loss of the old. Great Britain was still there, Mr Burn may say. In the facts of trade, yes: but not in the policy of trade. Great Britain had no imperial economic policy from 1846 to the time of Joseph Chamberlain; and now at very long last she has gone to Ottawa to try and secure freer trade within the British Commonwealth of Nations. We are learning to respect Russia, as we see her struggling through initial failure towards a planned economy. The British Empire would be stronger to-day if it had possessed in the nineteenth century a firmer faith in the potentialities of continuous policy. I agree that Cunningham went too far in his integration of Edward III, but, documents or no documents, I am profoundly dissatisfied with the version of history which reduces the influence of human policy to the reactions of bedevilment or distress.

CHAPTER IX

THE CORN LAWS AND SOCIAL THOUGHT

MR Wesley Mitchell gently reproves Tooke and New-march for their obvious delight in controversy, and their editor, Mr Gregory, for his pride in this good hating.[1] Yet gold and corn have ever roused men's passions. Over these there have been wars, not of words only: they have run the herring and the clove a close race. But a concatenation of cir-cumstances was required to give to the corn laws their passionate emphasis in the first half of the nineteenth century. In Adam Smith the problem is still mainly economic. He, the critic of the corn laws, was the country gentleman's friend. The popular enemy was not the landlord, but the middleman. But he had sown the seed of social hate. For at the outset of his work he wrote, "As soon as the land of any country has all become private property, the landlords, like all other men, love to reap where they have never sowed, and demand a rent even for its natural produce" (*Wealth of Nations*, I. 51). The nineteenth century forgot all other men and concentrated on landlords, developing Adam Smith's second lead, "The rent of land...is naturally a monopoly price. It is not at all proportioned to what the landlord may have laid out upon the improvement of the land or to what he can afford to take; but to what the farmer can afford to give" (*ibid*. I. 146). To the Ricardians such a thought was blasphemous.

An American scholar has convincingly shown that if the various allusions to rent and prices in the *Wealth of Nations* are studied *seriatim*, a duality of approach is revealed.[2] Where the rent of land for a particular use in competition with other uses is being considered, then rent is a part of the cost of production; but where land as a whole is being considered, it is not: it is then emphatically a result and not a cause: it does not enter then

---

[1] *Economica*, 1929, p. 215.
[2] *Ibid.* 1929, pp. 123 sqq.; D. H. Buchanan, *Historical Approach to Rent and Price Theory*.

into the cost of production. When Adam Smith was writing, the
land of England, and of Scotland even more, was very much in
the making. There was no suggestion of finality. Land usance,
therefore, did not suggest exclusive monopoly. There were
hundreds of square miles awaiting enclosure and cultivation,
even in island Britain. The sore spot was not the scarcity of land
as a whole but the desire of enclosing landlords for coveted
pieces—a problem as old as Naboth's vineyard.

Adam Smith's mantle fell upon Ricardo; and Ricardo was as
definitely a child of war as Adam Smith of peace. If Old England
then had been where New England was, with a great interior
beyond adjacent mountains, the Napoleonic war would have
precipitated an extension of cultivation westwards, and the
emphasis on economic theory would have been not on recourse
to less fertile soils but on movement to lands less favourably
situated, because further away. But England was a small island
on the edge of warring Europe. Seemingly by accident the
period when she embraced industrialism was also the period
when her own limits no longer sufficed to feed her. For a
vague instant Ireland hovered on the edge of England, as a new
source of domestic supply, but only during the abnormality of
war. For after 1815 Ireland settled down into a land teeming
with people and potatoes and barely sufficient to herself. Therefore the English landlord now stood in a new and sombre light.
He had a monopoly of all the land there was to have; and im-
piously he tried to augment this by shutting out the produce of
overseas.

A further circumstance, the peculiarity of English land
tenure, helped to fix the guilt. For in England there was neither
sub-letting, as in Ireland, nor metayage, as in France. Landlords let direct to substantial tenant farmers. The landlords drew
owner's rent, the tenant made farming profits. Moreover,
English landlords were progressive landlords who supplied
buildings and permanent improvements; and this invited the
distinction between the payment for improvements which
really was interest on capital outlay and the residuum due to the
properties of the soil, which was rent—pure rent, economic rent.
By 1900 these two elements in rural rent were distinguishable

only in thought; for through foreign competition and other causes the gross receipts of rural landlords, in the mass, did not yield even normal interest on the capital sunk in the property by themselves and their immediate predecessors. But before 1875 they yielded this and something more.

Ricardo was a financier, and it would be churlish to suggest that he had a townsman's prejudice against the country. On the contrary he loved the land and retired to a beautiful estate in Gloucestershire to work out his theories of political economy. More important far in the determination of his thought were the fundamental changes between Adam Smith's day and his—the generation of war, the experience of scarcity, the threat of starvation, the straining of the productive machine, the soil itself, to the full capacity of war-time pressure, the removal of all the cover that stood between landowning and farming for profit— of commoners, squatters, rural bye-industries and cultivable waste. Changes so profound invited a restatement of the relation between land (not particular land, but all land) and industry. It is tempting to speculate on what would have happened if Parliament in 1814 had returned to the moderation of 1773. The fundamental conditions of price and consumption would have been the same, but it may be doubted whether in this event three men almost at the same time would have been found to enunciate the Law of Diminishing Returns in Agriculture.

Among controverting minds this law speedily replaced Malthus' law of population, which was always more of a sermon than a law, the parson in it being greater than the mathematician. Diminishing Returns talked prices as well as amounts; and Malthus had to graft the new law on to his older stock. In 1798 political economy held up its hands in pious lamentation to Heaven—there was no more room at Nature's board: in 1815 it took to task a band of earthly transgressors. They and their selfishness were worth exposing: the poor at the park gates and in the cellars of the towns, it were better to forget or emigrate.

Of the three, Sir Edward West, a Fellow of University College, Oxford, is commonly considered to be the father of the law, as he himself strenuously claimed. In 1814 he wrote and early in 1815 he published (though not ahead of Malthus' *Rent*)

his *Essay on the Application of Capital to Land with observations
showing the Impolicy of any great Restriction of the Importation of
Corn and that the Bounty of* 1688 *did not lower the price of it*: by a
Fellow of University College, Oxford.[1] The copy in Cambridge
University Library is bound in a volume of Tracts on the Corn
Laws, an appropriate economy. West argued that "in the progress of the improvement of cultivation the raising of rude
produce becomes progressively more expensive, or in other
words, the ratio of the net produce of land to its gross ratio is
constantly decreasing" (*Essay*, p. 1). The idea was not new.[2] It
had been in the air ever since the Physiocrats began to write.
Turgot, for example (*Œuvres*, ed. Daire, 1. 420–1), compared the
returns from land to the increasing resistance of a spring as extra
equal weights are added to it. But West gave it a new emphasis
in a unique setting, the hubbub which accompanied the introduction and passage of the bill of 1815.

Parnell in his 1813 Report had urged that if his proposals were
accepted, the farmer, by being able to render his land more
productive in proportion as he improved it, and at a small
expense according as he made use of good implements, would
be able to afford to sell his corn at reduced prices. The economists took issue with him. Thus Malthus in his *Observations on
the Effects of the Corn Laws* (1814) attacked the ideal of self-
sufficiency on the ground that the higher cost of raising corn in
England was in large measure due to the necessity of cultivating
and improving poorer land to provide for the demands of an

---

[1] The order of publication seems to have been:
  I. Malthus, *Observations on the Effects of the Corn Laws*, 1814.
  II. Malthus, *An Inquiry into the Nature and Progress of Rent*: not later than
      the beginning of February 1815, possibly Jan. 31, 1815.
  III. Malthus, *The Grounds of an Opinion on the Policy of Restricting the Im-
      portation of Foreign Corn, intended as an appendix to "Observations
      on the Corn Laws"*: early in Feb. 1815 (see Malthus' letter to
      Sir John Sinclair of Jan. 31, 1815, *Sinclair's Correspondence*,
      1. 391–2).
  IV. West, *Essay on the Application of Capital to Land*: February 1815,
      certainly after Malthus' *On Rent*, and before Ricardo's *Essay*.
  V. Ricardo, *Essay on the Influence of a Low Price of Corn on the Profits
      of Stock*: end of February 1815.
[2] Cf. *Economic Journal*, 1892, E. Cannan, "The origin of the Law of
Diminishing Returns, 1813–15"; also E. Cannan, *Theories of Production and
Distribution*, pp. 147–182.

increasing population. And they found further support in the language of the Committees of 1814, which pointed to the way in which high prices had stimulated enclosure and to the obvious way in which low prices would throw out of cultivation the inferior soils. This gave West his chance—Indeed it would; and so much the better. Let freedom prevail and rents fall! Malthus, who was at heart a protectionist, could not go thus far. He followed up his essay of 1814 with *An Inquiry into the Nature and Progress of Rent* (1815), which contains the following (p. 39): "As the price of raw produce continues to rise, these inferior machines [he had likened different qualities of land to a 'gradation of machines'] are successively called into action, and as the price of raw produce continues to fall, they are successively thrown out of action".

And in the slightly later pamphlet, *The Grounds of an Opinion on the Policy of Restricting the Importation of Foreign Corn* (1815), he refers in a footnote to the argument of the *Inquiry into Rent*, saying, "In every rich and improving country there is a natural and strong tendency to a constantly increasing price of raw produce, owing to the necessity of employing, progressively, land of an inferior quality" (p. 21 n.).

Since the *Inquiry into Rent* and the *Grounds of an Opinion* both appeared some days before West's *Essay*, there can be no question of Malthus' taking anything from West. But whereas Diminishing Returns was West's main and all governing thought, and a most welcome argument against protection, to Malthus it was by no means the whole, and on the political side it was awkward for him as a protectionist. For he believed still that high rents were a sign of prosperity, and he lamented in *Grounds of an Opinion* the loss of agricultural capital and the general inquiry which would follow the removal of protection.

Therefore Ricardo, who was an out-and-out free-trader, entered the fray on the side of West in criticism of Malthus. In his *Essay on the Influence of a Low Price of Corn on the Profits of Stock*[1] (1815), he contended that higher rents would come out of

---

[1] The title continues, "shewing the Inexpediency of Restrictions on Importation with Remarks on Mr Malthus' two last publications 'An Inquiry into the Nature and Progress of Rent,' and 'The grounds of an Opinion on the Policy of Restricting the Importation of Foreign Corn'".

the pockets of manufacturers, merchants and farmers themselves. He agreed with West that with the progress of wealth, and in spite of improvements in agriculture, the returns from agriculture had diminished, and that this diminution was the historical reason of the fall in the rate of profit. He did not dispute priority with West. Indeed, in the preface to his *Principles of Political Economy and Taxation* (1817), he acknowledged that West and Malthus "presented to the world, nearly at the same moment, the true doctrine of rent"; and West in the introduction to a later essay, *The Price of Corn and Wages of Labour* (1826), claimed that he (West) was also the first to demonstrate in 1815 Ricardo's further point, that the diminution in the profits of stock was the necessary result of the diminution of the productive power of labour in agriculture.

Be that as it may, West was not Elisha. It was Ricardo who gave West's rendering of the problem the stamp of classical truth. None of West's argument, however, is really concerned with agriculture. His proof is *a priori*: if it were not so, something else admitted to be true could not be so—the something else being the fall in the profits of stock, which could not be due to wage earners getting more, because otherwise population would indefinitely increase. Here we recognise the real stuff, not a paltry economics of agriculture, but abstract strife-begotten law; and on it the classical economists, whose ardour for history was slight, contentedly pastured for the best part of a century. Cobden and Bright, of course, were too shrewd to try such mysteries upon their public. They talked their simpler statistical moralities. But the endorsement of political economy was at their service; and they assumed it, when calling down the wrath of Heaven upon landlords and landlords' monopoly. Adam Smith, the friend of the country gentleman, was now a "lesser light".

But in case the curious are interested to know what John Stuart Mill understood by this crucial law, let us recall the homage which he paid to it in his *Principles* of 1848. (i) It is a general law or principle; (ii) it does not come into operation at a very early date; (iii) it is liable to temporary supersession; (iv) it is one against which headway has been made throughout

the whole known history of England by the antagonising principle of civilisation; (v) nevertheless it is of immense importance,
"the most important proposition in political economy".[1] But
the corn laws had been repealed two years; and though Mill's
successors paid lip service to the law (or tendency—they preferred this word as the years went on), their hearts were not in
the matter. They transferred themselves to Diminishing Returns
per factor of production, having no corn bill to denounce: or, if
they had an urge to social reform, to the phenomenon of the
site values of large towns. Is it possible that wheat quota will
bring them back to their old stamping ground? Stranger things
have happened—revenue tariffs for example. Mr Wesley
Mitchell then will come to know why we in England are such
passionate economists.

Meanwhile, through war and peace, the great mass of England
toiled on, totally uninterested in Diminishing Returns, and interested only at second best in Corn Law Repeal. By 1838
their first hate was the New Poor Law, and their first love the
Charter, but what of olden days?

Behind every movement that has ever influenced the thoughts of
mankind, there is always some master mind, a Jesus of Nazareth, a
Wiclif, a John Wesley, a Darwin, a Tolstoy, or a Henry George; and
it is in the comparatively unknown Jerrard Winstanley that we shall
find the master mind, the inspirer and director of the Digger Movement.[2]

> With spades and hoes and plows, stand up now, stand up now,
>   With spades and plows and hoes, stand up now,
> Your freedom to uphold, seeing Cavaliers are bold
>   To kill you if they could, and rights from you withhold.
>   Stand up now, Diggers all.
>
> (*The Diggers' Song*, by Jerrard Winstanley, 1649.)

So writes Winstanley's biographer; so wrote Winstanley himself. Winstanley, like John Bright after him, was a Lancashire
man and a Quaker. Winstanley came from Wigan: Bright from
Rochdale. And indeed the Gracchi of England have mostly
come from north of the Trent—Winstanley: Bright: Thomas

---

[1] J. S. Mill, *Principles of Political Economy*, I. xii. § I.
[2] L. H. Berens, *The Digger Movement in the Days of the Commonwealth*,
p. 40.

Spence of Newcastle-upon-Tyne: William Ogilvie, the Aberdeen professor: Patrick Edward Dove, the Ayrshire laird: Richard Cobden, son of a Sussex farmer indeed but identified with Manchester and Stockport. Robert Owen, no Southron, was a Welshman who reached New Lanarck via Manchester. William Langland and Joseph Arch (to make a stride over six centuries) were Midlanders. Though the most famous community experiment of the nineteenth century was at Queenwood, Hampshire, yet it was concocted in the industrial North after the model of Orbiston, and in its performance it could not compare with the boisterous benevolence of Ralahine, county Clare. Finally, Henry George himself appeared from America to speak for Irish peasants and Scottish crofters. He was lionised in London, Miss Helen Taylor, Mill's stepdaughter, leading the way, but his real audience was in Irish cabins and Scottish crofts.

The greater freedom of the new North may be worn into a *cliché*. Some account thus for Birmingham, Manchester and Leeds; and say too little, though indeed one may say too much, about good water, humid air and grassy moors. But Scotland economically was newer than England, and there was no bondage in England comparable to that of the Scottish collier in the eighteenth century. We should say rather that the North was more rebellious and more intent on freedom, learning it from their residence in towns, which have been the soil of freedom since Domesday. Adam Smith, the Scotsman, bathed England in a liberalism which all but drowned its social sense; so that we do not know whether to be more grateful to him for his denunciation of the law of settlement or to the lordly engrossers of England for saving their dependents from starvation by the ignominious compromise of Speenhamland. It has been said of the People's Charter that it could not stand the journey from the provinces up to London. It was the peculiar achievement of the Anti-Corn Law League that, with the help of the railways, it journeyed to and from London until the corn laws were repealed. But when Philip Snowden tried to lash Parliament into righteous sympathy with the taxation of land values, the response he got was the forced response of party politics. His real audience no longer lived—levellers, corn-law rhymers, starving chartists,

Irish nationalists or unquenchable radicals from north of Berwick-upon-Tweed. Between socialism and land reform there is no natural affinity. The thing of which John Bright was persuaded, that landlordism is the common foe, was tenable only in the days of Bright. It was impossible in the age of Thomas Spence; for industrialism was then too young to be class-conscious. It was impossible in the age of Henry George; for by then socialism had passed beyond land reform altogether. The farms they still owned and operated, the co-operators of the 1880's could hardly have accounted for—so great was the gap between 1826, when villages of mutual unity and co-operation were in the dreaming, and 1886, when the vanguard of discontent was following Marx to the overthrow of capitalism and the bourgeoisie.[1] The landlords of 1886 were a minor hate. And the same disappointment awaited Henry George in his own country. He returned to America to find the first flame of the Granger movement spent and to be defeated in a stiff fight for the Mayoralty of New York. The Socialists, who should have supported him, insisted that *the* question was "not a land tax, but the abolition of all private property in the instruments of production".

Jerrard Winstanley's quarrel of 1649 was with "the old Norman Prerogative Lord of that Manor". (Indeed, he seems never to have forgiven "1066 and all that".) "Undeniably the earth ought to be a Common Treasury of Livelihood for all without respecting persons."[2] Therefore he and his disciples proceeded to sow roots and beans on the waste of St George's Hill in Surrey. But Fairfax and the Protector refused to see the Light: they thought the diggers a paltry nuisance, and suppressed them by soldiers armed with pike and bible. And this, in miniature, is the fate of all agrarian revolt in England. It has sometimes done damage: in 1830 it burnt many hayricks. But it has never made the country really afraid. It was formidable only when it was a revolt of native fenmen against Cornelius Vermuyden and his draining Dutch. The Bank of England has

---

[1] In 1886 *Das Kapital*, written 1867, first appeared in English. Marx died in 1883.

[2] Winstanley, *Watchword to the City of London*.

been barricaded many times, but never against dispossessed commoners. How very different was the fear of Chartism. Indeed, it is this impotence of rural discontent which makes the England of 1789 so vastly different from Revolutionary France. Suppose that not in 1789, but in 1688, landlordism had been abolished in England. Even then a peasantry would not have been established in its place; for even then such progress had been made in the extension of tenant farming, such slices had been cut in the pattern of communal agriculture, that the large majority of villagers would only have exchanged a new master for an old.

Throughout the eighteenth century enclosure was a burning issue, but no one who has traced with Gonner the extent of enclosure, county by county and soil by soil, will contend that it was a national issue. It was a long-drawn multiplicity of local battles, reconstructed into dramatic unity by the gifted correspondent of *The Manchester Guardian*. But in Lancashire itself there never was a regular system of open fields. We are sometimes asked to lament with Arthur Young that the villager was not salvaged in the Napoleonic age by the gift of five acres and a cow. It had as much chance of salvaging him then, as the allotment movement of the 1830's. He would have dug himself very soon into a potato standard. For either the small working farmer owns the land or he does not. If he owns it, there is no place for landlords as an institution. If he does not, five acres are a wage extra, a useful extra, but a wage. And without restrictive legislation they would have passed from his hands to the speculators, as swiftly as the land grants for soldiers in the early days of Canadian settlement.

Thomas Spence of Scottish ancestry was a schoolmaster of Newcastle-upon-Tyne, and he proposed in 1775 that the rent of all lands should be divided among the people; for "mankind have as equal and just a property in land as they have in liberty, air, or the light and heat of the sun".[1] He was provoked to demand this restoration of primeval right by the spectacle of the great moor outside Newcastle, which had just been enclosed and its rent divided among the freemen of the town. It was the cry

[1] Lecture, p. 9 (*Pioneers of Land Reform*, ed. M. Beer).

of a townsman; and the towns of England took it up, after the French Revolution had loosed their tongues. Spence supplied *Pigs' Meat* to Burke's "swinish multitude", and had just started *The Giant Killer* when in 1814 he died. The Cato Street conspirators of 1819 were Spenceans to a man, but it is doubtful whether in 1830 the revolting labourers of Hampshire and Kent so much as knew his name.[1]

Thomas Paine, the politician of land-law reform, William Ogilvie its "Euclid", Patrick Edward Dove, its scientist, were all true to type. Ogilvie published anonymously in 1781 his *Essay on the Right of Property in Land*, a considerable and closely reasoned work: Paine his *Agrarian Justice* in 1796, a brief tract, coming after the *Rights of Man* and *Age of Reason*, and very apposite, because it proposed to compensate every adult for the loss of his or her natural inheritance, out of a revolving fund as mysterious as Pitt's Sinking Fund of compound interest. Patrick Edward Dove was the contemporary of Cobden and Bright. He published a notable treatise on the Revolver,[2] and in addition pistolled society with some rebel economics. In *Elements of Political Science* (1854) he argued that historically private rent is misappropriated taxation. The allocation of rents to the nation would make one single tax in lieu of all customs and excise. It would unite the agricultural and manufacturing classes into one common interest. It would secure to every labourer his share of the previous labours of the community (this is an echo of the 1820's—the right of labour to the whole produce of labour). Landlords are the natural enemies of God and man. "As a class they are antagonistic to industry, enemies to freedom and to progress, barriers to the civilisation of the world, living on the fruits of other men's labours, yet hating the toil which alone endows them with wealth."[3] At this precise

---

[1] For the influence of Thomas Spence on American land reform, see *Documentary History of American Industrial Society* (ed. J. C. Commons, etc.), VII. 29–32, and in particular a letter of May 1844 to the Working Man's Advocate, from which the following is taken: "One, at least, of Spence's publications found its way to America, and, in all probability, led to the movement of the Working Men of New York in 1829" (*ibid.* p. 322). The letter sees in the land schemes of O'Brien and O'Connor a revival of "Spence's principles".

[2] Cf. the account in Morrison Davidson, *Four Precursors of Henry George*, p. 61.   [3] *Op. cit.* p. 328.

point rebel thought was halted and remained at rest as long as prices rose under the help of a metal found in California in 1848. In 1879, when the influence of the new gold from North America and Australia was about exhausted, Henry George, a printer of California, who in his youth had sailed before the mast, published *Progress and Poverty*. Within eight years two million copies of the work were sold or given away. Thought can be pickled. Mill proved this in one sphere, the disciples of Henry George in another. What was new enough to Henry George, being born directly from his Californian life, was old to England, which had repealed its corn laws in 1846. In 1882 Alfred Russel Wallace (who, like Darwin, had arrived through Malthus at organic evolution) followed with his book on *Land Nationalisation, Its Necessity and its Aims*: and England fought unreal battles for a few years—land nationalisation, just too late, because rents now were tumbling down—fair trade versus free trade, a whole generation too soon, because that free trade, which was almost as dear to Henry George as the single tax, had still many years of lusty life.[1] These unrealities misled the scholarly editors of the *Documentary History of American Industrial Society*, when they wrote, "What Fenianism was to Ireland and land nationalisation to England, so was greenbackism to America" (vol. ix. Intro. p. 33). For "land nationalisation" they should have written "The People's Charter", not forgetting O'Connorville.

But a straw showed which way the wind was truly blowing. The Royal Commission on the Housing of the Working Classes (1885) recommended a local tax of 4 per cent. on the selling value of vacant or inadequately used land, as a relief to general rates and a means of bringing down the price of building land by forcing new land into use.[2] The stage was now set for a real

[1] For George's conception of the relation between Free Trade and Single Tax, see his *Protection or Free Trade* (1886).

[2] The Royal Commission on the Housing of the Working Classes published its first Report in 1885. The first two signatories are Albert Edward, Prince of Wales, and Cardinal Manning. The paragraph (p. 42) in full runs: "In connexion with any such general consideration of the law of rating attention would have to be given to the following facts. At present, land available for building in the neighbourhood of our populous centres, though its capital value is very great, is probably producing a small yearly return until it is let

fight which, with imperfect success, is still being fought—the
fight to which Henry George with his memories of San Francisco
would have introduced England, if he had not been intoxicated
by Michael Davitt and his Fenians. In this fight the country-
side, *qua* country-side, and the corn laws have no part. We must
read up Cannan on the History of Local Rates, follow the Webbs
into the maze of Local Government and pretend at all events to
understand De-rating; and when our ennobled throwback to
radicalism, Philip Viscount Snowden, proposes a little something
at very long last, we must be prepared for a reproof from Mr
G. M. Trevelyan and other champions of the open space. In
our zeal to get level with landlords' monopoly we are forcing, so
they tell us, the overtaxed rural landlord to action which will
ribbon the country-side with petrol pumps and bricks. The social
will now desires fewer houses and more trees, which corn law
landlords all along would have been delighted to supply. How
very relative the social *Streitpunkt* is!

You may read for a month in the pamphlet literature of the
eighteenth century upon corn laws and enclosure without
finding anything of documentary importance to say upon the
relation between the two. I find support for this lean conclusion
in Mr Barnes' chapter VI, "The Enclosure Movement and the
Corn Laws". He first of all gives in summary the views of many
historians upon the consequences of enclosure, author by author
and school by school; and in his final page writes, "We now

---

for building. The owners of this land are rated not in relation to the real
value but to the actual annual income. They can thus afford to keep their
land out of the market, and to part with only small quantities, so as to raise the
price beyond the natural monopoly price which the land would command by
its advantages of position. Meantime, the general expenditure of the town on
improvements is increasing the value of their property. If this land were
rated at, say, 4 per cent. on its selling value, the owners would have a more
direct incentive to part with it to those who are desirous of building, and a
twofold advantage would result to the community. First, all the valuable
property would contribute to the rates, and thus the burden on the occupiers
would be diminished by the increase in the rateable property. Secondly, the
owners of the building land would be forced to offer their land for sale,
and thus their competition with one another would bring down the price of
building land, and so diminish the tax in the shape of ground rent, or price
paid for land which is now levied on urban enterprise by the adjacent land
owners, a tax be it remembered which is no recompense for any industry or
expenditure on their part, but is the natural result of the industry and activity
of the townspeople themselves".

come to the last and, from the standpoint of this study, the most important point to be decided: namely, the relation of enclosure from 1765 to 1815 to the Corn Laws ".[1] Then follows a fact, so general that no documentary reference is called for—enclosure, by eliminating the peasant, left the landlords without any backing, save that of the tenant farmers, after 1815. I would go further and say that but for enclosure England would have met the American avalanche of the 1870's by the device which all the countries of Europe adopted, a protective tariff. For all other countries possessed to a greater or less extent a class of cultivating peasants.

Similarly there are general things which one can say of the eighteenth century. Enclosures and corn laws testify jointly, the one locally, the other nationally, to the progress of improvement and the advent of industrialism. The corn laws, by encouraging agriculture, encouraged the enclosures which were the condition of an improved technique; and the enclosures by increasing output made the corn laws endurable. But the progress of enclosure was so piecemeal and secular that it cannot be related in pace or extent to the brief course of corn-law policy. At their best the corn laws were a serviceable stop-gap between an old agriculture that had no surplus to export and a new agriculture that found its entire market at home. At their worst they were an obstruction (in incidence and modes of circumvention not unlike the law of poor settlement) to the fluid supply of a fundamental want. Let those who will believe that without the corn laws there would have been no Tull or Townshend. But given Tull and Townshend the corn laws, as an aid to production, sink into the second order of magnitude.

Thus far of the producer. But the corn-law policy of the eighteenth century had two sides, regard for the consumer, as well as regard for the producer; and during the eighteenth century the industrial consumer, by petition and *émeute*, was slowly attaining to power. Examples of this in one very significant industry have been collected by Messrs Ashton and Sykes in chapter x of their *Coal Industry of the Eighteenth Century*. This, be it noted, was also the industry of royalties and way-

[1] D. G. Barnes, *History of the English Corn Laws*, p. 113.

leaves, of royalties which went not to the Crown, but to noble lords and the prince bishop of Durham. Describing "a small common not exceeding 300 yards over", a pamphleteer of 1779 says, "The herbage of the whole common is not, nor ever was, worth 20s. per Annum. For leave of a Way over this small pittance of ground, otherwise almost useless, the late Mr C., as I am credibly informed, received annually for some years, above 2500 l".[1] Mulcted as a producer by one class of landlord, the coal-miner, as a consumer, was starved by another.

In the dear years of the eighteenth century the miners came out on riot, attacking granaries as a variant on the detested turnpike—in 1709, 1740, 1753, 1757 (when most towns and trades were on riot), and sporadically from 1765 to 1773. Now they would board an export vessel or seize wagons on the way to the ship's side. Now their women would show the way: now they would show the way to their mates, the iron smelters, or the keelmen. On June 26, 1740, they entered Newcastle "in terrible numbers and with all sorts of weapons".[2] In 1757 in Northumberland, Carmarthen and Somerset there were clashes between the miners and the troops. After 1765, as years of unfavourable harvests and of war grew in number, corn riots became almost endemic. In 1789 in North Wales thousands of colliers were on the roads, and "gentlemen of the first rank were insolently called upon, in the most public manner, to lower their rents or take the consequences".[3] In the great scarcities of 1799 and 1800 the tumult was general. And when peace came in 1815, the insolent corn law of that year provoked disturbances in the country which have been graphically described by Samuel Bamford in the opening pages of his *Life of a Radical*. In their dismay the people turned to Cobbett and political reform. And after the reform bill of 1832 corn law repeal was politically possible.

But to have surrendered the corn laws to mutinous miners would have been as complete an abnegation of government as to have granted the Charter in 1839 and 1842. We have now to

[1] Ashton and Sykes, *op. cit.* p. 188.
[2] Ashton and Sykes, *op. cit.* p. 119.
[3] Ashton and Sykes, *op. cit.* p. 128.

trace the way in which hostility to the corn laws became respectable. This occurred before 1832 through a device of democracy which is peculiarly English: the examination of witnesses before Committees of Parliament and the publication of the evidence and report. When Huskisson assumed office, the merchants and manufacturers had a perfect avenue for the expression of their views. New interests were represented in England long before new towns or new classes. The schoolmaster of the Commons was Thomas Tooke, and he had for pupils men like Huskisson and Peel. As the editor of Tooke and Newmarch says, "No Parliamentary Committee of Inquiry into the Currency and the Bank acts, from the Resumption Committees of 1819 to the inquisitions into the working of the Bank Acts in the 'fifties was complete without an exhaustive and, at times, it must be confessed, an exhausting hearing of one or other of the two".[1] And he might have added "or into the Corn Laws and the State of Agriculture".

The instruction of a Parliament of Tory landlords began in 1814 when Isaac Solly explained the devious ways of the Polish corn trade. And Polish corn in return for Lancashire cotton before long became part of the furniture of free trade. In the 1820's a whole battery of mercantile talent was turned upon the agricultural citadel, Tooke himself, William Jacob, David Hodgson of the crop surveys, and others. From their evidence one might construct a very serviceable economics of the corn trade: the causes of fluctuation in supply; the rigidity of demand for a staple like wheat; the rôle and influence of speculation; why combination of producers is impossible; the objection to Government entering the market and becoming a dealer itself (Brougham's contribution to a proposal of this sort in 1824 was to recommend that the Government should affix three golden balls to the front of the Treasury); the switch from one cultivation to another, in response to price changes, and the difficulties of switching in time. Furthermore, the misbehaviour of the corn averages gave scope for refinements of criticism, such as Gladstone delighted to indulge when he was adjusting the duties on wines and spirits. While this and much else was being

[1] Gregory, Intro. to Tooke, *History of Prices*, p. 6.

told to Parliament, Tooke and others were turning it into substantial books. Between 1818 and 1838 there was, as it were, an Anti-Corn Law League of intellectuals; and they had already worn away half the defences of Huskisson and Peel before Manchester came into action. They had no particular master, unless perhaps it was Ricardo. But some were more emphatic than the rest, notably Colonel Robert Torrens, who came into notoriety in 1815 with an *Essay on the External Corn Trade*. At inordinate length and with tireless pleasure he exercises in the jargon of comparative costs, outdoing Ricardo. If the corn laws had not been in the offing, none would have listened to him, but until 1846 there was always an audience for comparative cost, with England as country A, Poland as country B, corn as commodity Y, and cottons as commodity Z. Mill lived in the thick of repeal, but he was always detached and he reserved his powder for the taxation of unearned increment of rent.[1] The academicals who talked corn laws in their theory were Nassau Senior and Thorold Rogers, both of Oxford. In them the substratum and antecedents of Corn Law Repeal are visible and both moved on its plane. Senior diverted economic thought from landlords' share in the gross produce to burdens upon real property, the cost of land transfer and the like. He gave evidence before the Committee of 1846 on the Burdens on Real Property, whose Report is the genesis of the tax theory embodied by the leading economists of England in the well-known *Memoranda on the Classification and Incidence of Imperial and Local Taxes* of 1899. Thorold Rogers, most irritating of learned men, dug out from the muniment rooms of Oxford colleges the price of wheat and the wages of agricultural labour from the beginning of things. This seemingly antiquarian research made a livelier appeal to the working-class imagination than the theory of tax burdens. Under Rogers the fifteenth century loomed up as the golden age of the agricultural labourer: after which came exploitation. The working men, whose sons will be in the W.E.A., studied him. The land taxers turned to him for quotations, "I contend that from 1563 to 1824, a conspiracy concocted by the law and carried out by parties interested in its success, was entered into,

[1] Cf. *Principles*, v. ii. § 5.

to cheat the English workman of his wages, to tie him to the soil, to deprive him of hope and to degrade him into irremediable poverty".[1] And again, "The labourers, as far as the will went, were better off under the rule of the Saints than under that of the sinners".[2] For the sinners of the Restoration framed the acts of Charles II, which are the starting-point of our Corn Law story. Perhaps Mr Gras knew his English history well enough to suspect that there must be a Stuart corn bounty somewhere!

When the League's lecturer came to Cambridge, he met, as we have seen, with a rude reception. When Henry George in the early spring of 1884 went to Oxford the atmosphere was not less tense. Marshall, then a lecturer at Balliol College, engaged him. He had already in 1883, while Professor of Political Economy at the University College, Bristol, delivered three lectures on *Progress and Poverty*: "Wealth and Want: do they increase together?" "Poverty and Wages", "The Nationalisation of Land". From lecture III, I treasure this, "For the sake of this [*sc.* the single tax] Mr George is willing to pour contempt on all the plans by which working men have striven to benefit themselves; he is willing arbitrarily to bring to ruin numberless poor widows and others who have invested their little all in land; he is willing to convulse society and run the dangers of civil war". It merits a front place in any collection of the "orphans and widows" argument. A lady who heard the lectures said that he reminded her of a boa constrictor, who first slobbered over his victim and then swallowed him.

At the meeting the atmosphere was electric. York Powell was in the chair. Ladies fainted, among them Miss Max Müller, the daughter of Henry George's host. In language that must be true, Henry George, the son, describes the scene:

Alfred Marshall, lecturer on political economy at Balliol College, was the first to rise. He observed among other things, that not a single economic doctrine in Mr George's book was both new and true, since what was new was not true and what was true was not new. He announced that he had repeatedly challenged anyone to disprove

---

[1] *Six Centuries of Work and Wages*, p. 398, quoted L. H. Berens, *Digger Movement*, p. 89.
[2] *The Economic Interpretation of History*, p. 241, L. H. Berens, *op. cit.* p. 110.

this, but that no one had come forward. Moreover, he was of opinion that Mr George in his book had not understood a single author whom he had undertaken to criticize, but he (Marshall) offered no censure, because Mr George had not had the special training necessary to understand them. Interspersed with assertions of this kind was a shower of questions.

The lecturer's chief reply was that he was willing to subject "Progress and Poverty" to Mr Marshall's test—that it contained nothing that was both new and true. Because, said Mr George, the book was based upon the truth; and the truth could not be a new thing; it always had existed and it must be everlasting. He endevoured to pick out and answer a number of Marshall's questions, and he really succeeded in winning the support and applause of a considerable number of the audience. But there were cheers from others for the Balliol man, and he, after rising very often and engaging much time, turned to his supporters and answered that the lecturer had failed to meet his queries; whereupon he sat down.[1]

It is reported that during the meeting Henry George got rather angry.

And the dear old *Dictionary of Political Economy* is not less superb. After committing the elementary blunder of attributing George's theories to the slums of New York, and saying nothing about the gold mining, the railroad barons and the building booms of California, from which *Progress and Poverty* directly issued, the article quotes a few of George's most challenging sentences, such as "What I propose as the simple yet sovereign remedy...is to appropriate rent by taxation"; and concludes, "The danger of these opinions has become more apparent as time goes on".

Lest this should not suffice, an added unsigned column to the article on Land Nationalisation concludes:

The principles Mr George advances would be equally valid against the existence of any property at all, and, however the inequality of wealth may menace civilisation, the destruction of all wealth would be fatal to human progress.

Nowadays we say all this with the single word, Bolshevism.

Three hundred years ago, the City Companies kept granaries of corn for the provision of London's poor; and as late as 1890

[1] *Life of Henry George by his son Henry George Junior* (1900), pp. 435–6.

Sir William Crooks threatened mankind with eventual starvation. To-day, however, we are asking the question, Is it more painful to grow wheat or to run the risk of lacking it? The modern problem is brought home by a letter such as that received from an unknown correspondent in Canada, which runs:

Kipling, Sask., Canada.

Jan. 18, 1932.

I have just read an article of yours *re* Stamp Report on Wheat Pool. I doubt whether you or anyone else over there realizes what we are up against here. We have had three years of droughts and low prices combined. Some have had no crop at all for 3 years, we ourselves had our seed back for 2 years, this year we have nothing. I have been here 28 years and have still assetts supposed to be worth about 24 hundred £. Like the rest of the farmers I have some debts. The result is that my assetts are not assetts any more, but rather Liabilities. 2 years ago we got 10*d.* per bus. for barley, last year 5*d.*, this year no crop. Wheat is, one Nor; 1*s.* 9*d.* or 1*s.* 8*d.* at the most, at the present time, and I think when they have oats and barley to sell, they will get no more than 10*d.* per bus. at the most, as we are 700 to 1000 miles from Fort William and prices are based on these. Butter is 5*d.* lb., cockerels 5*d.* each, hides 1*s.* 8*d.* for a 50 lb. hide. Wool thrown out, a neighbour of mine was offered one halfpenny per lb. for a dressed carcass of beef. Pork is 2*d.* per lb. the best quality. We had no crop, no vegetables, and like thousands of others we are going on relief, yet we have 8 horses, 10 cattle, 9 sheep besides poultry. If you should care to know further about conditions I will be glad to send you newspaper clippings as you will learn from them and I am anxious to let my fellow countrymen know the truth about things here, I am quite sure they would be appalled.

Yours,

(etc.).

A mad world, my masters! Abundance beyond the dream of the Hungry Forties, yet distress such as they perhaps never knew. It is not pleasant to see too closely into the heart of things, neither into the agonies of war nor into the depressions of peace. We cannot always rouse ourselves to the high pitch of corn law orators or ranting Chartists; and yet that quivering under-life, which now and then under social strain comes out into the daylight of events, furnishes some of the most poignant chapters in the history of mankind. Is it surprising that numerous workers in the Old World and the New speak of the breakdown of capitalism and passionately desire a new state of society? Is it surprising that those who are very close to the earth murmur about a financial conspiracy in high places and subscribe to Major Douglas or one of the numberless variants upon him? For such as these are the true children of Henry George, as Henry George was the true child of Cobden and Bright.

TWO SPEECHES OF SIR ROBERT PEEL
TRANSCRIBED FROM HANSARD
(For *précis*, see p. 213 *et seq.*)

I

Introducing the Corn Bill of 1842

[Feb. 9, 1842

CORN LAWS—MINISTERIAL PLAN.] Sir R. Peel rose, and moved that the paragraph in her Majesty's Speech relating to the Corn Laws be read.

The motion being agreed to,—

The Clerk at the Table read the following paragraph in the Speech from the Throne:—"I recommend also to your consideration the state of the laws which affect the import of corn, and of other articles, the produce of foreign countries".

Sir R. Peel next moved, that the House resolve itself into a Committee to consider the laws relating to the import of corn.

The House accordingly resolved into Committee, and Mr Greene, the chairman of committees, having taken the chair,—

Sir *R. Peel* again rose, and spoke as follows:—Sir, I rise in pursuance of the notice which I have given, to submit to the House the views of her Majesty's Government with respect to the modification and amendment of those laws which regulate the import of foreign corn. I should consider it a reflection on this House were I to prefer any claim on its patience and indulgence. Whatever demands I might have to prefer, and however unqualified I may be to relieve a subject necessarily one of detail, necessarily abstruse, by any illustrations of fancy, yet I am convinced that the paramount importance of the subject itself will induce the House to lend me that patient attention for which, under other circumstances, I might have deemed it necessary to appeal to its indulgence. I am aware of the difficulties which encompass the subject I am about to bring under the consideration of the House. With regard to a matter in respect to which such adverse opinions prevail, it is difficult to discuss it without making statements or admissions which will be seized on by those who entertain opposite opinions; but I feel that the best course I can pursue is to submit to the House the considerations which influenced the judgment and decision of her Majesty's Government, and to leave them to be decided on by the reason, moderation, and judgment of Parliament. I am confident that the course which her Majesty's Government have pursued in bringing forward this measure, whatever may be the differences of opinion as to its nature—I am confident that that course at least will meet with general approbation. If her Majesty's Government deemed it right to submit a measure of this character to the consideration of Parliament, it was due to the importance of the subject that the attention of Parliament should be called to it in the Speech from the Throne. It was due also to the importance of the subject that her Majesty's Government should undertake, on their own responsibility, to propose a measure for the adjustment of this question, and that no interval which could be avoided should be allowed to elapse between the recommendation contained in the Speech from the Throne, for consideration of the subject by Parliament, and the proposal of the measure itself. The only object which I shall aim at, in bringing this subject under the consideration of the House, will be to state as clearly and as intelligibly as I can the considerations which have influenced her Majesty's Government in reference to the nature of the measure I am about to propose. One other object I shall aim at—namely, to discuss this question, affecting such mighty interests, in a temper and spirit conformable with its great importance, bearing in mind how easy it is, on each side, to raise exaggerated apprehensions, and find inflammatory topics by which the feelings of the people may be excited. Her Majesty's Government have deemed it their duty to consider the Corn-laws with a view to their modification and amendment. They undertake the consideration of this question at a period when there is commercial distress, and when there exist great suffering and privations connected with that distress. But I feel it my duty, in the first place, to declare that, after having given to this subject the fullest consideration in my power, I cannot recommend the proposal which I have to make by exciting a hope that it will tend materially and immediately to the mitigation of that commercial distress. While I admit the existence of commercial distress—while I deplore the sufferings which it has occasioned, and sympathise with those who have unfortunately been exposed to privations, yet I feel bound to declare that I cannot attribute the distress—to the extent in which it was by some supposed imputable—to the operation of the Corn-laws. I do not view with those feelings of despondency, with which some are inclined to regard them, the commercial prospects of this country.

I do not believe that the resources of our commercial and manufacturing prosperity are dried up. I do see a combination of causes, acting concurrently and simultaneously, sufficient, in my opinion, to account, in a great degree, for the depression which has unfortunately prevailed among the manufacturing and commercial interests of this country; and I have that reliance on the native energies of this country, and I have had such frequent experience of preceding depressions and revivals almost as sudden and extraordinary as the depression which has recently occurred, that I do entertain a confident hope and belief that we may still look forward to the revival, by the operation of natural causes, of our commercial and manufacturing prosperity. It is impossible, I think, to take a review of the causes which have affected that prosperity without perceiving that there have been in operation, during the last four or five years, several causes, the separate effect of which would have been considerable, but the concurrent effect of which is sufficient to account for the depression which has taken place. If you look at the stimulus which was given, partly, I think, by the facilities of credit, to great undertakings in 1837 and 1838; if you look to the connection which existed between the directors and parties concerned in joint-stock banks and the manufacturing establishments; if you look at the immense efforts made for the increase of manufactories and for the building of houses for the reception of those who were to labour in those manufactories; if you look at the immigration of labour from the rural districts into districts the seats of manufactures, and the immense increase of mechanical power which took place in consequence in the years 1837 and 1838, you will hardly be surprised to find that the result which has before attended similar excitement and stimulus should again ensue. The same causes which operated here to produce depression operated also in the United States at the same time. The derangement of the monetary affairs of the United States has acted powerfully on the demand for our manufactured produce, and, concurrently with the depression in this country, has had the effect of diminishing the demand for British manufactures. There has been at the same time an interruption of our amicable relations with China, which has been the cause of a considerable deficiency in the exports to that country of our manufactured goods within a recent period, as compared with previous periods. There have been also up to a recent period an alarm of war in Europe, and that stagnation of commerce which, in some degree, is inseparable from such a state of things. The united effect of these causes goes far, in my opinion, to account for that depression in our prosperity, which has created so much regret. I am admitting the extent of that depression; and I am equally disposed to admit the extent of the privations and sufferings which have resulted; but I feel bound again to declare that I cannot recommend the measure which I am about to propose, by exciting a hope that any alteration of the Corn-laws will be a remedy for some of the evils which, in a great manufacturing country like this, seem inseparable from the system. Extend your foreign commerce as you may, depend on it that it is not a necessary principle that the means of employment for manual labour will be proportioned to the extent of your commerce. Whatever may be the extent of your commercial prosperity, whatever may be the demand for your manufactures, it is impossible not to feel that coincident with that general prosperity there may exist in particular districts the severest partial distress.

This must have been the case at periods of the greatest commercial and manufacturing prosperity. The necessary consequence of the sudden employment of machinery, diminishing the demand for manual labour, must be to expose in certain districts of the country those who depended for support on manual labour to great privations and suffering. You find hundreds of persons occupied in a great manufacturing establishment. Their reliance for subsistence has been placed on their labour in that establishment; but by an exercise of ingenuity some improvement in machinery is suddenly devised, and copied by others, which has the effect of depriving those who have relied on manual labour for subsistence of employment. This has been the case with the handloom weavers, and with many parties engaged in manufactures. It is the hard condition, inseparable from a manufacturing country, that there must be such revulsions in the demand for manual labour; and it is not an impeachment, therefore, of any commercial system that great privations and sufferings exist. Let it not be supposed that I am deprecating the exercise of skill and the improvement of mechanical power. It would be madness to attempt to check them. It would be folly to deny that in the aggregate this country has derived a great source of strength from such improvements in manufactories. The attempt to obstruct them would have the necessary effect of encouraging competitors and rivals, already too formidable. In referring to instances of distress, inseparably connected as it appears to me with such development of skill and improvement in machinery, I do not do so for the purpose of impeaching that skill or deprecating that improvement, but for the purpose of discouraging the too sanguine hope that any extent of legislative interference can exempt you from the occasional recurrence of distress. In proportion to the manufacturing excitement—to the *stimuli* to which I have referred—the *stimuli* of speculation—of facilities for undertakings created by undue advances and credit— in that proportion must you expect that in certain districts those privations to which the attention of Parliament has been called will occur. But looking at the general state of the commerce of this country, I neither see grounds for that despondency, with which some are in the habit of viewing it, nor can I see any ground for imputing to the operation of the Corn-laws, as some do, any material share in the evils at present existing. I think we are too apt to assume that there must be a constant and rapid increase in the amount of our exports to other countries, and we are too apt to despond when we find any occasional check in the amount of our exports. We decline to compare the extent of our commerce in the last year with a period of time more distant than the preceding year. We insist on comparing it with the year immediately preceding; and if there appears a decline we are too apt to apprehend that the sources of our prosperity are dried up. At all periods of our commercial history there have been these alternations of prosperity and depression. The latest period to which the returns respecting our trade are fully made up will include the year 1840, and comparing the state of trade in 1840 with its condition in preceding years, during the operation of the Corn-laws, I see no ground for the inference sometimes drawn, that the Corn-laws are the cause of our misfortunes, and that the repeal or alteration of them will supply an immediate remedy. In 1840 the exports of British produce and manufactures to all parts of the world exceeded the exports of 1837 by 9,355,000*l.* I am speaking now of declared value. The exports of 1840 exceeded those of 1838 by 1,345,000*l.* and fell short of the exports of 1839 by 1,827,000*l.*, a falling off sufficient no doubt, to create anxiety and unpleasantness. But the causes of that falling off are amply accounted for, by referring to the state of commercial transactions with the United States—a country with whose prosperity our own was so intimately interwoven. There, during that period, there were causes operating, connected with the monetary derangement, sufficient to account for the cessation of the American demand. I have stated that in 1840 as compared with 1839, there was a deficiency in our general exports of 1,827,000*l.* declared value. But in 1839 there was an export to the United States of goods to the value of 8,839,000*l.*, whereas, in 1840 the total amount of exports to that country was only 5,283,000*l.* thus showing a diminution of our exports to the United States in 1840, as compared with 1839, to the extent of 3,556,000*l.* That fact, therefore, is sufficient to account for the falling off in the general amount of exports in the year 1840 as compared with 1839. The falling off in the amount generally was greatly less than that in the amount taken by America, and the difference was consequently made up by an extension of our commerce with other parts of the world. It is very satisfactory, Sir, for example, to view the progress of our colonial trade. In 1837 the exports to the colonies were 11,208,000*l.* in value; in 1838 they were 12,025,000*l.*; in 1839 they were 14,363,000*l.*; in 1840 they were 15,497,000*l.* Let us look also to the state of our commercial transactions with those countries in Europe which are the chief sources of our supply of food. Let us look at the state of our export trade with Germany, with Holland, and with Belgium. In 1839 the value of our exports to those three countries, the chief sources of our supply was 8,742,000*l.*; in 1838 it was 9,606,000*l.*; in 1839 it was 9,660,000*l.*; in 1840 it was 9,704,000*l.* So that even with respect to those countries from which we derive our chief supply of grain, when we stand in need of it, which are supposed to be such formidable competitors in manufactures, and from which the demand for British produce and manufactures is supposed to be so rapidly diminishing, on account of our exclusion of their products, it still appears, on the whole, that there has been a progressive increase in the amount of our commerce carried on with them. I cannot, therefore, infer that the operation of the Corn-law is to be charged with the depression which is at present so severely felt in many branches of trade; I see other causes in operation which are sufficient, in a great degree, to account for the evils no one can deny to exist. In considering then, Sir, those modifications of the Corn-laws which it may be desirable to effect, it is important to review the proposals that have been made for this end. Various opinions are entertained with respect to the Corn-laws. There are some who will admit of no modification whatever in those laws as they now exist. My firm belief is, that that party in this country is exceedingly limited in number. I do believe that among the agriculturists themselves there is a prevailing feeling that the Corn-laws may be altered with advantage.

So far as I can collect that feeling from the communications which have been made to me, I must say I think that the impression among the agriculturists is in favour of modifying those laws in certain respects. There are others who entertain a decidedly opposite opinion, who will not hear of a modification, but insist on the immediate and absolute repeal of the Corn-laws. Sir, it is impossible not to feel that those who advocate the repeal of every impost of every kind upon the subsistence of the people are enabled to appeal to topics which give them a great advantage—to urge that there is a tax upon bread, a tax upon the subsistence of the people—to urge that that tax is maintained for the protection or advantage of a separate class. He who urges arguments of this kind must, of course, make a considerable impression upon those who listen to him. A comparison is made between the dearness of food in this country, and the cheapness of food in some other countries, and the inference is immediately drawn, that the people of this country ought to be placed upon the same footing in respect to the articles of subsistence, and that their condition will be benefited by the reduction of the price of food to that rate at which it can be purchased in other countries. Sir, it appears to me that any conclusion founded upon such a position will be altogether erroneous. The question is, can you infer the comfort and ease of the people from the price which they pay for their food? Reference is made to the price of food in Germany, and to the facility which the low price of sustenance gives for the establishment of manufactures; and the inference is hastily and unwisely drawn that the people of this country would be placed in a situation of greater comfort if the price of food should undergo a corresponding reduction, if it should be equalized with the price prevailing in Germany. Now, I apprehend the true question is, not what is the price of food, but what is the command which the labouring classes of the population have of all that constitutes the enjoyments of life, whether these be necessaries or luxuries, partaking, in point of fact, from the universal prevalence of consumption, of the nature of necessaries. Now let us compare the condition of the labouring classes in this country, under the operation of the Corn-laws, with their condition in other countries in which, I admit, the price of provisions is greatly less. There is nothing to impede the cultivation of corn in the Prussian states, in which its price is greatly lower than in this country. But can it be thence inferred that the condition of the people in the Prussian states is preferable to the condition of the people in this country, or that the consequence of an immense reduction in the price of various articles, and particularly in the price of food, must necessarily lead to a great increase in the comforts and enjoyments of the labouring classes in this country? Sir, there are means, from sources I apprehend of unquestionable authority, for forming a judgment as to the comparative degree of comfort enjoyed by the people of the two countries I have mentioned; and, before you determine that a low price of provisions is necessarily essential to manufacturing industry, general consumption, or to the comforts and enjoyments of the people, it will be well to weigh the materials of which you are possessed for forming a judgment on the subject.

Sir, in the report of the committee which sat for the revision of the import duties, there is evidence upon this point given by the hon. Gentleman, the Member for Bolton, whose attention has been directed to this subject, who has collected the materials of information and comparison, and who, before that committee, as well as in the report which he made on the Prussian League, on the state of our commercial relations with Prussia, and the laws which exist in that country with reference to trade, has made statements as to the comparative consumption of the people of this country and the inhabitants of the Prussian states. Let us look to the great articles of consumption. I will begin by admitting that meat is dear in this country; that corn is dear; and that the other great articles which constitute the sustenance of the people and add to their comforts are dear; that they are much higher in price in this country than in Prussia; but, as I said before, it appears to me that the true test is not the comparative lowness of price, but the command which the people have over all that constitutes comfort and enjoyment. I will begin, then, with meat, and I will quote no authority which can be suspected—I will take my information from a perfectly unobjectionable source. I will refer to one who differs entirely from me with regard to the operation of the Corn-laws, and who is a decided advocate for their repeal. Dr Bowring's calculation with respect to the consumption of meat was made in 1840, and given in his report on the Zollverein. The hon. and learned

Gentleman spoke on a state of things in this country when the Corn-laws had been in operation for nearly thirty years, affecting, as they must have done, if it was their tendency to produce such effect, the comfort of the people, and consequently the means of consumption within their power. Dr Bowring then says, that in Prussia,—and I beg the House will remember that the means of ascertaining the exact proportion are believed to exist,—14,000,000 inhabitants consume in one year 485,000,000 lb. of meat, that is, 35 lb. per head. The hon. and learned Gentleman says again, that in this country 25,000,000 persons consume 50 lb. per head yearly; that the quantity cannot be less than 50 lb.; and that it has been frequently estimated at 100 lb. I take the lowest calculation, from which the House will observe it appears that while the inhabitants of Prussia consume but 35 lb. per head, those of the British empire consume at least 50 lb. I am not attempting to deny, by the quotation of these facts, the severity of that distress which prevails in many parts of the country. I could not have attended the discussions which have taken place without feeling a perfect conviction that in Paisley and many other places there is a fearful amount of distress. Do I mean to say, for instance, that the 17,000 persons in Paisley who are supported by charitable contributions consume meat to any thing like the extent I have stated? Not at all; but it is impossible to argue on this subject without drawing general inferences from general statements. I must not be taunted with the remark that individuals at Paisley, Stockport, and other places do not consume 50 lb. of meat per year. I admit they do not; but in drawing general conclusions, with reference to legislation, you have no other alternative than to deal with general averages and general results. I ask you again, before you determine that high prices are necessary evils, to compare the consumption of sugar in this country with that of other European States. I rely entirely on the authority of the hon. and learned Gentleman. The hon. Member states the consumption of sugar in France at 4¾ lb. per head annually; I will say 5 lb., as there may be some increase which he has overlooked. In the States of the German League, it is 4 lb.; in Europe generally, 2½ lb.; while the consumption of Great Britain is calculated by the hon. Gentleman at 17 lb. per head. Taking next the consumption of wheat, I find that Mr Deacon Hume, a gentleman whose loss I am sure we must all sincerely deplore, states the consumption of this country to be one quarter of wheat for each person. Dr Bowring calculates that 24,000,000 of inhabitants in Great Britain consume 45,000,000 quarters of all kinds of grain. I beg the House to recollect, that I take the estimate of two gentlemen possessed of ample means of information, and entertaining views on this question which free their testimony from all suspicion. Mr Hume, then, made our consumption one quarter of wheat per head. The hon. Gentleman (Dr

Bowring) allows nearly two quarters of grain to each individual. In the Prussian states, he says, 14,000,000 of inhabitants consume 13,000,000 quarters of grain, being less than one quarter to each person. Again, while Mr Hume allows one quarter of wheat per head in England, the hon. Gentleman calculates that of the one quarter of grain which he assigns to each individual in Prussia, three fourths at least consist of rye. Throughout the Prussian states, the consumption of rye to wheat, he says, is in the proportion of from three and four to one. In 124 towns of the League he estimates the consumption per head of 65 lb. of wheat, and 241 lb. of rye; that is to say, each individual consumes very little more than one bushel of wheat, instead of one quarter. In England, the hon. Gentleman states the consumption of tea at 1 lb. per head, annually; in the Prussian states at only $\frac{1}{4}$ lb. The consumption of salt, he says, is $16\frac{1}{2}$ lb. in Prussia, and $22\frac{1}{2}$ lb. in England. The annual consumption of cotton goods in Prussia, he says, is about $4\frac{1}{3}$ lb. for a family of five persons, which is about half the amount supposed to be used in England. The consumption of woollen cloth in Prussia amounts, he says, to $2\frac{1}{6}$ ells for each individual; in Great Britain, it has been estimated at $5\frac{3}{4}$ ells. The consumption of tobacco appears to be greater in Prussia than in England, it being 3 lb. per head in the former country, and 1 lb. in the latter. Of butter 2 lb. per head are used in Prussia, and only 1 lb. in England. But, taking the other great articles I have enumerated, it is shown, that the consumption of them by each individual in this country, for the year 1840, was very much greater, although, in that year, the price of corn was exceedingly high, compared with the price in Prussia. So that, looking to the command enjoyed by the laborious classes, of the necessaries and comforts of life, it is found to exist to a far greater extent in England than in Prussia, although there, the price of grain scarcely exceeds half that which it bears in this country. I do not mean to say, that this forms any argument against increasing that amount; I do not wish to push my conclusion further than the point to which it can be legitimately brought. My argument goes to show, that it is not fair to appeal to the diminished price of food in other countries as proving increased comfort in the people in proportion as the article is low priced.

Additional information has been very recently laid on the Table, with respect to the condition of the working classes in Belgium. I invite the attention of the House to the prices of manual labour there, as stated in this document. The average prices of labour are, for agricultural labourers, 11*d*. a day; for weavers, 1*s*. a day; for masons, 1*s*. 3*d*. a day; for locksmiths and carpenters, 1*s*. 3$\frac{3}{4}$*d*. a day; for operatives, working in manufactories, 1*s*. 3*d*. a day; for operatives, working in quarries, mines, &c., 1*s*. 4*d*. a day; for jewellers, goldsmiths, and others, 1*s*. 8*d*. a day. That is the rate of wages in Belgium. Now, what is the price of corn in that country? Last year, at Ostend, wheat was from 51s. 9d. to 53s. a quarter; at Antwerp, it was 51s. to 51s. 2d. a quarter. Taking the general average prices of labour in Belgium, and comparing them with the amount of wages received by the labourers, it does appear to me, that notwithstanding the amount of the manufacturing wages, and notwithstanding the amount of the agricultural wages, which are received there, it does, I say, clearly appear to me, that those wages do not give the labourer there such a command of subsistence, as that given him by the rate of wages usual in this country. I refer to this for the purpose of confirming my impression, that to look for any rapid or great change in the condition of the working population of this country from any extensive change of the Corn-laws, would subject you to great disappointment. My firm belief is—I am now speaking with reference to those who wish for an absolute repeal of these laws—that if the House of Commons should be induced to pledge itself to a total repeal, which we on this side of the House deprecate so much, without relieving permanently the manufactures of the country, you will only superadd the severest agricultural distress. Any such disturbance of agriculture as must follow from a total repeal of the Corn-laws would, in my opinion, lead to unfavourable results, not only with respect to the agriculturists themselves, but also to all those numerous classes who are identified with them in interest.

There is, however, another portion of those who wish for an alteration of the existing laws who would not go the length of total repeal, but desire a substitution for the present, at least, of a fixed duty. With respect then to the ground as thus narrowed, they who are favourable to a fixed duty on corn admit that the agriculturist of this country is entitled to some protection, and therefore they seek to impose a duty invariable in its amount on the importation of foreign corn. Now, with respect to this proposition, it must be remembered that whatever odium attaches to the imposition of a variable duty must apply with equal force to the imposition of a fixed. (A cry of "No, no," from the Opposition benches.) Hon. Members do not seem to apprehend my meaning. I was not saying that exactly the same objections apply to a variable as to a fixed scale of duty. I was only saying, that so far as odium attaches on the imposition of any duty at all, to that extent odium attaches to the imposition of a fixed duty. There might possibly be advantages in a fixed duty which did not apply to the case of a variable duty, but the argument against the imposition of any duty whatever on the importation of the subsistence of the people applies equally to the imposition of a fixed duty. Either the one or the other is imposed on the ground that the agriculturist needs protection. On principle, however, the imposition of a fixed duty rests on the same grounds, and must on principle be defended by the same arguments, as the imposition of a variable duty. Together with my Colleagues, and in concert with them, I have given to the question of a fixed duty the fullest and most patient attention; and if I could have come to the conclusion that for the variable scale of duty it would be better to substitute a fixed duty, I hope I should—considering the obligations under which I act as Minister of the Crown—I hope I should have had the moral courage to avow my conviction, and to propose a fixed duty for the adoption of the House: but, under the actually existing circumstances of the country, I cannot reconcile it to myself to propose to the House that measure for its adoption. But I do not see how to propose such a fixed duty as shall be sufficient for the protection of the agriculturists of this country. I agree that for the last four years the average supply of this country has been unequal to the demand; but in considering this question it becomes important to ascertain what is the probability that this country from its own resources can be able to supply its own population. Now, I am not prepared to admit that this country is unable in ordinary years to supply its own population. If I formed my judgment from the circumstances of the last four years, I should have been compelled to conclude that we were dependent on foreign supply for a great proportion of our consumption; I should have been compelled to come to this conclusion, because the average of the last four years importation of foreign corn into this country was 2,300,000 quarters. But if we take a longer period—if we take twelve or thirteen years, then it would appear, that on the whole, the annual average importation of foreign corn was very considerably smaller. In proof of this I beg to state, that taking the quantities of wheat and wheaten flour imported in those years, it appeared that the whole did not amount to more than 12,000,000 or 13,000,000 of quarters. I will state it more particularly since the year 1828. From July the 5th, 1828, to January the 1st, 1841, the whole quantity of wheat and wheaten flour entered for home consumption was 13,475,000 quarters; and thus I think it must be admitted, that if you take any period of ten years, or taking a somewhat shorter period even, you cannot hope for any period of anything like ten years to pass without seasons occurring within it during which you must be dependent on foreign supply. You cannot hope for an absolute freedom from all dependence on foreign supply some time in the course of a period of ten years, and therefore in that sense you are not now independent of foreign supply. Looking, then, at the question from this point of view, I retain my opinion, which I expressed some time ago, that it is of the utmost importance to the interests of this country, that you should be as far as possible independent of foreign supply. By this I do not mean absolute independence, for that, perhaps, is impossible; and nothing I think would be more injurious than to pass such laws as would give rise to a general impression that it was intended to keep this country in absolute independence of foreign supply; but, speaking generally, I say that it is of importance in a country like this, where the chief subsistence of the labourer consists of wheat, if we resort to foreign countries for supplies, to take care that those supplies should be for the purpose of making up deficiencies rather than as the chief sources of subsistence. Again, if I draw my inference from the last four years, I should be bound to admit, that this country, on account of the increased population, was dependent on foreign countries for a considerable amount of annual supply, because, as I said before, the amount derived from foreign countries in those years was as much as 2,300,000 quarters. But take the last ten years, and what do we find? With respect to the first six years, the produce in those years was sufficient to supply the consumption, or very nearly so; for, in the first six years of the last ten, the average annual importation was only 137,000 quarters. Taking, however, the years 1832, 1833, 1834, 1835, 1836, and 1837, it would be too much to infer, that the population has so rapidly increased with reference to the production of subsistence, that you must abandon altogether the hope of deriving your supplies from your own fields. Within the last ten years the increase of population has exceeded any thing that has ever hitherto been known in this country, and during the last four years the demand for foreign corn has been much greater than usual; but for the greater part of the ten years, the produce of the country has been found equal to its necessities. Therefore I cannot bring myself to the conclusion, that there must be periodical, or even an annual importation of foreign corn, in order to supply the wants of the country; and therefore, in determining our course on this occasion, we have to provide for the case of the produce of comparatively abundant years, as well as for years of comparative scarcity. Now, six years of good harvests may again recur consecutively, in which the produce of the country shall equal its necessities. If they do occur, then, what I fear from your fixed duty would be, that the unlimited right of import at a given amount of duty, which you could always maintain in periods of scarcity, would expose this country to great suffering and distress from producing by excess too great a fall in the prices of agricultural produce, and the remuneration of agricultural labour. It has been observed by writers of great authority, that favourable and unfavourable seasons return in certain cycles; that a year of abundance does not follow a year of scarcity, but that you will find five or six years of the one followed by five or six years of the other. Now, the effect of a fixed duty will be at all times, and under all circumstances, to admit foreign corn to our markets, the produce of a favourable harvest on the continent generally corresponding with that of a favourable harvest here. The great producing countries are within the same parallels of latitude, and are affected by the same causes, and you will generally find that an abundant harvest here has been contemporaneous with an abundant harvest in most countries on the continent. Now, whenever there is an abundant harvest, a slight addition to the amount of corn brought into the market produces a difference in the price very disproportionate to the extent of such addition.

Mr Tooke, in his *History of Prices*, lays down the position that prices vary in a ratio very different from the variation in quantity, and that the difference of ratio between quantities and prices is liable to alter according to the nature of the commodity, but is greater probably in the case of corn than in that of most other articles of extensive consumption. Mr Tooke also institutes a comparison between the produce of deficient and productive harvests on the continent, and states that a deficient harvest here is accompanied generally by a deficient harvest in the countries from which our supplies are usually derived, and that an abundant harvest here is usually accompanied by an abundant harvest there. If that be so, then, when the harvest in this country is sufficient, or very nearly sufficient, to afford a sufficient supply of food, clearly we shall not stand in need of importation from abroad; but if there comes a series of deficient harvests, in that case it appears to me, that there will be such discouragement given to the national agriculture, as must ultimately lead to that dependence for subsistence on foreign supply which I should most earnestly deprecate. But it is argued on the other side by the advocates of a fixed duty, that a fixed duty will prevent these great alternations, and that though it might be difficult to support the fixed duty in times of scarcity, yet the tendency of this duty will be to preserve the country against the occurrence of such contingencies, during which, it is admitted, it would be difficult to maintain it. Now, it appears to me, that such fluctuations of prices are continually taking place, in consequence of the variations of the seasons, as it will be impossible to provide against by legislation, and that no law which you could pass for the establishment of a fixed duty would, in case of a deficient harvest here and on the continent also, prevent a rise to such prices as would render it impossible to maintain the fixed duty. Look to the case of the United States; they are not subject to Corn-laws, yet there you will find fluctuations in the prices, arising out of the variation in the seasons, altogether as great as takes place here. In Prussia, I find that the price of rye, a grain not subject to the operation of the Corn-laws, is liable to fluctuations as great as wheat is subject to under the operation of those laws. In fact, fluctuations in price, must depend so much on the seasons that no law, in my opinion, can guard against the occurrence of high prices. But, if high prices occur, will you maintain your fixed duty? If you impose a fixed duty of 8s. or 10s., and if you

do not authorise some relaxation in periods of scarcity, then, supposing prices to rise to 80*s.* or 90*s.*, I retain the opinion which I
expressed last Session, that no Government in such a case could
undertake to enforce the payment of the duty. If that be admitted,
then you must make some provision for a relaxation of the duty; but
if you intrust this power to the Executive Government, you introduce
uncertainty into the system, you introduce a power difficult to
exercise, and liable to abuse; and you destroy altogether the grounds
for looking forwards to permanence of mercantile arrangements,
which is the great secret of commercial success. I have again, therefore, after considering this subject with the fullest attention, come to
the conclusion that it would not be advisable for Parliament to
legislate on the principle of applying a fixed duty to the importation of
foreign corn.

The alterations of the law which I shall propose will proceed on the
principle of retaining a duty upon corn, varying inversely with the
price of the article in the home market—i.e. the principle of the
existing law. The retention of that principle necessarily involves the
maintenance of a system of averages. It has, indeed, been said that
there would be a great advantage in sweeping away altogether the
system of averages. It is quite obvious that whether it may or may not
be desirable to abandon the system of averages with respect to the
imposition of a duty on corn, you must nevertheless maintain a
system of averages because the whole of your proceedings under the
Tithe Commutation Act are founded on the system of averages. It is
impossible for you to abolish the system of averages, because the
annual payments on account of tithes are founded on calculations
connected with it; and it does appear to me, that as the averages must
be maintained for the purpose of the payments under the Tithe
Commutation Act, it would not be expedient to adopt any other
system of averages materially varying in principle from that for
determining the duty on corn. I hope I shall not be misunderstood.
I am not saying, that because there is a system of averages for fixing
the payments to be made under the Tithe Commutation Act, therefore
you must apply a system of averages for the purpose of determining
the duty on corn. That is not my argument. I am merely stating that
you cannot dispense with a system of averages while your present
Tithe Commutation Act continues in force. The averages must be
taken in order to determine the payments under the tithe law; and I
say, that as you have to determine the amount of payment applicable
to tithe by averages, and also the amount of duty to be imposed on
corn, it would be inconvenient on the one hand to have two systems
of averages prevailing in the country at the same time; while on the
other hand, it would be inconvenient and unjust to depart materially
from that principle on which the averages with respect to tithes are

determined. I propose, therefore, as a necessary incident of a varying duty, to retain a system of averages. Now, there is a very general impression throughout the country that there have been very great frauds in respect of the averages. There is a very general impression, particularly on the part of the agricultural body, that very great frauds have been practised with regard to the averages, a very extensive combination being supposed to have been entered into for the purpose of influencing the averages, and procuring the release of corn at a lower rate of duty than it ought to have paid. I am not disposed to deny, that such a combination may, in some cases, have been entered into, and that in some instances frauds may have been practised; but I very greatly doubt, whether they have been practised to any such extent or with any such effect as is generally supposed. It is generally supposed, that the returns for London unduly influence the averages, and that in Leeds, Wakefield, and other great towns in Yorkshire there have been great and successful combinations for the purpose of unduly influencing the averages. As I said before, I am inclined to think that the impression on this subject may not be altogether without foundation, but still the apprehensions entertained have been greatly exaggerated. Taking the aggregate averages of the kingdom for the six weeks in 1841, ending August the 6th, 13th, 20th, 27th, September 3rd and 7th (*sic*), the price of wheat was 73*s*. 1*d*.; and if I exclude the London market from the averages altogether, the general average would be 72*s*. 8*d*. in place of 73*s*. 1*d*. If I exclude the Yorkshire markets, the average would be 71*s*. 10*d*. It is possible that by raising the price in London, or some of the great corn markets, you create an influence which will raise the price in the other markets of the kingdom; but, so far as you can judge from figures and returns, I think the apprehension that there have been extensive frauds with respect to the averages is, as I said before, if not altogether unfounded, at least very greatly exaggerated. The difference in the aggregate averages, excluding London, amounts in these six weeks to only 5*d*.; excluding Wakefield and the other Yorkshire markets, the difference in the average is only 1*s*. 3*d*.; and if London, Leeds, and Wakefield be excluded, the difference is 1*s*. 1*d*.

Lord *J. Russell*: These differences would make a material alteration in the rate of duty to be paid.

Sir *R. Peel*: Undoubtedly the difference, although so very slight, would affect the amount of duty; but the price of corn in London is much higher than in the country; and therefore I maintain that it is not necessarily to be taken as a ground for the imputation of fraud that the London average exceeds the country average. I will now take the average in 1838; from the 13th of August to the 7th of September the weekly aggregate average of the kingdom was 73*s*. The exclusion of the London market would have made no difference. In 1840, the aggregate average from July 24th to August 28th was 72s. 1d.; the average, exclusive of the London market, was 70s. 11d.; but that difference greatly affected the amount of duty, because when the price is 72s. and under 73s., the duty per quarter is only 2s. 8d., while the exclusion of the London market would have raised the duty to 10s. 8d., the price being above 70s. and under 71s. At the same time, as I said before, we cannot, I think, fairly infer fraud from the higher average of the London market. Now various proposals have been made with respect to the amendment of the law of averages— proposals which have received the utmost consideration from her Majesty's Government. I think there will be a general agreement in this, that whatever system be devised, fraud should as far as possible be excluded, and that all should be fair and legitimate. It is advised by some that returns should be made by the growers only. That proposal has been made by many. I think it impossible to adopt such a suggestion. At present Irish and Scotch corn are admitted into the averages of this country; it would be impossible, therefore, to have in these cases a certificate from the grower, and the exclusion of Irish and Scotch corn from the averages would have a material effect in raising the price of corn. I must also state that I think we ought to guard as far as we can against fraud, but I do not think we ought to attempt to increase protection by any indirect operation. If a certain amount of protection be requisite, and if the Legislature will consent to give it, let it be given directly and openly. It would not be fair to procure an indirect protection and encouragement for domestic agriculture by any suggestion with respect to the averages which had not immediately in view the prevention of fraud and collusion. Various alterations in the law of averages might be made which would have that effect, and which, if they are necessary for the pur- pose of guarding against fraud, ought, in my opinion, to be intro- duced, but for the purpose of getting an indirect protection for agriculture I would not be a party to the proposal of any. It has been suggested by some that the seller should be required, under a penalty, to make a return of the corn sold. It is difficult to foresee what might be the effect of an enactment of that kind, requiring under a penalty every party who might sell a certain proportion of corn to make a return of the quantity sold. The great and only effectual security against fraud in the averages is to take away the temptation to commit it. If you deprive the parties of any motive of self-interest to combine, you take the best and most effective security against the commission of fraud. The proposal of her Majesty's Government with respect to the taking of the averages will be this:—They will propose to take the average in the present mode from the factor, miller, and purchaser of corn—the party who, under the existing law, makes a return at the close of each market day of the whole of the purchases he has made during the preceding week. Upon the whole, we can see no advantage in departing from that principle in taking the averages—making the buyer of corn return the amount of sales of the preceding week, and trusting to the alterations we may make in the levying of the duty for the purpose of effectually preventing fraud. We shall propose that the duty of collecting the returns shall be devolved upon the excise. The excise is perfectly competent to undertake it. That department has an officer employed in each market town—an officer qualified for the discharge of the duty—an officer who has other important cognate functions to perform, and who will be enabled at a very small comparative increase of expense to overtake this additional duty; while his general ability, his habits of business, and the responsibility he incurs from being a public officer, afford a greater security against fraud than could be taken by intrusting the duty to private individuals. We propose, therefore, that the averages should be taken as at present; that they shall be returned to an excise officer acting under the authority of the Board of Excise. Another security we propose to take is to widen the range from which the returns shall be received. At present there are 150 towns named in the Corn Act from which returns are received. From that number of 150 many considerable towns are excluded, in which, since the passing of the present Corn-law, markets have grown up, where considerable quantities of grain are disposed of. We propose, therefore, not to give a discretionary power to any executive officer for the purpose of adding towns from which the averages should be collected; but in the bill which we shall introduce, we propose to name specifically the towns having corn markets to be admitted within the range, but which are now excluded from the list of 150.

It appears to me, that the more you widen the range from which you collect the corn returns, the greater security you take against the averages being influenced by combination and fraud. The best means of determining what is the real average of corn, is by ascertaining its price in a greater number of markets. At present the towns selected are towns in England and Wales, and although I propose to add to their number, I should still restrict them to towns in England and Wales.

Lord *Palmerston*: Can you state the number to be admitted?

Sir *R. Peel*: At present there are 150. I propose to enlarge the range by adding others where corn markets have grown up, and the towns to be so admitted, shall be specifically named in the act. The precautions we propose, appear to us most effectual against combination for the commission of fraud. Our first proposal is to widen the range from which the averages shall be taken; the second is to employ a responsible officer, acting under the authority of a public department, for the purpose of collecting the returns; but the main security we rely on as a prevention of fraud, is such an alteration of the duty as shall diminish the temptation to commit fraud. I trust I have made sufficiently clear to the House the nature of the alterations we shall propose with respect to the taking of the averages. I now approach that more important—by far the most important—part of the subject viz., what is the amount of protection we propose to give to corn the produce of this country, and the manner in which we propose to levy the duty upon foreign corn. At present the House is aware, that the duty payable upon corn is levied in this manner. At 59s. and under 60s., the duty is 27s., diminishing 1s. with 1s. increase of price, until corn arrives at the price of between 66s. and 67s., when the duty is 20s. 8d. The duty then falls 2s., when corn is between 68s. and 69s. At 69s. the duty is 16s. 8d.

Lord *J. Russell*: Not exactly so. Between 69s. and 70s. the duty is 13s. 8d.

Sir *R. Peel*: I am reading from a printed statement, and I believe it to be correct. Between 70s. and 71s. the duty per quarter is 10s. 8d. It then falls 4s., when the price is between 71s. and 72s. It falls 4s. more between 72s. and 73s. and when the price of wheat reaches 73s., or upwards, the duty is 1s. only. The objection to that mode of levying the duty, which has been urged in various quarters, is this— that the reduction of duty is so rapid that it holds out the temptation to fraud; for instance, at 60s. the duty is 26s. 8d., at 73s. the duty is 1s. only; therefore between 60s. and 73s. there is an increase of 13s. and a decrease in duty of 25s. 8d., operating as an inducement to retain corn, or combine for the purpose of influencing the averages, if parties are inclined to combine, amounting on a single quarter of corn to 38s. 8d. So far as pecuniary inducement can go, it is im- possible to be placed higher, either to retain corn, or practise on the averages. Take again prices which are nearer to each other. At 66s. the duty is 20s. 8d.; between 66s. and 73s. the inducement to retain corn is 7s. rise in price, and 19s. 8d. in duty, being a total amount of pecuniary inducement to retain corn of 26s. 8d. Take prices still nearer, between 66s. and 70s. At 66s. the inducement to retain corn in the hope of its rising to 70s. is 4s., and 10s. in duty, forming a total pecuniary inducement of 14s. Again, between 70s. and 73s. there is, besides the difference of 3s. in price, 9s. in respect of duty, forming an inducement of 12s. to retain corn at 70s., in the hope of its reaching the price of 73s. Now it has been argued that the consequence of that very rapid decline of the duty is injurious to the consumer, to the producer, to the revenue, and to the commerce of the country. It is injurious to the consumer, because when corn is at a high price (between 66s. and 70s.), and when there would be public advantage in the liberation of that corn for the purpose of consumption, the joint operation of increased price and diminished duty induces the holders to keep it back, notwithstanding the already high price and pressure in the market, in the hope of realizing the price of upwards of 73s., and paying a duty of only 1s. It operates injuriously to the agricultural interests, because it is a temptation to keep back corn until it can be suddenly poured in at the lowest amount of duty, and when agriculture loses the protection which the law intended it should possess. It is said to be injurious to the revenue, because, instead of corn coming in when it must under a fixed duty or other modifications, have been entered for home consumption, it was retained until it could be introduced at 1s., the revenue losing the difference between 1s., and the amount of duty which would otherwise have been levied. It is also said to be injurious to commerce, because where the corn is grown at a distance, in America for instance, the grower is subject to this disadvantage, that before his cargo arrives in this country, the sudden pouring in of wheat at 1s. duty from the countries nearer England, may have so diminished the price, and increased the duty, that his speculation may have turned out, not only a failure, but ruinous. These objections have been urged against the rapid transition and decline in the duty inversely with the price of wheat. Now our object will be, in applying the scale of duty to corn, as far as it may be possible, consistently with the principle for which we contend, to diminish the temptations to fraud, or undue holding back of corn. And the agricultural interest ought to observe what has been the effect of the law permitting the importation of corn at certain prices, at a duty of 1s. the quarter. In 1838, the total amount of wheat taken for home consumption was 1,728,000 quarters in the course of the year. Of that amount 1,261,000 quarters were entered at a duty of 1s. In 1840, the total amount of wheat entered for home consumption was 2,020,000 quarters, of which 1,217,000 quarters were taken at a duty of 2s. the quarter. But it is important that we should observe, not only the amount of corn taken in these years at the low duties of 1s. and 2s. the quarter, but also the period of the year at which this took place. In 1838, the corn so taken at that duty of 1s. was taken out one week following the 13th of September. In 1840, the corn taken out at 2s. 8d. the quarter was taken out on the 3rd of September. In each of those two years by far the greater portion of the wheat taken out was at the low rates of 1s. and 2s. 8d.; but it was also at that critical period of the year, just when the farmer in the greater part of the counties of England had thrashed his corn; it was for the purpose of meeting the British farmer in the market when he was thrashing, or had thrashed his corn, for the purpose of producing his rent.

And this tells unfavourably, more especially to the farmer in Yorkshire, who, while compelled to defer the sale of his corn to a later period, is exposed to the disadvantage of the sudden influx of corn whenever the price shall be such as to admit it at the lowest rate of duty. This consideration alone ought to prevail with those most determined in favour of the protection to agriculture to listen with favour to any proposal that has for its object the modification of the existing laws; for it appears to me that some modification of those laws in this respect would be equally as advantageous to the agricultural interest as to any other class. I will now, with the permission of the House, proceed in the course of a few moments to read the scale of duties which I propose should be applied to corn. That scale, Sir, has been devised with a sincere desire to afford to agriculture and the agricultural interest every protection which they can legitimately expect. It has, at the same time, been devised for the purpose, when foreign corn shall be required, of facilitating, as far as possible, commercial intercourse with respect to corn, and subjecting the dealing in corn, as far as possible, consistently with the principle on which the duties are to be levied, to the laws which regulate ordinary commerce. Nothing can be more difficult than to attempt to determine the amount of protection required for the home producer. I am almost afraid even to mention the term "remunerating price", because I know how necessarily vague must be the idea which is attached to it. The price requisite in order to remunerate the home-grower must necessarily vary; a thousand circumstances must be taken into account before you can determine whether a certain price will be a sufficient remuneration or not; and the same difficulty occurs when we attempt to determine on adjusting the scale of duties. The two great points to determine, if we wish to give a just and sufficient protection to domestic agriculture, are, first, what is the price which, on the whole, taking a comprehensive view of the circumstances attending the growth of corn, and viewing the general production of the country, may be supposed to constitute a sufficient encouragement to the growth of wheat or any other kind of agricultural produce. Another element of that consideration and of that determination must necessarily be the price of foreign corn brought into the country, under competition with domestic produce. To attempt to draw any accurate conclusion on both of these two elements of the question must be difficult, from the various opinions that prevail, and the conflicting nature of the details. I have drawn a conclusion as well as I could, without being able to say, that I feel it to be completely accurate. But with regard to the price of wheat in this country, there are some elements, at least, towards determining what may be considered a fair average, speaking of the country at large. Now, if we take the average of prices of wheat which determines the commutation of tithes, the principle on which the Tithe Bill passed, taking the average of seven years, we find the price of wheat during those seven years to have been 56s. 8d.

If we take the average of wheat for the last ten years, we shall find

that the price has been about 56s. 11d. But in that average is included the average of the last three years, when corn has been higher
certainly than any one would wish to see it continue. Allowing for
that excess of price, however, 56s. 11d. was the average price for the
last ten years. Now, with reference to the probable remunerating
price, I should say, that for the protection of the agricultural interest,
as far as I can possibly form a judgment, if the price of wheat in this
country, allowing for its natural oscillations, could be limited to some
such amount as between 54s. and 58s., I do not believe, that it is for
the interest of the agriculturist that it should be higher. Take the
average of the last ten years, excluding from some portion of the
average the extreme prices of the last three years, and 56s. would be
found to be the average; and, so far as I can form an idea of what
would constitute a fair remunerating price, I, for one, should never
wish to see it vary more than I have said. I cannot say, on the other
hand, that I am able to see any great or permanent advantage to be
derived from the diminution of the price of corn beyond the lowest
amount I have named, if I look at the subject in connexion with the
general position of the country, the existing relations of landlord and
tenant, the burdens upon land, and the habits of the country. When
I name this sum, however, I must beg altogether to disclaim men-
tioning it as a pivot or remunerating price, or any inference that the
Legislature can guarantee the continuance of that price; for I know
it to be impossible to effect any such object by a legislative enactment.
It is utterly beyond your power, and a mere delusion, to say, that by
any duty, fixed or otherwise, you can guarantee a certain price to the
producer. It is beyond the reach of the Legislature. In 1835, when
you had what some thought was a nominal protection to the amount
of 64s., the average price of wheat did not exceed 39s. 8d., and I
again repeat, that it is only encouraging delusion to hold out the
hope that this species of protection can be afforded to the agriculturist. To return, however, to the subject; I again say, that nothing
can be more vague than to attempt to define a remunerating price.
The different qualities of land, and a thousand other considerations
enter into the question; and I must say, that the same difficulty exists
to a much greater extent as to determining exactly the rate at which
foreign corn can be brought into this country. Here, again, you must
first ascertain the quality of the corn, the cost of freight, the distance
of the country the corn is brought from; all these considerations
ought to enter into the calculation; and, therefore, it is almost impossible to determine what should be the exact price at which foreign
corn shall be admitted into the market. With these observations I will
now at once proceed to read the scale of duties which her Majesty's
Government propose as a substitute for the existing scale. We
propose that when corn is at 50s. and under 51s. in price, a duty of

20s. shall be taken, but that in no case shall that duty be exceeded. We propose that when the price is 51s. and under 52s., the duty shall be 19s.; and after this we propose that there should be what I should call a rest in the scale. That at the three next items of price the duty should be uniform. Thus it would be:—When the price is 52s. and under 53s. the duty should be 18s.; when 53s. and under 54s., 18s. and when 54s. and under 55s., still 18s. When the price is 55s. and under 56s., we propose that the duty shall be 17s.; when 56s. and under 57s. that it shall be 16s.; when 57s. and under 58s., that it shall be 15s.; when 58s. and under 59s., that it shall be 14s.; when 59s. and under 60s., that it shall be 13s.; when 60s. and under 61s., that it shall be 12s.; when 61s. and under 62s., that it shall be 11s.; when 62s. and under 63s., that it shall be 10s.; when 63s. and under 64s., that it shall be 9s.; when 64s. and under 65s., that it shall be 8s.; and when 65s. and under 66s., that it shall be 7s. At the three next items of price I propose another rest in the scale similar to the former. I should propose upon the next three a duty of 6s., that is to say, when the price is 66s. and under 67s., when it is 67s. and under 68s., and when it is 68s. and under 69s.; in each of those cases the duty would be 6s. When the price is 69s. and under 70s., I propose a duty of 5s.; when 70s. and under 71s., a duty of 4s.; when 71s. and under 72s., a duty of 3s.; when 72s. and under 73s., a duty of 2s.; and when 73s. and upwards, a duty of 1s. the quarter. When that price is arrived at, I propose that the duty should altogether cease. The sum of the proposition then, is this, that when corn in the British market is under the price of 51s. the quarter, a duty of 20s. shall be levied, which duty shall never be exceeded, for I am quite satisfied that it is useless to take any greater amount of duty. ["*Hear, hear,*" *from the Opposition benches*.] I mean when British corn is under 51s. the quarter, that duty of 20s. the quarter shall be an effectual protection to the home grower; not, of course, excluding the taking for home consumption some small portion of foreign corn, but taking care that the protection shall be a valid one. Thus, when the price is 56s. and under 57s., the duty will be 16s., and when 60s. and under 61s., the duty will be 12s. Now, it is apparent that this scale will have the effect of diminishing the temptations to practising on the averages, and producing a fall of the duty, as its operation will be gradual; and when corn shall have arrived at 60s. or 61s., there will be no inducement to the holding back of corn for the purpose of getting higher prices. It is when markets are rising, and when under the present system there is a prospect of being able to force corn up to a price of 73s., that alone the inducement exists to keep corn back in order to obtain additional prices. I have attempted to remove altogether that inducement to fraud by rendering it useless; and the scale is so regulated that there shall be no inducement to parties to combine to hold back corn and defraud the revenue for the sake of being able to produce a sudden reduction of the duty. I will now call the attention of the House to what has been the effect, with regard to the articles of oats and barley, of having applied the principle of more gradually reducing the duty as the price rises. In the case of wheat, where the fall of the duty was so rapid, the temptation to hold back until the lowest amount of duty shall have been realized has been very effectual, and by far the greater part of the wheat has been taken out at the least amount of duty.

In the case of barley and oats, where the fall in the amount of duty was more gradual, the same results have not occurred. In the case of oats, of 3,513,000 quarters, 248,000 quarters were taken at a duty of 1s. 9d., 695,000 at a duty of 3s. 3d., 243,000 at a duty of 4s. 9d., and 940,000 at a duty of 6s. 3d. That was the effect of a gradual fall of 1s. 6d. in the scale of duties, the same principle which I propose to apply to wheat, with the exception that in no case will the fall in the duty on wheat exceed 1s. I consider that there is a fair ground to entitle me to assume, that, by applying that principle of the gradual fall of duty to wheat, there is a fair prospect that wheat, like oats, will be taken out at a higher rate, that the revenue will profit proportionably, and that the consumer and the agriculturist will be equally benefited by corn being taken out when the legitimate demands of the market may require it, and not to answer the objects of speculators. With respect to the other articles of grain, I propose to adopt the proportion of value and duty which I find in the present law. Valuing wheat in the proportion of 100, barley in that of 53, oats in that of 40, and rye, peas, and beans in that of 58; if it be assumed that at the price of 56s. for wheat the duty would be 16s., then the duty on barley, when at 29s. would be 9s.; on oats, at the price of 22s., there would be a duty of 6s. 3d.; and on rye, peas, and beans, at 32s., there ought to be a duty of 10s. 3½d. These are the proportions under the existing law, and I am not aware of any reason for altering them with respect to the other kinds of grain. For this reason, in adjusting the scale of duties applicable to these other kinds of grain, the proportions under the existing Corn-law will be adopted, and the scale itself will correspond with that in the relation of price. In the case of foreign oats, I should propose a *maximum* duty of 8s. (I do not need to enter into all the details)—that it should fall with the increase in price to 7s., and then continue at 6s. for three items of price, that is to say, 22s., 23s., and 24s. When the average price reaches 25s. it will be reduced, as the price increases, by 1s. The extremes of duty would be 8s. on the one hand, and 1s. on the other, the duty of 1s. being the *minimum*, and continuing so long as the price of oats exceeds 28s. In the case of barley, when the price is under 26s., the duty I propose is 11s. per quarter, that being the *maximum* price. When the price is

26s. and under 27s., I propose that there shall be a duty of 10s.; that when the price is 29s., and under 30s., the duty shall continue at 9s.; that when the price is 30s. and under 31s., the duty shall be 8s., and so on till the price is 37s. and upwards, the duty decreasing 1s. for each gradation in price of the same amount. With regard to rye, the same proportion will be observed.

And now I must enter into a short explanation respecting colonial wheat. The law with respect to it is to this effect—that British colonial wheat and flour shall be imported into this country at a duty of 5s. whenever the price of British wheat is below 67s.; that when the price of British wheat exceeds 67s., it shall then be admissible at a duty of 6d. I propose to give the same advantage to colonial wheat, respecting the reduction of prices at which it shall be admissible, as is given to other descriptions of wheat. But, considering that the sudden drop in the prices from 5s. to 6d., on account of the difference of 1s. in the price, is at variance with the principle of the law, which seeks to establish as equable and uniform a reduction of duty as possible, we propose to make this arrangement respecting colonial wheat—that when the price of British wheat is under 55s., the duty upon every quarter of British colonial wheat shall be 5s.; that when at 55s. and under 56s., it shall be 4s.; when at 56s. and under 57s., it shall be 3s.; when at 57s. and under 58s., 2s.; and when at 58s. and upwards, it shall be 1s., thus taking away that sudden fall in the amount of duty levied upon colonial wheat which takes place under the existing law, but giving to the colonial wheat that advantage in the reduction of the price which is given to other descriptions of wheat. With respect to flour, I propose to maintain the same calculation as exists with respect to wheat, so as to allow it to be admitted upon the same relative terms. I believe the House is now in full possession of the nature of the proposal which it is the intention of her Majesty's Government to submit. If you compare the reduction in the amount of duty with the existing duty you will find that it is very considerable. To those who have appeared to think that the modification which I propose to make in the existing law is of no importance, I shall only say, compare my scale of duties on the admission of foreign corn with the existing scale of duties. When corn is at 59s. and under 60s., the duty at present is 27s. 8d. When corn is between those prices, the duty I propose is 13s. When the price of corn is at 50s., the existing duty is 36s. 8d., increasing as the price falls; instead of which I propose, when corn is at 50s., that the duty shall be only 20s., and that that duty shall in no case be exceeded. At 56s. the existing duty is 30s. 8d.; the duty I propose at that price is 16s. At 60s. the existing duty is 26s. 8d.; the duty I propose at that price is 12s. At 63s. the existing duty is 23s. 8d.; the duty I propose is 9s. At 64s. the existing duty is 22s. 8d.; the duty I propose is 8s. At 70s. the existing duty is

10s. 8d.; the duty I propose is 5s. Therefore it is impossible to deny, on comparing the duty which I propose with that which exists at present, that it will cause a very considerable decrease of the protection which the present duty affords to the home-grower, a decrease, however, which in my opinion, can be made consistently with justice to all the interests concerned. If the agriculturist fairly compares the nominal amount of duty which exists at present with that which I propose, he must perceive, that he will still be adequately protected, notwithstanding that the reduction which I propose is considerable. I certainly feel bound to say, that I think the agricultural interests of the country can afford to part with a portion of the protection they now receive, and that it is only just that that protection should be diminished. Whatever arrangement can be made, tending to facilitate the introduction of corn when corn is required, consistently with the ordinary principles of commercial intercourse, it ought, in my opinion, to be made. The protection which I propose to retain, I do not retain for the especial protection of any particular class. Protection cannot be vindicated on that principle. The only protection which can be vindicated, is that protection which is consistent with the general welfare of all classes in the country. I should not consider myself a friend to the agriculturist if I asked for a protection with a view of propping up rents, or for the purpose of defending his interest or the interests of any particular class, and in the proposition I now submit to the House I totally disclaim any such intention. My belief, and the belief of my colleagues is, that it is important for this country, that it is of the highest importance to the welfare of all classes in this country, that you should take care that the main sources of your supply of corn should be derived from domestic agriculture; while we also feel that any additional price which you may pay in effecting that object is an additional price which cannot be vindicated as a bonus or premium to agriculture, but only on the ground of its being advantageous to the country at large. You are entitled to place such a price on foreign corn as is equivalent to the special burdens borne by the agriculturist, and any additional protection you give to them I am willing to admit can only be vindicated on the ground that it is for the interest of the country generally. I, however, certainly do consider that it is for the interest of all classes that we should be paying occasionally a small additional sum upon our own domestic produce, in order that we might thereby establish a security and insurance against those calamities that would ensue, if we became altogether or in a great part dependent upon foreign countries for our supply. My belief is, that those alternations of seasons will continue to take place, that whatever laws you may pass you will still occasionally have to encounter deficient crops, that the harvests of other countries will also at times be deficient, and that if you found yourselves dependent upon foreign countries for so important an amount of corn as 4,000,000 or 5,000,000 of quarters, under these circumstances, and at a time when the calamity of a deficient harvest happened to be general, my belief is, that the principle of self-preservation would prevail in each country, that an impediment would be placed upon the exportation of their corn, and that it would be applied to their own sustenance. While, therefore, I am opposed to a system of protection on the ground merely of defending the interests of a particular class, I, on the other hand, would certainly not be a party to any measure the effect of which would be to make this country permanently dependent upon foreign countries for any very considerable portion of its supply of corn. That it might be for a series of years dependent on foreign countries for a portion of its supply—that in many years of scarcity a considerable portion of its supply must be derived from foreign countries—I do not deny; but I nevertheless do not abandon the hope that this country, in the average of years, may produce a sufficiency for its own necessities. If that hope be disappointed, if you must resort to other countries in ordinary seasons for periodical additions to your own supplies, then do I draw a material distinction between the supply which is limited, the supply which is brought in for the purpose of repairing our accidental and comparatively slight deficiency, and the supply which is of a more permanent and extensive character.

This is the proposal I am authorized on the part of her Majesty's Government to submit to the House. This is the proposal which, taking a review of the whole question, looking to the extent of the protection which, for a long series of years past, the laws of this country have afforded to agriculture, adverting to those Acts of Parliament which have assumed a given price of wheat as the basis of rent, and the foundation of great legislative propositions, considering also the importance of deriving your supply, as far as you can, from domestic sources—this, I say, is the proposal which her Majesty's Government, prompted by no other interest but that of the country at large, driven by no other pressure than that of their own judgment, consider it most for the advantage and welfare of the people should meet with the sanction of the Legislature. Sir, this is not altogether an unfortunate period, in my opinion, for the adjustment of the question. In the first place, there is no such amount of foreign corn available to the supply of this country as need excite the alarm of those who dread an excess; and, in the next, there has been, during the period which has elapsed since the separation of Parliament, concurrently with great commercial distress, as much of moderation, of calm, and of disposition to view with moderation and calmness a proposal for the adjustment of this question, as could possibly have been anticipated. There may have been excitement—there may have been attempts to inflame the minds of the people—but this I must say, that the general demeanour and conduct of the great body of the people of this country, and of that portion of them who have been most exposed to sufferings on account of commercial distress, have been such as to entitle them to the utmost sympathy and respect. There is no difficulty, then, in the shape of violence interposed to the settlement of this question; and it appears to me to be perfectly open for legislation at the present moment. I earnestly trust that the result of the proposal which I now submit to the House, whether it be acceded to or not, will at all events be to lead to some satisfactory adjustment of the question. The adjustment we propose, we propose under the impression and belief that it is the best which, upon the whole, and looking to the complicated state of the various relations and interests in the country, we could submit for the consideration of the House, consistently with justice to all classes of her Majesty's subjects. If it is the pleasure of Parliament to affirm that proposal, it will, of course, pass into a law. If it be the pleasure of Parliament to reject it, I still hope that the question may be adjusted. Whatever may be the determination of Parliament with respect to it, I shall conclude by expressing my most earnest and solemn hope that the arrangement, whatever it may be, may be one most in concurrence with the permanent welfare of all classes, manufacturing, commercial, and agricultural, in the country.

II

Adjourned Debate on Corn Importation Bill of 1846
[March 27, 1846]

SIR ROBERT PEEL said: Sir, the hon. Gentleman who spoke last[1] appears to have repented of the neutrality which he observed on a former occasion, and to have determined to make up for that neutrality by the sharpness of his present attack. I have heard, indeed, from one hon. Gentleman, the Member for Newark, a young Member of this House, that I have been treated with marked forbearance during the discussion upon this measure. I think, then, that under the circumstances I might have expected a little more indulgence from the hon. Member for Winchester. I did, it is true, present two petitions, one from Manchester, and one from Liverpool; and the hon. Gentleman is so captious, that he finds even in the performance of that duty grounds for making an attack upon me. All I did, however, was to state the prayer of these petitions. The petitioners are connected with the manufacturing and commercial interests of the country; and I

---

[1] Mr H. St. J. Mildmay, Southampton.

think that the hon. Gentleman, considering the community of occupation between himself and the petitioners, might have allowed them unquestioned to speak for themselves. The petition from Manchester was signed by the President of the Chamber of Commerce—a body entertaining strong political opinions, and many of whom have been connected with the agitation for the repeal of the Corn Laws. In order, however, to show the unanimity of opinion which prevailed upon this question, the petition was also signed by the President of the Commercial Association—a body holding political opinions of an opposite tendency to those entertained by the Chamber of Commerce; but they, notwithstanding, on this subject came to the same conclusion. To the same conclusion came all the bankers of Manchester; as did also, I believe, the vast majority of the inhabitants of that town connected with great manufacturing establishments. These parties concurred in addressing a petition to this House; and they concurred in attributing the stagnation of trade to the prolongation of the debates; and expressed their opinion that the stagnation will continue until the decision of this House shall be finally pronounced upon the question: praying, therefore, that the House will, at as early a period as may be consistent with mature deliberation, come to a decision upon the subject. Sir, the hon. Gentleman is a proof of how exceedingly difficult it would be to devise any measure connected with the Corn Laws which shall please all parties. But I think the hon. Gentleman stands almost alone in this House upon this question. The hon. Gentleman who so violently attacks the measures of the Government, says, if we had proposed a cautious measure of this nature—that the scale of duties which I propose to exist for three years should be carried into execution, and at the end of that period there should be a fixed duty—he would have been inclined to vote for such a proposal. He has not quite made up his mind whether he would vote for it or not; but still he is so favourably disposed towards it that he thinks he should have been inclined to adopt it. Well, I think he is the only man in the House who would have supported that proposition. The hon. Gentleman makes another charge against me, at which I am somewhat surprised. He says, that every Irish Member ought to be indignant with me for interposing delay, instead of relieving the distress which prevails in Ireland. Indignant with me! I am not conscious of occasioning any delay. Circumstances may have interposed obstacles for which I feel regret; but that the hon. Gentleman has any right to rouse the indignation of the Irish Members against me for interposing delay in the way of extending relief to the distress which prevails in Ireland, I entirely deny; and it is a charge which I think cannot be fairly made against me by any hon. Member of this House. I am extremely unwilling, at this protracted stage of the debate, to refer to personal matters;

and were I a private individual, I would pass by all such accusations as I have heard made against me. I am so conscious of having acted throughout from pure and honourable motives, I am so supported by the conviction that I have abandoned no duty, and betrayed no trust —[*Interruption*]—well, if it be your impression that I have, at least after the accusations which have been preferred, you will concede to me the privilege of defence, and will listen with patience to the answer which I have to give you. Observe, throughout these debates I have not quarrelled with any man for offering his opposition to the opinions which I now profess. I have respected in others the maintenance of their former opinions. I knew not by whom the measures which I proposed would be supported on this side of the House. I can say with truth, that I have attempted to influence no man. I have listened to the attacks made upon me with sorrow, but not with anger. I admit it is natural that hon. Gentlemen should retain their opinion; but if they do not respect in me that privilege which I concede to them, at any rate I entreat them, from a sense of justice, to hear with patience my defence. As I said, if I were a mere private individual, strong in the conviction that I have acted from nothing but a sense of duty, and from pure and honourable motives, I would have let these accusations pass by; but I am not in the situation of a private individual, and it is right that, as Minister of the Crown, I should vindicate from the attacks made upon it my conduct as a Minister of the Crown. I have been asked—it is not, I know, quite regular to refer to former debates, and I shall not encroach upon the rule of the House by express reference to the debates—but the House will permit me to refer in general to the questions which were put, and to the charges which were made, since I have had an opportunity of last addressing the House. It was said then, in the course of the late debate, that I had expressed an opinion that the charge of this measure for the adjustment of the Corn Laws would have been committed with much greater propriety to other hands than mine. And yet it was observed that I had proposed to the Cabinet to undertake the conduct of this measure, and that if the Cabinet had been unanimous the conduct of it would have been committed to my hands. Further, it was remarked that there was thus an apparent inconsistency between the opinion that it would have been better to submit the proposition to other hands, and my undertaking, had the Cabinet concurred with me, to propose the permanent adjustment of this question, as a consequence of the temporary suspension of the law. Sir, I did pronounce an opinion that it would have been better, under any ordinary circumstances, that others more entitled than I am to the credit of the success of this measure, should have had the conduct of it. And yet it is true that in the Cabinet I did propose, if the Cabinet concurred with me, to undertake the task of submitting the proposi-

tion to Parliament. On the 1st of November, I proposed, in concurrence with my right hon. Friends the Secretary at War and the
Secretary of State for the Home Department, upon the ground of the
reports from Ireland, to take that precaution against impending
danger which I thought was a natural precaution, namely, the suspension, either by an Order in Council or an Act of Parliament, of
those laws prohibiting the importation of foreign corn. I renewed
that proposition at the close of the same month. I believe, had the
measure proposed been simply the suspension of the Corn Laws, with
a guarantee that the existing system should revive, I believe—I have
no grounds for not believing—that there would have been no very
serious difference of opinion on the subject. There might have been a
difference of opinion as to the extent of the danger in Ireland; but had
the measure been merely a suspension with a guarantee of revival, or
at least that I would propose the continuance of the existing law, I am
not sure that we should have had any difference of opinion on the
matter. But I did distinctly refuse—I here admit it—I did distinctly
refuse to undertake a guarantee for the revival of the existing law at
the end of the period of suspension, and I did it upon these grounds.
As I said before, I thought that suspension was a becoming and
necessary measure. The right hon. Gentleman the Recorder of
Dublin says that we were deluded by accounts from Ireland. He
admits, however, that he was alarmed at the outset, and that the
prevailing feeling through Ireland was one of alarm; but then he
talked of as unfounded the reports made from time to time by official
bodies in Ireland. It is very easy for an individual to neglect those
reports; but those responsible for the well-being of the country—
deeply responsible should famine and disease come without precautions being taken to meet them—what are they, what is a Government to do—a Government receiving reports from all quarters—
from the highest authorities—from private parties the most disinterested—what, I ask, would be the position of a Government which
should meet such warnings with neglect? The alarm may turn out to
be unfounded, and the precautions, therefore, superfluous; but do
you think that when there is good ground, probable ground, for
expecting a general and wide-spread famine, do you think that a
Government ought, in such a case, to neglect to take precautions, even
should those precautions turn out to be superfluous? Are you to
hesitate in averting famine which may come, because it possibly may
not come? Are you to look to and depend upon chance in such an
extremity? Or, good God! are you to sit in Cabinet, and consider and
calculate how much diarrhœa, and bloody flux, and dysentery a
people can bear before it becomes necessary for you to provide them
with food? The precautions may be superfluous; but what is the
danger where precautions are required? Is it not better to err on the

side of precaution than to neglect it utterly? I say that, with the reports received by Government, in my opinion we should not have been justified in neglecting that precaution. Of course, then, the question arose, "What will you do when the period of suspension shall have terminated?" Will you guarantee the revival of the law? That question was put to me. I said at once I cannot, and for many reasons. In the first place, in the last Session of Parliament I expressed a decided opinion that you could not long continue to apply different principles in respect to agriculture from those you had applied to other articles of commerce. I am told I made a sudden turn—that I surprised every one. Well, hear my defence. Speaking on the Corn Law, in the course of last Session, on the Resolution of the hon. Member for Wolverhampton, while I opposed that Resolution, I stated that I could not defend the existing law on many of the grounds on which it had theretofore been defended. I could not say that I thought the rate of wages varied with the price of corn. I could not defend the law on the ground that we ought to be independent of foreign supply. I stated expressly then, that in my opinion the same principle which formed our ordinary commercial policy must also be applied to agriculture. I was followed by the noble Lord the then Member for Sunderland (Earl Grey), who began his speech by stating expressly that I had made no objection to the first Resolution of the hon. Member for Wolverhampton. Here are his words—he said—

"In Sir Robert Peel's speech there had not been one word uttered attempting to contradict the two first Resolutions of his hon. Friend the Member for Wolverhampton. Had the last Resolution been worded to the effect ' that it was expedient that all restrictions on the importation of corn be gradually abolished,' the right hon. Baronet's speech would have been an unanswerable speech in support of the hon. Member's Motion."

Such was the speech of the noble Lord. Now what was the resolution of the Protection Society in the month of December? Hear it, and say whether the late declaration of opinion in my case can be considered as so sudden or surprising. The Protection Society, I say, came to this resolution:—

"That, in consequence of the declarations made by several leading Members of Government during the last Session of Parliament, it was evident that a further reduction would be attempted in the already greatly diminished amount of protection now afforded to agriculture, and that, in consequence of such interpretation being put on these declarations, an impression, well or ill-founded, is circulated, calculated to destroy all confidence in the stability of the present Corn Laws, and to arrest the progress now making in the improvement of inferior lands."

should undertake after the suspension to propose to Parliament the adjustment of the Corn Laws. I did undertake it, and under these circumstances: As I could not propose the revival of the existing law —as I thought any slight alterations in the details of the present sliding-scale, any slight modifications, would be utterly unavailing for the permanent adjustment which would be the legitimate consequence of suspension: I did undertake to do that which in ordinary circumstances I certainly think ought to have been undertaken by others, and I did engage to meet the existing emergency, and to become responsible for all the consequences of suspension. I drew up then, and I read to my Colleagues, the memorandum I hold in my hand previously to the dissolution of the Cabinet.—The right hon. Baronet then proceeded to read the following document:—

" I cannot consent to the issue of these instructions, and undertake at the same time to maintain the existing Corn Law. Slight modifications of the existing law, as the consequence of these instructions, or immediately following them, would, in my opinion, answer no good end. The proposal of them would add to the difficulty of defending that portion of the Corn Law which it was sought to maintain. I think we ought to suspend the operation of the existing law for a limited period. There is conflicting evidence as to the degree of pressure from the scarcity of food; but there is that probability of severe pressure a few months hence that would in my opinion amply justify the precautionary measure of unrestricted import. We have written authority which would justify it, written authority which, should the anticipations of those from whom we receive it prove correct, would impose on us a heavy responsibility for having neglected a precaution which has been taken in former periods of scarcity in this country, and by some countries in Europe within the last week. But, independently of these considerations, the issue of these instructions fully justifies, if it does not require the temporary removal of impediments to the free import of corn. They contain a proof not only that the crisis is great—not only that there is the probability of severe suffering from the scarcity of food; but the proof that we are ourselves convinced of it. It appears to me that the suspension of the Corn Law would be the course most consistent with these instructions. I will not refer to the preceding discussions in the Cabinet; but the issue of these instructions, placing on record our deliberate conviction as to the possible extent of the evil with which we have to contend as a new event. By acting now, the lapse of time since we last met in Cabinet would be accounted for. I am prepared for one to take the responsibility of suspending the law by an Order in Council, or of calling Parliament at a very early period, and advising in the Speech from the Throne the suspension of the law. I conceal from myself none of the difficulties that attend a suspension of the law. Suspension of the law will compel a very early decision on the course to be pursued in anticipation of the period when the suspension would expire. Suspension will compel a deliberate review of the whole question of agricultural protection. I firmly believe that it would be better for the country that that review should be undertaken by others. Under ordinary circumstances I should advise that it should be so undertaken; but I look now to the immediate emergency, and to the duties it imposes on a Minister. I am ready to take the responsibility of meeting that emergency, if the opinions of my Colleagues as to the extent of the evil, and the nature of the remedy, concur with mine."

I, therefore, Sir, thought that the adjustment of the Corn Laws would be the natural consequence of the suspension of the laws. I felt that it would be inconsistent with my duty to suspend the law, and then to run away and leave it to others to deal with the consequences. I was prepared then to propose an adjustment of the question of duties on foreign corn—I was prepared to do so had my Colleagues agreed with me, notwithstanding the declaration which I made then, and which I repeat now, that under ordinary circumstances I should have preferred that the task should have been left to other hands than mine. If there be any inconsistency in that, I am ready to incur the blame of it; but I confess I think the course I adopted, the natural and fitting course for a Minister in my position. I was, however, in a minority in the Cabinet. When there was no longer unanimity amongst my Colleagues, I despaired of success in carrying the measures I intended, and therefore the Cabinet was dissolved. My hon. Friend the Member for Dorsetshire blames me very much because, after resigning, I wrote a letter to Her Majesty stating the course I intended to pursue. He says that was a most unconstitutional and a most unusual act. Unusual I admit it to be, but the circumstances were altogether unusual. Unconstitutional I cannot admit it to be. That a Privy Councillor should state to his Sovereign what course under very peculiar circumstances he was prepared to pursue, I cannot admit to be unconstitutional. A Peer has a right to seek an audience of Her Majesty, and tender his advice; a Privy Councillor has a right to do so also. True, my official relation to Her Majesty had terminated; I was no longer a Minister, but being a Privy Councillor I conceived I had a perfect right to intimate to Her Majesty—I did it with a view of preventing embarrassment—having advised certain measures, having been prepared to propose them as a Minister, I had a right to state what those measures were, and that, as a private Member of Parliament, I would give to them a cordial support. And what were the circumstances under which that assurance was conveyed? My hon. Friend says that I prevented the formation of a Conservative Government—of a Protection Government, I mean. I did no such thing. [Mr BANKES: What I said was, that you prevented a dissolution of Parliament.] The circumstances under which I wrote that letter, which my hon. Friend complains of as unconstitutional, were these—[Mr G. BANKES—I beg pardon, I to the great and fundamental point of the succession to the Crown, was a breach of treaty and an act of usurpation."

Then, Mr Pitt asked, if they turned to Ireland herself, what would they say to the Protestant Parliament that destroyed the exclusive Protestant franchise, and admitted the Roman Catholics to vote, without any fresh appeal? Mr Pitt went on:—

"What must be said by those who have at any time been friends to any plan of Parliamentary Reform, and particularly such as have been most recently brought forward, either in Great Britain or Ireland? Whatever may have been thought of the propriety of the measure, I never heard any doubt of the competency of Parliament to consider and discuss it. Yet I defy any man to maintain the principle of those plans, without contending that, as a Member of Parliament, he possesses a right to concur in disfranchising those who sent him to Parliament, and to select others, by whom he was not elected, in their stead. I am sure that no sufficient distinction, in point of principle, can be successfully maintained for a single moment; nor should I deem it necessary to dwell on this point in the manner that I do were I not convinced that it is connected in part with all those false and dangerous notions on the subject of Government which have lately become too prevalent in the world."

Mr Pitt contended, therefore, that Parliament had a right to alter the succession to the Throne, to incorporate with itself another Legislature, to disfranchise its constituents, or associate others with them. Why, is it possible for a Minister now to advise the Crown to dissolve Parliament, on the ground that it is incompetent to entertain the question what this country shall do with the Corn Law? There could not be a more dangerous example, a more purely democratical precedent, if I may so say, than that this Parliament should be dissolved on the ground of its incompetency to decide upon any question of this nature. I am open to the charge, therefore, if it be one, that I did advise Her Majesty to permit this measure to be brought forward in the present Parliament. Now I am not aware of any other matter of mere personal character brought forward against me; there is no one part of my personal conduct of which I am not ready to give a full explanation; if I have omitted any, it has been unintentionally, and if any hon. Member has any question to put to me, I will answer it. Then I come to the question itself—Is it for the public interest—is it advisable, that, under the present circumstances of this country, in the present state of public opinion, we should now either refuse to modify the law, in order to meet the case of Irish distress, or that, having modified it, we should have a new Corn Law, or that we should try to adjust permanently this question? The hon. Gentleman who spoke last says—

"You might have dealt with maize and nothing else; maize is the
food the Irish people require, and why not admit maize and nothing
else?"

Why, if you want to undermine this Corn Law effectually, it will be
done by taking such a course as that—by holding out to a people
suffering under severe privation that maize is food good enough for
them, and that the law as to maize shall be altered, but that as to
wheat, barley, and oats you will not permit a letter of the law to be
touched. If you were to venture to make such an experiment upon
public opinion, you would rouse a storm of indignation against the
law you attempted to maintain such as would make it impossible to
maintain it. And what is it you would do with respect to maize?
There is a duty of 8s. on it now. Our doctrine is, that the Government
cannot support the people of Ireland; that we can do nothing without
earnest local exertions; we all say that those local exertions ought to
be made, that the duties of charity are imperative though they cannot
be legally enforced, that it is the duty of the landlords of Ireland, and
of all classes possessing property, to co-operate with us in mitigating
the evils of this great calamity. It is all very well for us to pay the
duty upon maize or oats, paying with one hand and taking with the
other, as we distribute it to the people; but what are we to say to
those whom we are inciting to acts of charity? Are we to say to them
that potatoes are failing, and other food must be supplied, but that
they shall pay an 8s. duty upon maize, and an 18s. upon wheat, and
there shall be no relaxation of that law? Say what you will, about this
Irish distress, mitigate it as much as you please—do you think it
would be possible (even with the extent to which you cannot deny
that it exists), to vote half a million of money from the English
Treasury for the support of the Irish people, and to incite Irish
proprietors to acts of charity, and to the purchase of food for the
support of the famishing people; and yet, in the face of every country
in Europe that is at this moment threatened with scarcity, Holland
and Belgium, the Russian provinces, and within these four or five
days the whole kingdom of Bavaria, and after they have adopted that
which the heart of every man tells him is the natural precaution to
take, namely, the removal of impediments to the free import of food;
yet, say that you will make no relaxation whatever in the existing
Corn Laws? I believe that would be hardly possible. The right hon.
Gentleman the Member for the University of Dublin (Mr Shaw) says
he cannot deny that there does exist a great scarcity in Ireland. I took
down his words. What said he? He said—

"I cannot deny that there is a great scarcity, and also that there is
great danger of disease; but these are common things in Ireland—this
is the normal state of Ireland. A large portion of the Irish people,"

said he, "are always living on the verge of destitution. There has been no year in my recollection when the same statement as to disease might not be made."

Well, be it so; that, you will say, goes some way to nullify the argument in favour of the present proposition. But, in the face of that declaration, will you tell me that this is a labourer's question? Will you say that the maintenance of protection is for the benefit of the Irish agricultural labourer, if protection has brought him to this? In that part of the United Kingdom, which is almost exclusively agricultural, which may be said to depend on agriculture, has protection brought you to this—that, speaking of the agricultural labourers, a large portion of the Irish people are "always living on the verge of destitution?" Is it true, "that there has been no year within your recollection when the same statement might not have been made?" Well, be it as you say. Admit that this is the permanent, the usual state of Ireland—does that afford any strong argument for the maintenance of the existing Corn Laws? But you will answer, if that has been the permanent state of Ireland, why did not you introduce this measure before? Surely, however, that is no reason against our doing it now. You are so pressed by the force of the argument, that the only answer you can make is, "Why did you not do it before?" Well, no doubt we might have done it before. Perhaps we have neglected at former periods our duty; but is that any reason why we should neglect it at present? If you have a potato-fed people, and consequently many millions depending on the supply of an article of food like the potato, subject to such diminution of quantity and deterioration of quality as we have been visited with in this year—if that be the permanent state of Ireland, does it not afford a paramount reason for attempting to effect some permanent change, and not merely supplying a temporary remedy? I think to do nothing would be impossible. To modify the existing law—to propose as a permanent system such a change in the law as that proposed by the hon. Member for Southampton (Mr Mildmay)—a sliding-scale for three years and then a fixed duty—such a change as that would only encourage agitation on the one hand, while by the agricultural body it would be rejected with scorn—laughed at—scouted. Such an arrangement would effect no good, produce no benefit. Then what is left? Is there any alternative but trying to lay the foundation for an ultimate adjustment, by repealing those laws? My firm conviction is, that it is for the interest of all, of the agricultural interest in particular, that this in the present state of affairs is the safest course. The hon. Member for Newark asked me repeatedly whether I meant to ruin the agriculturist interest? Sir, I attach the utmost importance to the prosperity of the agricultural interest. ["Oh!" *and ironical cheers from the protection benches*.] Why, I don't know for what reason I have not as much right to feel an interest in the prosperity of agriculture as any of those who received that sentiment with scorn. Why, what possible interest can I have to injure that interest? I attach the utmost importance to it. I think, for great political reasons, it is of the utmost importance that the agricultural interest should have great weight and authority in the government of this country. I think, with Burke, that land is the safest basis of political power. He says, "All the writers,"—and he quotes Aristotle as speaking of the Grecian States, and Cicero as speaking of Rome—"All the writers on politics have attached the utmost importance to land, and have declared that it is the safest basis of a sound and permanent Government." I concur in that opinion, and deeply should I deplore the day when the landed interest of this country should be excluded from its full share in its councils and legislation. But Burke adds, with equal truth, that, fortunately for this country, land has directed its councils, the reason being that the landed aristocracy and the landed proprietors have never been as a class dissociated from the general interest, but subjecting themselves to the influence and the progress of public opinion, and proving their unity of interest with all. Why, that is just the question. By what means shall we secure the continuance in the just influence of the landed interest of this country? Is it by maintaining your privileges on the ground of the exclusion of food? ["No!"] Well, then, on the ground of taxation on the importation of foreign corn? I will call it by which name you wish; it is not, certainly, the "exclusion" of food. But the question is, will it more conduce to the permanent, just, and legitimate influence of the land in this country that these Corn Laws should at length be repealed, or that they should be continued in all their integrity? Now, my firm conviction—accuse me of treachery if you please—is, that you will fortify and maintain the influence of the land by this arrangement, rather than, in the present state of public feeling, by pertinaciously insisting on maintaining the present laws. Look, for example, at the tax on butter. That, at any rate, is not a tax of 400 or 500 years' standing. The taxes on butter and cheese were introduced within a few years. Why should the removal of those taxes be construed into any assault on the privileges of the landed interest? Let us consider the bearing of this question of the Corn Laws on the great interests of this country, upon the land and the landed aristocracy, the legitimate influence of which I hope to see maintained for ever. We have to deal with a population which by the last census, that of 1841, consisted of about 19,000,000 people. [An hon. MEMBER: Twenty-seven.] I am excluding Ireland; if I were to include Ireland in my present calculation I should greatly fortify my position. In this country we have 19,000,000 of people. Now, how are they divided? You have of persons engaged in or connected with the agricultural interest about

1,500,000, not including women and children; of landed proprietors, farmers, and occupiers of land, and persons above and under twenty years of age, employed in agriculture, about 1,500,000; you have of labourers engaged in other occupations about 761,000, including all those classes who labour in mines and quarries, and so on; of persons engaged in trade and manufactures, including all the commercial and manufacturing classes, you have 3,111,000; 200,000 persons belonging to the learned professions, including educated persons following miscellaneous occupations; 511,000 persons independent or living on their fortunes; and 200,000 paupers, lunatics, and so on. Now, just consider what a vast proportion of that great mass of people, 19,000,000 altogether—what a vast proportion of that mass consists of people who earn their subsistence by manual labour, and must subsist upon wages under 30s. a week. And just consider how taxation, wholly apart from the tax on food—just consider, I say, how taxation for the State presses on that class of the community. You raise about 32,000,000l. of taxes by the Customs and Excise. Take those articles which enter into the consumption of a family, the head of which earns less than 30s. a week. I have returns here of those articles which are in weekly use by families of that class. Now, what are these articles, independent of bread? They are butter, cheese, a little meat, bacon, lard, candles, soap, and a little tobacco. Hardly any one of those articles is free from being taxed. Let us see what is the influence of taxation on that class of the community. It is inevitable, with a system of indirect taxation, that they must pay heavily; but I know, if the burden presses unjustly upon them, it is from no want of sympathy on the part of the gentlemen of England; it is, however, inevitable: we must raise a great part of our taxation by indirect taxes, and the burden will be unequally distributed. You have, and my belief is, that you have established a just claim to the confidence and the gratitude of this country, relieved those classes to some extent. You did take upon yourselves the burden of raising 5,000,000l. a year by means of the Income Tax, not only to supply a deficiency, but to relieve the labouring classes from some of the taxation that pressed too heavily upon them. In order that I may be perfectly accurate, I will here state, from documents which I hold in my hand, the actual consumption of a labourer, earning 10s. a week in summer, and 9s. a week in winter, he having a wife and one child. This is an actual return of the consumption of this one individual and his family. He bought four gallons of bread—but put that out of the question at present—he bought 1½ lb. of cheese, some bacon, some salt meat, some butter, some tea and sugar, some candles, and some soap. Now, with the exception of candles, the duty on which was removed very recently, all these things are taxed. By the Tariff now proposed, we remove the duty from bacon and from salt meat, and

we diminish the duty on butter and on cheese. Can you repent that I
have made that proposition? The man died, leaving a widow and a
child. The widow earned 4*s.* 6*d.* a week, and the guardians allowed her
1*s.* 6*d.* for the child; and this was her weekly expenditure—rent,
1*s.* 6*d.*; candle and soap, 4½*d.*; butter, 2¾*d.*; tea, 1½*d.*; sugar, 2*d.*; and
with her expenditure for bread she was left with only 1*s.* 8*d.* for
firing, shoes, clothes, &c., all of which it was very difficult for her to
buy out of that sum of 1*s.* 8*d.* Even in that case the soap and the
candles, the butter, the tea, and the sugar, all were taxed. Now, Sir,
let me take the case of a Yorkshireman spending more money,
living on better fare, and earning more wages. This, too, is a *bona fide*
return of actual expenditure. This man earned 15*s.* or 16*s.* a week, out
of which he spent 14*s.*, and the expenditure was thus—meat, 2*s.*;
sugar, 7*d.*; cheese, 7*d.*; soap and candles, 3½*d.*; butter, 8*d.*; tea and
coffee, 1*s.* 6*d.*; and oatmeal, 7½*d.*, making altogether 6*s.* 3*d.* What was
the expenditure of that man for wheat flour? No less than 8*s.* a week
out of 14*s.* Every week he had to buy three stone of flour, which, for
the last few years, had ranged at 2*s.* 8*d.* a stone. Six shillings he spent
upon all other necessaries, but wheat constituted the great part of his
expenditure—on wheat flour he was compelled to spend more than
one-half of his wages. Now, supposing the abolition of the law were
to cause some reduction in the price of wheat flour—just ask yourselves this—suppose it does cause some reduction, are you not most
materially adding to the comfort and the enjoyment of those classes?
This is by far the most important aspect under which you can view
the question. I know the real sympathy you have for the condition of
the working classes. I do not agree with those who throw imputations
upon your humanity. I know that the gentlemen of England are most
sincere in their sympathy for the suffering of the poor, and earnestly
desire to better their condition. I know that that desire actuates you
as much, if not more, than any other class of the community; and
I ask you to consider the expenditure of a working man, which I have
laid before you. You cannot increase direct taxation with any
advantage—I believe you would if you could. You raise 7,000,000*l.*
by stamps, 5,000,000*l.* by the Income Tax, and 4,000,000*l.* by the
assessed taxes. You may add to the Income Tax without at all
benefiting the poor, as there are limits to this direct taxation. You
may carry the tax upon capital to too great an extent, and although it
falls at first upon the rich, it would end by more seriously injuring the
poor than indirect taxation. Adam Smith says, "The first maxim
with respect to taxation is, that every man shall contribute to the
taxation of the State in proportion to the amount of property he
enjoys under the protection of the State." Now, are you able to
apply that maxim to the case of the Yorkshireman whose expenditure
I have given you? I much doubt whether taxation does not fall

much heavier on his class than upon us. The poor cannot resort to other countries where the scale of taxation is less than here. They are fixed as it were to the soil. They are tied to the labour from which they derive their subsistence, and undoubtedly taxation falls more heavily upon them than upon us. If you increase the assessed taxes, or the stamp duties, or the income tax, it does not follow that you will benefit the labourer. Indirect taxation may be more beneficial than direct taxation; but look how many of the articles which enter into the consumption of the poor man are heavily taxed; and then comes the question of bread, the expenditure on which consists of more than one-half of his income. When you say there will be a reduction in the price of corn, and that the danger is there will be some reduction in rent as a consequence, you certainly have no sympathy for those with whom corn constitutes the greater part of their weekly expenses. The noble Lord the Member for Lynn required me to state what was my calculation with respect to the future price of corn. Well, I have repeatedly declined; and I know not how it is possible for any human being to make a calculation with regard to the probable price of corn hereafter. But the noble Lord said, "Well, if you will not answer that question, there is another question which you shall answer, and to which I pin you." In 1835 the price of wheat, on the average of the year, was 39s.; and the noble Lord says, "I insist upon your telling me what would have been the price at which foreign corn might have been imported, supposing there had been no duty upon corn in the year 1835." I say to the noble Lord, I am not prepared to admit that there would have been a reduction in the price of corn; I am not prepared to admit, as a necessary consequence, that if there had been established for some time previously a free trade in corn, there necessarily would have been in the year 1835 a lower price than 39s. That is my answer, which the noble Lord thinks a monstrous one, because the noble Lord has got a list of some few cargoes of corn bought at Dantzic and other places, and brought into this country at a profit for less than 39s. [Lord G. BENTINCK: They were returns which I read.] I do not doubt the accuracy of the return, but I say it is completely beside the question. It is no sort of proof whatever, because in 1835 some cargoes of corn were brought here, having cost at Dantzic 20s., that if you had established a permanently free trade in corn, the price of wheat in this country would necessarily have been below 39s. I will give the noble Lord my reason for maintaining my proposition in opposition to his. I say there is no arguing from the price of corn upon the Continent in any given year, when the market of this country was not fully and fairly open to importation; and as the noble Lord says he relies upon Parliamentary returns, I also will rely upon Parliamentary returns. You sent Mr Jacob, a man of great knowledge and great experience with respect to the Corn Law, in

1827, to the Continent to report upon the state of foreign corn, and you find in Mr Jacob's report this principle laid down. He says:—

"In consequence of your excluding foreign corn by your high duties, there has been an accumulation of corn in many foreign markets."

He then says:—

"It is this accumulation which depresses the agricultural interest, by the exaggerated representation of its amount when we have an abundant harvest, and by the too rapid influx whenever the harvests are deficient."

I cannot think that in the years 1822 and 1823 wheat could have sunk so low as 38s. per quarter, if the ports had been open to foreign grain, and the surplus of continental Europe had been sent to this country as it was required.

"The penning up of wheat (continues Mr Jacob) in countries of small extent soon creates a glut in such countries, although the quantity really accumulated there may be very minute, and such as, if distributed here, would produce no sensible decline in price. A few thousand quarters of wheat, for instance, in Holstein, Mecklenburgh, or Denmark, for which there was no foreign market, would reduce the price even below the half; the seller must take what is offered, and the reluctant buyer will offer a very low rate. A small sale fixes the price in such cases."

And that is the true state of the case. I apprehend that if you encourage production abroad by the hope of an extravagant price, and a good harvest causes a great accumulation on the Continent, then you will have wheat at a very low price; the needy seller will sell, and the cunning buyer will buy, and there will be profit though the price be very low; and the noble Lord argues that this exception is the universal rule, and that under a free trade the price of corn will necessarily fall. I differ from the noble Lord, and that is my reason for saying that I am not prepared to admit that if you open the ports, and have a regular dealing in corn with foreign markets, it will necessarily follow that the price of corn will be below 39s. As the noble Lord has referred to returns, I may also refer to them. The Consuls in the different corn-producing countries were required to state what quantity of corn, of each kind, could be exported to England from the country in which they resided, if the trade in corn was made constantly free at a moderate duty. What is the answer of the Consuls? The general average of price 40s. 6d., free on board. The general average of freight 4s. 9¾d. The average, free on board, of wheat, from St Petersburgh, was calculated, by the British Consul, to be 39s. 1d.: freight from 4s. 6d. to 5s. At Dantzic, the price of wheat, in all ordinary years, the ports of England being open, was calculated at 40s., and the price of freight from 3s. 6d. to 4s. I am not including now the prices of landing and shipment in this country. I am only speaking of the average price of wheat and the average freight. The price at Stettin was calculated at 40s., freight from 4s. to 5s.; at Hamburgh, 35s. to 46s., freight from 2s. 6d. to 5s. 6d. Relying, then, upon the opinion of Mr Jacob, that if you obstruct the trade in corn there will be occasional accumulations and very depressed prices, and that you will have the means of bringing it into the market on account of the accumulation at a low rate, and relying also upon the returns of your own Consuls as to what would be the probable cost of wheat in this country free on board, and the probable freight, provided there was free admission—relying upon these two Parliamentary Returns, the argument of Mr Jacob, and the facts furnished by the Consuls, I again repeat that I am not prepared to admit that, with a free trade in corn, the price of wheat would be reduced below the 39s. 5d. which it bore in the year 1835. What was the fact? In the year 1822, of which Mr Jacob speaks, and in the year 1835, you had no foreign import whatever; you had completely excluded foreign corn: it was not foreign competition that depressed your prices; but with full protection you had in 1822 a price of 38s., and in 1835 a price of 39s. There is no pretence for saying that the price of foreign wheat had depressed prices here. In 1822 you moved for a Committee on agricultural distress. It was stated that the agricultural interest was suffering so severely that it was necessary to inquire what remedies could be applied; and, therefore, observe, the complete exclusion of foreign corn does not ensure you either from depression in price, or from severe agricultural distress requiring the appointment of a Parliamentary Committee. Then, in 1835, the other year to which the noble Lord referred, you had no foreign competition; you had a price of 39s. 1d.; but the depression of price was entirely caused by the abundance of your own harvest. In 1836, following the example of 1822—it being impossible to allege that foreign corn had, in either case, depressed your price or caused your distress—in 1836, as in 1822, a Parliamentary Committee was appointed, for the purpose of considering what remedy could be applied to agricultural distress. I have been attempting to show, looking at the population, looking at the bearings of taxation, what immense masses of people depend for the subsistence of their families upon their weekly earnings—taking those weekly earnings at less than 30s.—what enormous masses there are in this country who so earn their subsistence, and to whom the price of wheat is of the utmost importance in their domestic economy. I have shown you that it constitutes more than one-half of the expenditure in those cases where wheat is consumed; and I ask you, could you do anything more to benefit the social condition of that class than give them an assurance that they shall have wheat at a moderate price in this country? There might be a great depression in price; but if free trade in corn gives you a guarantee against such low prices as you have had under protection, a guarantee against such high prices as you have also had under protection, would be of inestimable advantage to the working classes. Suppose the price of corn were not depressed below 50s. or below 54s., or any other sum that you can name—if you take a guarantee, by extending the sources and ranges of your supply, that it should not rise to 70s. or 80s., by that act alone you would be conferring an inestimable advantage on the working classes of this country. Surely, no hon. Gentleman can now share in the alarm that, by widening the sources of supply, we shall establish a dependence on foreign countries, because he has shown you that the more you extended the area from which you drew cotton and indigo, the more you reduced the price and equalised the supply. We are about to admit maize and many other articles of subsistence besides wheat. Suppose wheat should fail. If you suppose that foreign countries would enter into a combination not to give us their wheat, still, by the law which we propose, we should have maize to rely upon, rice to rely upon; and I confess, if the two Tariffs shall pass and receive the sanction of the Legislature, I think it impossible for any one to entertain an apprehension that, by any combination of foreign nations, we shall be in danger of being exposed to an enormous rise in the price of corn. Taking the whole of these measures together, I do not apprehend the existence of any scarcity from a reliance upon an increase of the foreign supply of corn. I have hitherto been referring to the manufacturing class; and I think Gentlemen cannot deny that those who are connected with commerce and manufactures, and who earn their subsistence by their daily labour—I think it cannot be denied that they have a direct and immediate interest in a moderate price of wheat. But it may justly be said, that to their interests the interests of the agricultural classes ought not to be sacrificed. I admit it—I admit it. I think the position of the farmer, the position of the agricultural labourer, ought to be a subject of equal concern at least with that of any other class in the country; and if we could, with truth, say that under a system of protection we had been able to exhibit a prosperous and contented class of agricultural labourers throughout the country, then I should be disposed to acknowledge that you had made out some valid objection to the proposed change. But, can we say, with truth, that throughout this country the position of the agricultural labourers has been such as I have described? [Colonel SIBTHORP: Yes.] The gallant Colonel says "yes." I say no. And I will now deal with that position —that the rate of wages of the agricultural labourer varies with the price of food. In manufacturing districts, I again say, it is my firm impression that his wages are more likely to vary inversely to the price of food, than directly. I am prepared to contend, and I think to prove, that there is no direct connexion between the wages of the agricultural labourer and the price of wheat. [A MEMBER: Yes.] If there is, then, how do you account to me for this? If the wages of the agricultural labourer vary directly with the price of wheat, why is it that wages are 8s. in Wiltshire, and 13s. in Lincolnshire? Take an agricultural county. I admit that in Lincolnshire wages are about 13s. In Kent too, for some reason or other, wages are high—they are not generally less than 13s. But take the case of those labourers who are most removed from the influence of manufactures. Take Somerset-shire, Dorsetshire, Wiltshire, Cornwall—take Devonshire too. In the first place, I say that as you advance from purely agricultural districts to manufacturing districts, you find the wages of the agricultural labourer increased. But how direct is the sympathy between manufacturing prosperity and agricultural? The fact which you admit is, that in Somersetshire, Dorsetshire, Wiltshire, Devonshire, and those counties of England which are depending upon agriculture, wages are low; and in proportion as you advance to Northampton-shire and the midland counties, and on to Warwickshire, Staffordshire, Yorkshire, and Lancashire, you find the wages of the purely agricultural labourer increase as you approach the manufacturing towns. Is not this a very strong proof that the prosperity of manufactures increases the demand for agricultural produce? But see the position of the agricultural labourer, and see the lesson which we ought to derive from the gradual increase of his wages. Take a purely agricultural county—Dorsetshire, Somersetshire, or other counties in the south-west of England. If there is any direct connexion between the rate of wages and the price of wheat, why are wages in those counties at the existing rate, and why are they 13s. or 14s. in the midland counties? Because great skill and industry are employed in the latter districts. That is just what I want to prove. I am trying to show that a country naturally not fertile may be brought into fertility by the use of manure and the application of skill and capital, and that the effect of these is the same as that produced by the approach to a manu-facturing town—to raise the wages of the agricultural labourer. I am trying to show that there are two causes of a high rate of wages for the agricultural labourer—the application of skill and capital, as, much to the credit of the agriculturists of Lincolnshire, those means are employed in Lincolnshire, or the approach to a manufacturing town. [Colonel SIBTHORP: They get a remunerating price for their corn.] A remunerating price for their corn! There is as remunerating a price in Wiltshire and Devonshire as in Lincolnshire. In those counties the farmer has equally the protecting duty of 18s.; at present that does not vary, but the rate of wages does. The gallant Colonel must see, without much stress upon his logical faculties, that there is some other cause for the variation of the wages of the agricultural labourer. Well, but how can we say that, with protection, the position of the agricultural labourer, in a purely agricultural county, is one which we approve of. You know you cannot. Do you not admit to me that in the social condition of the millions in the manufacturing districts, who earn their subsistence by the sweat of their brow, the price of wheat is of the first importance, and has become an object of the deepest interest? Have you read the Reports on the Health of Towns? Are you not deeply convinced that some effort ought to be made to improve the social condition of the masses of the population, who earn their subsistence in the manufacturing towns? It seems to me that the first foundation of any such improvement is, that there should be abundance of food. You may talk of improving the habits of the working classes, introducing education amongst them, purifying their dwellings, improving their cottages; but believe me the first step towards improvement of their social condition is an abundance of food. That lies at the bottom of all. It is in vain, if the people are suffering under scarcity, or if any apprehension of scarcity prevails; the suffering, or the apprehension of it, so depresses the spirits, that it is vain for you to inculcate lessons of cleanliness, or to improve dwellings, until the people are provided with abundance of food. The experience of the last three years, and the experience of the three preceding years, has taught us a lesson which we ought never to forget as to the effects upon the social condition, the moral habits, and the happiness of the working classes, of an abundance of food. Is it possible to resist this conclusion from the observations that have been made? In a purely agricultural district, is it possible to say the rate of wages of the agricultural labourer has any direct connexion with the ratio of the price of wheat?—[An hon. MEMBER: Yes!] Well, now I will demonstrate that it has not. Observe, I do not mean to say that there may not be some increase in wages when prices rise. I do not mean to say that when wheat is very high, there is not an occasional increase of wages; but I think I can demonstrate that the rate of wages does not bear any proportion to the increase of price of food. I have here a return, and I will quote no figures which I am not prepared to communicate to any Gentleman connected with the counties to which they refer. They are the best test of the condition of the labourer, and communicate information which may be relied upon. I will take the variations in the price of wheat from the year 1837 down. I requested to have an account made up from the wages actually paid to agricultural labourers on particular farms from 1837 to 1844 inclusive. I begin then with the wages of agricultural labourers for eight years, from 1837 to 1844 inclusive, in the Sodbury Union, in the county of Gloucester. The labourer received money as well as beer. Here, then, is an account of the wages for the summer and winter weeks. Since 1837, the price of corn has varied very much.

Why, in the present year it has varied from 45s. 1d. to 58s. 3d. I will read the price of wheat since 1837:—

In 1837 the price was 53s. 10d.

1838	,,	64s. 7d.
1839	,,	70s. 8d.
1840	,	66s. 4d.
1841	,,	64s. 4d.
1842	,,	57s. 3d.
1843	,,	50s. 1d.
1844	,,	51s. 2d.

Therefore, the price of wheat had varied from 70s. 8d. to 50s. 1d. within this period of eight years. Now, I dare say you will say, as writers upon political economy have already said, that the ultimate tendency of wages is to accommodate itself to the price of food. I must say that I do not believe it. But I should like to know what consolation it would be to the poor agricultural labourer to be told that the increase in the price of corn would have a tendency to increase his wages in perhaps a period of ten years? What consolation is it to tell him in 1839, that although he paid 70s. 8d. a quarter for his corn, he might be able to purchase it in 1843 for 50s. 1d., when it was likely there would be a close approximation in the amount of his wages within that year? But I do not believe that there is that tendency. I tell you, now, what I think is more natural, namely, a tendency rather to substitute potatoes for wheat among the people of this country. I do not mention this fact with a view of using any acrimonious language in reply to acrimonious observations. I am dealing with matters of the deepest import. The allotment system has been much extolled; the adoption of which has been very extensively recommended from, I admit, the most benevolent motives. Taking individual cases, the possession of small allotments is no doubt of very great advantage to the labourers. I believe that every one admits that within certain limits the greatest advantage would be conferred upon the poorer classes, by the adoption of this system. That it would give them great comfort, independent of the physical advantage that they would derive from it. It would also give him an interest in the soil, a healthful occupation, and by making him a landed proprietor, it would give him great social advantages. But after all, what is the tendency of such a system, if extensively carried out? Is it not to create a kind of Irish peasantry, by the substitution for their food of potatoes for wheat? You will find that this would be the case—that potatoes would be substituted for wheaten bread. According, then, as this system increases, you will be also increasing the dangers probably of such calamities as the people of Ireland are now suffering under, although, no doubt, in a much more mitigated state. Now, I should think it would be a very great calamity indeed, if we were to see potatoes used here instead of wheat. I believe that the higher the kind of food is which we introduce among the labourers, the security will be the greater for their permanent happiness and contentment. What is the fact? Just in proportion to the depressed condition of the labourers, is there a tendency amongst them to substitute potatoes for wheat. The labourer who has no allotment must depend for his subsistence upon wheat almost exclusively; and, therefore, the greatest proportion of his earnings goes for the purchase of wheat. The possession of an allotment has a tendency, no doubt, to improve immediately the condition of the labourer; but I am only speaking of the danger of carrying this system out to a very great extent, by inducing the substitution of potatoes for wheat. I have read the variations of the price of corn for several years. I will now refer to the variations in the price of labour. I do not mean that these quotations are the total amount of wages, because in harvest time there are always some additional allowances made; but these allowances are made in every year, so that we may strike these additions altogether out of our consideration. In the union to which I have referred, the price of wages averaged in summer 9s. a week, and 1s. for beer. The total average per week, including beer, for winter and summer, was—

In 1837	...	...	10s. per week.
1838	...	...	11s. ,,
1839	...	...	11s. ,,
1840	...	...	11s. ,,
1841	...	...	11s. ,,
1842	...	...	11s. ,,
1843	...	...	10s. ,,
1844	...	...	10s. ,,

so that while the price of wheat varied from 50s. 1d. to 70s. 8d., the price of wages in the same union within a like period varied only from 10s. to 11s. a week. From Blandford, in Dorsetshire, we had this reply:—

"The statement on the other side was given me by four different yeomen. It is only the first-rate labourer that gets 9s. in these parts, unless at piece-work or extra times, and then if the extra hours were reckoned up which the men work at piece-work, I do not think it would average more than 8s. to 9s. with the best men."

Now, at that place the average wages were—

In 1837 the price of wages was			7s. per week.
1838	,,	,,	8s. ,,
1839	,,	,,	8s. ,,
1840	,,	,,	8s. ,,
1841	,,	,,	8s. ,,

1842	,,	,,	8s.	,,
1843	,,	,,	8s.	,,
1844	,,	,,	8s.	,,

Therefore, whilst the price of corn had varied from 70s. 8d. to 51s. 1d., it was 48s. 6d. in 1836; wages have only varied from 7s. to 8s. a week. There were extra earnings, such as piece-work, harvesting, &c., as I am aware; but those, for the reason I have given, I do not reckon; they might probably amount to 1s. more each week. That is the statement of one of these yeomen near Blandford. Another farmer states that wages in 1837 were 7s.; in 1838, 7s.; 1839, 8s.; 1840, 8s.; 1841, 8s.; 1842, 8s.; 1843, 8s.; 1844, 8s.—a variation of only 1s. in the rate of wages, notwithstanding the great variation in the price of wheat during the same period. I will take the rate of wages again, in Cornwall: from the Union of Bodmin, a person writes—

" In reply to your letter of the 8th instant, I beg to state that the rate of wages in this union has not varied from 1837 to 1844. Labourers have been in the habit of receiving 8s. or 9s. per week, during the whole of this period. Those who have had 9s. per week, have been supplied with wheat by their employers at 8s. per imperial bushel, and barley at 4s.; whilst those who have received 8s. per week have had to pay 6s. 8d. for wheat, and 3s. 4d. for barley, whatever may have been the price of grain."

Then from Barnstaple there is this communication:—

" I have inquired of several farmers residing in various parts of this union the amount of agricultural wages during the years 1837 to 1844 inclusive, and have ascertained that, in general, the sum paid was 8s. a week; some few farmers gave 9s.; but a much greater number only 7s. No rise or fall appears to have taken place during the eight years in question, except that in very dear seasons some employers supplied their labourers with corn at a reduced price; but I am inclined to think that they were not very numerous."

I will now take East and West Suffolk; and first, East Suffolk:—

" The variation of wages in this neighbourhood has been from 8s. to 10s. a week from 1835 up to the present time; and within that period the price of flour has varied from 1s. 3d. to 2s. 10d. the stone of 14 lbs."

That is to say, the wages increased one fifth, while the price of flour had more than doubled. The communication proceeded—

" The supply of labour is greater than the demand in this neighbourhood, and the price of labour is, in fact, what the farmer chooses to give; but he invariably raises his wages and lowers them with the price of corn, though never in the same proportions. Consequently the poor are better off with low than with high prices. You will at once see that 8s. a week with flour at 1s. 3d. is better than 10s. a week with flour at

2s. 10d., supposing the man's family to require from two to three stone of flour weekly."

Now, that is the state of things in East Suffolk. Next I will give you West Suffolk. The writer says—

"The general wages paid by the farmers of this parish have fluctuated from 9s. to 10s. per week; but the men employed at task work, such as thrashing, &c., have earned from 1s. to 2s. per week in addition. The variation in the rate of wages has certainly been caused by the fluctuations in the price of corn; but when wheat was selling at 20s. per coomb"—[a coomb is half an imperial quarter]—"I do not remember that wages were below 9s. per week; and when the farmers were realizing 35s. per coomb, 10s. per week was generally the amount of wages given. The result of my experience is, therefore, to show that although wages fluctuate, in a trifling degree, with the price of corn, they do not rise or fall in proportion to such price, and, therefore, that the labourers are best off when the prices are low."

There are occasionally extraordinary additions made to the labourer's earnings, and in harvest time his earnings are always increased; but these additions apply to all years alike, and therefore I have not reckoned them. Have I not then proved that it is impossible to gainsay that the present generation—the existing race of labourers—cannot be benefited in any way by the slow adjustment between the price of food and the rate of wages? Again, I say, I doubt the position that ultimately even there is any tendency between the two to approximate. But if I have shown that in these eight years—a long period in a labouring man's life—no rise at all in wages has taken place proportionate to the rise in the price of corn, I think I have shown so far that the rate of wages has no such connexion with the prices of food as to rise with them, but rather directly the reverse. I think I have succeeded in demonstrating that the rise in price of wheat operates almost immediately in favour of the agricultural interest. I put this to you in perfect good faith and sincerity. Do you think that you can maintain this system of protection much longer? and, above all things, are you not assured that we cannot maintain the existing law upon the ground of its being advantageous to agriculture? Adam Smith, whose name has been so often mentioned in the course of these discussions, tells his readers, and probably to the satisfaction of every impartial and intelligent man, that the rate of wages depends upon the country being in a prosperous condition. When there is abundance of capital, large profits, an active and healthy condition of agriculture, manufactures, and commerce, then will the rate of wages be high; and when the opposite state of things happens to prevail, then will the rate of wages be in a depressed state, and the working classes reduced to comparative poverty. General prosperity, and not legal enactments, produce a practical effect upon the rates of wages. It is by removing restrictions on manufactures and commerce that you create a demand for labour, and not by raising the price of food. Make the sustenance of mankind difficult of attainment, and you take a guarantee against the rise of wages. But remove restrictions upon agriculture, manufactures, and commerce—pass this measure—and then you at least save yourselves from the necessity and the odium of constant interference for the purpose of regulating the supply of food. And what is it that you relinquish? Well, I could prove to you, by returns from different parts of the country, not such as my right hon. Friend read to you, showing to you the extent of disease and distress, that there has been at least no panic in the price of food. I can adduce instances to you which would demonstrate this—I can point to eleven farms in Roxburgh that have become vacant since this measure was proposed, and in every one of these cases there has been an increase of rent—I can prove to you that enormous prices have been given for land in Scotland, and that where there is great capital and skill, there is no apprehension entertained as to the consequences of this measure. Even in Lincolnshire I can show you that farms have been let at an increased rent. I might, too, take the different counties, and show you that where there is the most agricultural skill there is the least alarm felt, and there is the greater tendency to take farms at an increased rent. Would you then, I ask, have a law maintained for bad farming and insufficient capital—that for them protection should be permanent; whereas for good farming and competent skill protection should not be required? I ask you, could such a law be justified? It is my firm belief that no general injury would follow from this measure. There may be, of course, individual cases of suffering. There will, and there must be, the suffering of property which is encumbered with tenants having insufficient capital. There may be these individual cases; but it would be most unfair from these to draw an inference against a general law. But, admitting these few cases, let us compare the advantages which you will have in the security against ruinously high prices for food; and there will be to you the advantage and the comfort that you will not be responsible for that high price in times of scarcity of food—that these afflictions will be the results of the operations of nature and not of human laws. Leave trade free, and you will not be held responsible for untoward events over which we have not, and of necessity cannot exercise, any control. Looking, then, at the compensation which this measure furnishes; I do not mean compensation in the way of small equivalents, but, on the contrary, I refer to the security and the permanency of the law—looking to the advantages which the change now proposed must confer upon the labourer—looking to the benefits it will confer upon yourselves; I mean not merely the more obvious advantages likely to arise to your estates, but the less evident effects on the improvement of your position—seeing that you will be elevated by making this concession—I think I am not acting as the enemy of that interest, with which my own is so intimately connected, when I recommend this Bill to the acceptance of the House. I repeat that that which I advise is for the true interests of every class. I ask you, do you feel secure; and if you foresee that the present system cannot long be maintained, why will you not take advantage of a favourable time for effecting a change that very soon must come? You say that the present time is one of prosperity. Is not that a most powerful reason for making this concession? At the present moment you are free agents. An hon. Member said, that there was nothing to apprehend this year nor anything next year. Then you will not go the length of saying that you are safe for more than two years. Can there be a better proof that the present is not an unfavourable moment for effecting the alteration which this measure is intended to accomplish? Again I ask you how long do you think you can maintain the system of protection? I know, and we all know, that it cannot be made permanent consistently with that degree of good-will and harmony without which a nation cannot be happy or prosperous. No doubt the immediate cause of this measure is the sad calamity which has befallen Ireland. It has forced upon you the consideration of the corn question. But suppose that you suspended the Corn Laws, what could you have done when the time of suspension was at an end? I have not overlooked the circumstance that, respecting this Bill it has been said to be a good political manœuvre on my part. The letter of the noble Lord the Member for London, has been described as a good political manœuvre on his part. Now, I ask what possible advantage can a Bill like this confer upon me as an individual? I know that I have been taunted, and have more than once been told, that my days as a Minister are numbered. But I have introduced this measure, not for the purpose of prolonging my Ministerial existence, but for the purpose of averting a great national calamity, and for the purpose of sustaining a great public interest. I am quite aware of the fact that more than once I have been asked how long I can reckon upon the support of those hon. Gentlemen opposite, without whose votes I could not hope to carry this Bill through the House—how long, in fact, I can reckon upon enjoying their support with respect to other subjects? I know, as well as those who taunt me, that I have not any right to the support or confidence of those hon. Members. I acknowledge, and I admit that acknowledgment with perfect sincerity and plainness, that they have supported me in passing this measure, if it will pass into a law. I do not say this as a private man—I do not on private grounds attach importance to it; but I feel and acknowledge every proper obligation to them as a public man, for the support which they have given to this measure, and for studiously avoiding everything calculated to create embarrassment to its progress; but then our differences remain the same. I have, Sir, no right to claim their support nor their protection, nor, I will fairly admit, shall I seek it, by departing in the slightest degree from that course which my public duty may urge me to adopt. If this measure pass, our temporary connection is at an end; but I have not the slightest right to expect support or forbearance from them; still less have I, after the declarations that have been made, a right to expect forbearance or support from this side of the House. Well then, that being the case; it being the fact, that there are but 112 Members to support me, then I may be asked what great measure of national policy I can expect to pursue with these 112 Members, constituting as they do but little more than one-sixth of the House of Commons? I am not, I say, surprised to hear hon. Members predict that my tenure of power is short. But let us pass this measure, and while it is in progress let me request of you to suspend your indignation. This measure being once passed, you on this side and on that side of the House may adopt whatever measures you think proper for the purpose of terminating my political existence. I assure you I deplore the loss of your confidence much more than I shall deplore the loss of political power. The accusations which you prefer against me are on this account harmless, because I feel that they are unjust. Every man has within his own bosom and conscience the scales which determine the real weight of reproach; and if I had acted from any corrupt or unworthy motives, one-tenth part of the accusations you have levelled against me would have been fatal to my peace and my existence. You may think that we took too great precautions against Irish famine in the month of November. You are mistaken. Events will prove that those precautions were not superfluous; but even if they had been, as our motive was to rescue a whole people from the calamity of possible famine, and consequent disease, I should be easy under the accusation. I do not say whether this measure will be effectual for that or not. I speak only of the motive. What weight would your accusation have then even if the precautions be superfluous? I, with the information we had, and the prospects which were before us, repeat the accusation that we took superfluous precautions; and I will reply, as Mr Burke did, when labouring under similar obloquy, and in circumstances not dissimilar: "In every accident in life, in pain, in sickness, in depression, in distress, I called to mind that accusation; and was comforted." No, never—no reproach will attach to me even if it be proved that our precautions were superfluous. Before the month of July—[OPPOSITION: May]—it will be established to the conviction of every man, that the precautions we took were not superfluous, and that our motives were not impure. I am not speaking of a temporary measure; I am speaking of a permanent measure. When I do fall, I shall have the satisfaction of reflecting that I do not fall because I have shown subservience to a party. I shall not fall because I preferred the interests of party to the general interests of the community; and I shall carry with me the satisfaction of reflecting, that during the course of my official career, my object has been to mitigate monopoly, to increase the demand for industry, to remove restrictions upon commerce, to equalize the burden of taxation, and to ameliorate the condition of those who labour.

PRÉCIS

Speech I

Peel admitted that his proposals would have no marked effect in mitigating the present economic crisis. But the distress was not due to the Corn Laws, and past experience showed that a revival of trade could be confidently expected through the operation of natural causes. He enumerated the forces at the root of the present trouble, and illustrated from the effect of industrial inventions on the demand for labour the powerlessness of government to prevent distress (159). The trade returns for a period of years, however, gave no ground for pessimism and certainly did not show that the depression was due to the Corn Law (160).

There were those who, in demanding Corn Law repeal took the example of Prussia, where the common articles of consumption admittedly were cheaper than in England. Yet reliable statistics showed that the consumption per head of such necessaries as meat and bread was considerably lower in Prussia than in England, so that it was wrong to infer from the high prices ruling in this country that its inhabitants were poorer than elsewhere (162–4). He was opposed also to those advocates of protection who desired to substitute a fixed for a variable duty. For, despite the phenomenal increases of population, the country could still grow enough corn for its needs (166–7). The fixed duty would merely expose England to the fluctuations of prices elsewhere, seeing that harvest conditions here usually coincided with those abroad. The rigidity of a fixed duty would destroy its efficacy (168–9).

The Government proposed to retain the principle of a sliding scale. This meant continuing the system of averages, which had been attacked because it was believed to be open to abuses. These, however, were exaggerated. Various checks against fraud had been put forward; and the Government had decided to retain the present method of collecting the averages, but to extend the number of towns in which the information was obtained, and to put the duty of collection in the hands of the excise officers (169–73).

As to the mechanism of the sliding scale: at present the duty fell so rapidly with each increase of price that there was an inducement to hold back supplies in the hope that prices would rise until the duty was at a minimum. This injured all parties and particularly the British farmer (173–5). He hoped that the proposed alterations would secure a just price to the home consumer, and also permit the importation of foreign corn when that was necessary. Here Peel read out the revised scale (177). It was graduated less steeply than the existing one, and would, he thought, end the practice of holding back corn. He then dealt with his proposals for other grains and for colonial wheat (178–9); and he concluded with the hope that, while his proposal would substantially reduce the scale of duties, nevertheless the time would be far distant when the country would depend for its existence on foreign supplies. He sought from Parliament the measure "most in concurrence with the permanent welfare of all classes, manufacturing, commercial, and agricultural, in the country" (182).

Speech II

Peel defended himself against the accusation that he had betrayed a trust in that, having stated previously that he did not consider himself a fit person to introduce a bill repealing the Corn Laws, he had nevertheless undertaken the task (184). But reports from Ireland had become so grave that he had no alternative but to take every possible precaution. "Good God! are you to sit in Cabinet, and consider and calculate how much diarrhoea, and bloody flux, and dysentery a people can bear before it becomes necessary for you to provide them with food?" (185). Nor could he guarantee that the Corn Laws would be revived at some future date. The sliding scale had been unable to survive the first strain put upon it, and public opinion had advanced too far to permit this re-enactment (188). Here he read out the Memorandum to his Cabinet of Nov. 26, 1845, in which his position was clearly stated (189–90).

Peel then described the situation which arose when he resigned and the motives which prompted him to take office again (191). The present Parliament was competent to deal with the situation, and there was no reason for a dissolution. He quoted as a constitutional precedent the statement of Pitt at the time of the Irish Union (192–3).

It was no argument for the Corn Laws that the Irish peasants had always been poverty-stricken; rather was it an argument against them. Nor was it fair to oppose repeal by asking why it had not been accomplished before. The removal of the Corn Laws would strengthen rather than weaken the landed classes. And illustrating from the last census tables the preponderance of the labouring classes in the country, he showed how heavily indirect taxation pressed upon the poorer members of these (196–8). Peel then examined the probable effect of Repeal upon the price of corn. It was argued that, since the continental price was lower than the English, the removal of Protection would depress the latter (199). But the exclusion of foreign corn was itself a factor tending to reduce prices abroad by causing accumulations there (200–1): and Protection had not always ensured high prices here. Free Trade in corn would be a guarantee against both the low and the high prices ruling under Protection (202).

As to the agricultural labourer: it was argued that his wages varied with the price of corn. But this was not so. Wages were high in areas which were close to manufacturing centres or where labour was highly skilled and much capital had been put into the land (203). He took the wages of labourers in the Sodbury Union of Gloucestershire, 1837–1844. Corn had fluctuated widely in this period (205), but wages were almost stationary (206). There was the same lack of correlation in other districts (206–8). High wages depended on general prosperity, and this could only be obtained when restrictions on trade had been swept away.

In his closing words Peel said he realised that his period of office was drawing to a close and that he had no right to rely for support on his political opponents. But he had no regrets, because he was clear in his own mind that his action had been right and would be of lasting benefit to the whole nation.

INDEX

Acts of Parliament

Corn Laws:

1660. Export of Wheat (12 Charles II, c. 4), 13
1663. Export of Wheat (15 Charles II, c. 1), 12, 14, 31, 54, 55 n.
1670–71. Export of Wheat (22 and 23 Charles II, c. 13), 1, 12, 14
1672. Bounty on Corn (25 Charles II, c. 1, s. 37), 13
1685. Improvement of Tillage (1 James II, c. 19), 14
1688. Bounty on Wheat (1 William and Mary, c. 12), 1, 12
1698–9. Poundage on export (11 and 12 William III, c. 20), 13
1707. Export of Oatmeal (6 Anne, c. 8 (Scotland), c. 24 (England)), 2
1710. Price of flour (8 Anne, c. 19), 46
1753. Corn debentures (26 George II, c. 15), 27
1757–8. Flour (31 George II, c. 29), 46
1772. Selling of Corn (12 George III, c. 71), 9, 54–5, 55 n.
1772–3. Duty on Corn (13 George III, c. 43), 2, 10, 29, 32, 33
1780–1. Inspector of Corn Returns (21 George III, c. 50), 63 n.
1789. Inspector of Corn Returns (29 George III, c. 58), 63 n.
1790–1. Duty on Corn and Corn Returns (31 George III, c. 30), 30, 55, 63
1796–7. Allowance to bakers (37 George III, c. 98), 46
1803–4. Duty on Corn and Corn Averages (England) (44 George III, c. 109), 30, 63

1805. Corn Averages (Scotland) (45 George III, c. 86), 64
1813–14. Export of Corn (54 George III, c. 69), 38
1814–15. Importation of foreign wheat (55 George III, c. 26), 65, 67
1814–15. Assize of bread (55 George III, c. 99 (local)), 46
1819. Abolition of Assize of bread (59 George III, c. 36), 52
1821. Corn averages (1 and 2 George IV, c. 87), 66
1822. Disposal of corn in bond (3 George IV, c. 60), 81
1824. Re-exportation of corn (5 George IV, c. 70), 82
1824. The Imperial Bushel (5 George IV, c. 74), 70
1825. Canadian wheat (6 George IV, c. 64), 126
1825. Warehousing of grain (6 George IV, c. 65), 82
1826–7. Importation of corn (7 and 8 George IV, c. 57), 67, 83
1827. Corn Averages (7 and 8 George IV, c. 58), 67
1828. Sliding Scale (9 George IV, c. 60), 83
1836. Weighing of bread (6 and 7 William IV, c. 37), 48
1842. Sliding Scale (5 and 6 Victoria, c. 14), 83
1843. Canadian preference (6 and 7 Victoria, c. 29), 126–7

Other Laws:

1552. Forestalling and Engrossing (5 and 6 Edward VI, c. 14), 53, 55 n.
1662. Frauds and Abuses in His Majesty's Customs (14 Charles II, c. 11), 15
1750–1. Calendar (new style) (24 George II, c. 23), 13 n.

Age of Reason (Paine), 145
Agrarian Justice (Paine) (1796), 145

Agricultural distress, 149, 201
Agricultural Protection Society, 91
America, 37
  and policy of land settlement, 117
  export of corn from, 114, 120
*American Treasure and Andalusian
  Prices* (Earl Hamilton), 20
Anti-Bread Tax Circular, 101
Anti-Corn Law Almanac, 93, 107
Anti-Corn Law Association, founda-
  tion of, 5, 90
  in Manchester, 90
Anti-Corn Law Circular, 91, 107
Anti-Corn Law League, and propa-
  ganda, 107
  foundation of, 87
  its strength, 100–3
  petition to Queen, 95
Arch, Joseph, 142
Ashley, Lord, 98
Assize of Bread, abolition of, 52, 62
  and Standard Bread controversy, 5
  Arthur Young on, 68
  original Assize of bread, 53
Australia, 128

Bamford, S., 149
Baring, 39, 41
Barley, and corn bounty Act of 1688, 1
  consumption of, 3
  duty on, 178, 194
Barnes, D. G., and corn bounty, 16
  and enclosures, 147–8
  and Repeal, 108
Barnstaple, 207
Beans, 178
Belgium, 160, 164
Bentinck, Lord George, 98, 99
Blandford, 206
Board of Excise, the, 172
Bowring, Dr John, and Prussia, 163
  on effect of Corn Laws, 109
  speech in Manchester, 89
Branston, Mr, 97
Bright, John, and landlordism, 143
  and Select Committee on Game
    Laws, 97–8
  election for Durham, 95
  genius of, 101
British North America, 122, 123
Brittany, 10–11
Brockwood, Nathaniel, 59
Brougham, Lord, 150
Buckingham, Duke of, 97
Burke, Edmund, 30, 36
Burn, D. L., 132–4

California, 119
Cambridge Chronicle, 92
Cambridge Historical Journal, 132
Canada, and Act of 1843, 127, 130
  and colonial preference, 122
  and Governor Grey, 128
  and wheat crop, 10, 154
  effect of Repeal of Corn Laws on,
    131–2
Cannan, E., 55 n.
Canning, 82
Carlisle bushel, 74
Carlyle, Thomas, 100
Cato Street conspirators, the, 145
Chamberlain, Joseph, 134
Chartism, 144
China, 158
*Coal Industry of the Eighteenth
  Century* (Ashton and Sykes), 148
Cobbett, 149
Cobden, Richard, and Corn Law
    Agitation, 96
  and Free Trade, 90
  and land drainage, 102–3
  and Manchester Free Trade Hall,
    92
  election for Stockport, 93
  genius of, 101
Coke of Holkham, 11
Colbert, 9
Complete Suffrage Movement, 101
Continental System, the, 113
Corn Bounty, the, and Act of 1804, 63
  history of, 12–27 *passim*
  its effect on prices, 16–20
  its lapse after 1773, 31
Corn Exchange, the, 56
Corn Laws, the, and corn deben-
    tures, 27
  and Repeal, 141, 196
  and Sir R. Peel, 184
  effect of 1815 corn law, 78–9
  history of, 7
  modification of, 157–8
  policy to 1815, 9–10
Croker, Mr, 42, 100
Crookes, Sir William, 154
Cunningham, and corn bounty, 16,
    27
  and economic policy of Edward III,
    132, 134

Danzig, port of shipment to Eng-
    land, 113–14, 119
  price of wheat in, 115, 199
Darwin, C., 146

Davitt, Michael, 147
Dictionary of Political Economy (Palgrave), 153
Diminishing Returns in Agriculture, Law of, 137, 141
Disraeli, Benjamin, 93, 99
Documentary History of American Industrial Society (Commons), 146
Douglas, Major, 155
Dove, Patrick Edward, 142, 145
Dundas, Charles, 69
Durham, Earl of, 102, 130

Economic History of England (Lipson), 16
Eden (F. M.), 4
Elcomb, William, 98
Elements of Political Science (1854) (Dove), 145
Elgin, Lord, 133
Elliott, Ebenezer, 121–2
Ernle, Lord, 12
Essay on the Application of Capital to Land with observations showing the Impolicy of any great Restriction of the Importation of Corn and that the Bounty of 1688 did not lower the price of it (West), 138, 138 n.
Essay on the External Corn Trade (1815) (Torrens), 151
Essay on the Influence of the Low Price of Corn on the Profits of Stock (1815) (Ricardo), 138 n., 139
Essay on the Right of Property in Land (1781) (Ogilvie), 145

Fair Trade, 146
Fairfax, 143
Finlay, Mr, 42
Fitzwilliam, Earl, 102
Flood, Sir Frederick, 42
Foundations of Agricultural Economics (Venn), 70
Fox, C, J., 100–1, 192
France, 136
Free Trade, and Canada Corn Bill, 127
and failure of Continental harvests, 110
and Fair Trade, 146

Galpin, W. F., *The Grain Supply of England during the Napoleonic Wars*, 112 n.
Gee, Joshua, 24

George, Henry, 142
and Alfred Marshall, 152–3
and California, 147, 153
author of *Progress and Poverty*, 146
George junior, Henry, 152
Gladstone, John, 71
Gladstone, W. E., 87, 105, 150
Gonner (E. C. K.), 144
Gooch, T. S., 80
Graham, Sir James, 94, 97
Granger Movement, the, 102, 143
Greg, R. H., 92
Grenville, Lord, 43
Grey, Governor, 128
Griffith, Talbot, 26
Grounds of an Opinion on the Policy of Restricting the Importation of Foreign Corn (1815) (Malthus), 139

Hamilton, Earl, 20
Handloom weavers, 159
Herbert, Sidney, 97, 100
Hincks, Francis, 130
Historical Inquiry into the Production and Consumption of the Precious Metals (1831) (Jacob), 80
History of Prices (Tooke), 150, 168
History of the English Corn Laws (Barnes), 16, 24
Hodgson, David, 80, 150
Holland, 11, 160
"Hop Pole," Ollerton (Notts), 44
Horner, Francis, 112
Hume, Joseph, 93
Hume, J. Deacon, 93, 163–4
Hungry Forties, the, 154
Huskisson, William, and Canada, 125–6
and colonial preference, 123–4
and corn law of 1815, 78
and prohibition of export of raw wool, 39
and Repeal, 100
and sliding scale, 82–5
and Tooke, 150
as Minister of Woods and Forests, 121
Hutt, William, 128, 129

Imperial bushel, the, 70
Income tax, 197–8
Industry and Trade, 24
Inquiry into the Nature and Progress of Rent (1815) (Malthus), 138 n., 139

Inspectors of Corn, 62
Ireland, and Pitt, 193
  and sub-letting, 136
  effect of 1815 corn law on, 79
  export of oats from, 2
  remission of corn duties in, 98
  suffering in, 185, 194–5

Jacob, William, 62, 80, 116

Keble's Statutes, 13
Keith, Dr Skene, and duty on corn, 71
  and graded bounty, 84
  and nation's food supply, 4
King, Gregory, 20
King v. Rusby (1800), Case of the, 55, 61
Kinnaird, Lord, 102
Kitson Clark, G., 108
Knatchbull, Sir Edward, 93, 97

Land tenure, 136
Land Nationalisation, Its Necessity and its Aims (1882) (Wallace), 146
Langland, William, 142
Letter from Governor Pownall to Adam Smith (1776), 21
Life of a Radical (Bamford), 149
Lipson, E., and corn bounty, 16, 22–4
Liverpool, and sale of corn, 75
  inadequacy of corn returns in, 65
Liverpool and Manchester Railway, 121
Liverpool, Lord, 42
Local Government, 147
London Flour Company, 59
Lowe, Robert, 99

Maize, 194
Malthus, T. R., and alterations in corn laws, 33
  and law of population, 137
  and self-sufficiency, 138–9
Manchester, and Anti-Corn Law Bazaar, 107
  and price of bread, 52
Manchester Guardian, 144
Marshall, A., and Henry George, 152–3
  and price of wheat, 24
Marx, Karl, 143
McCulloch, J. R., and corn trade, 119
  and sliding scale, 86–7

Melbourne, Lord, 89
Memoranda on the Classification and Incidence of Imperial and Local Taxes (1899), 151
Miles, Mr, 47
Mill, J. S., 140–1
Mitchell, Wesley, 135, 141
Morning Herald, 91
Müller, Miss Max, 152

Napoleon, and blockade, 122
  and Continental supplies of corn, 113
  and struggle with England, 8
National Library, Dublin, 3
Natur-Wirtschaft, 114
Navigation Laws, the, 6, 122
Necker, 10, 34
Newcastle, 149
Newmarch, 118

Oats, and Act of 1773, 2
  and corn law of 1670, 1
  and Ireland, 194
  duty on, 178
  imports of, into Great Britain, 59–60
Observations on the Effects of the Corn Laws (Malthus), 138, 138 n.
O'Connorville, 146
Ogilvie, William, 142
Ontario, 122
Orbiston, 142
Order in Council, 187
Owen, Robert, 81, 142

Paine, Thomas, 145
Palmerston, Lord, 172

Parliamentary Papers

Agriculture:
  Commons Committee on Petitions complaining of Agricultural Distress (1820), 64, 71
  Commons Committee on the distressed State of Agriculture (1821), 13, 114
  Commons Committee on Agriculture (1836), 86

Bakers:
  Commons Committee on Petitions of certain Country Bakers (1813), 50

Bakers (cont.):
Commons Committee on Allowances granted to Bakers by 53 George III, c. 116, in those places where an Assize of Bread is set (1824), 49

Bread:
Commons Committee on the Assize and Making of Bread (1800), 6, 111
Commons Committee on Laws relating to the Manufacture, Sale and Assize of Bread (1815), 45, 46, 48
Commons Committee on Existing Regulations to the making and sale of bread (1821), 47

Corn:
Commons Committee appointed to take into consideration the present High Price of Corn (1795–6), 5th Report, 71
Commons Committee appointed to consider Petitions relating to the Corn Law of 1804 (1805), 64
Commons Committee on Petitions relating to the Corn Laws of the United Kingdom (1814), 40
Commons Committee to enquire into the Present Practices of selling corn throughout the United Kingdom with a view to the better regulation thereof (1834), 71–2, 73
Commons Committee on Corn Sales (1893), 74–6

Corn Trade:
Commons Committee on the Corn Trade of the United Kingdom (1813), 3, 32, 39

Flour:
Commons Committee on Methods practised in making Flour from Wheat (1774), 45

Game Laws:
Commons Committee on the Operation of the Game Laws (1845), 98

Grain:
Lords Committee on the Growth, Commerce, and Consumption of Grain and Laws relating thereto (1814), 41

Housing:
Royal Commission on the Housing of the Working Class (1885), 146

Import Duties:
Commons Committee on Import Duties (1840), 93

Provisions:
Commons Committee on the High Price of Provisions, 2nd Report (1800), 7th Report (1801), 6, 61, 71

Trade:
Committee of the Council on Trade (1790), 13, 14 n., 20, 125

Parnell, Sir Henry, and Corn Committee of 1813, 38, 123, 138
and protective duty, 40
and sliding scale, 84
Paulton, Mr, 90
Peel, Sir Robert, and Catholic Emancipation, 81
and defeat of Whig government, 93
and imperial trade, 129
and sliding scale, 83–4
and Tooke, 150
his achievements, 108
his death, 121
his resignation, 99–100
Peel senior, Sir Robert, 42
Peel and the Conservative Party (Kitson Clark), 108
Peel, Sir Robert (Ramsay), 108
People's Charter, The, 142, 146
Phillips, 41
Physiocracy, 10, 138
Pigs' Meat (Spence), 145
Pitt, W., and Necker, 35
and the Act of Union, 192–3
Poland, 113–14
Poor Law, New, 141
Poor Law Settlement, 67
Population Problems of the Age of Malthus (Griffith), 26

Potato disease, 188
Poulett Thomson, C. E. (Lord Sydenham), 89, 90, 130
Powell, York, 152
Pownall, Governor Thomas, 30
Price of Corn and Wages of Labour (1826) (West), 140
Principles of Political Economy and Taxation (1817) (Ricardo), 140
Privy Council, 112
Progress and Poverty (Henry George), 146, 152
Protection, 118
Protection to Agriculture (Ricardo), 81, 82, 186
Prussia, 162–4

Quarterly Review, 108

Ralahine, 142
Ramsay, A. A. W., 108
Receiver of Corn Returns, 62
Redford, Dr A., *Some Problems of the Manchester Merchant after the Napoleonic War*, 120 n.
Rent, 135
and the Single tax, 145
Ricardo, David, and Adam Smith, 136
and fixed duty on corn, 81, 82
and high rents, 139–40
Richmond, Duke of, 97
Rights of Man (Paine), 145
Robinson, F. J., Viscount Goderich, 41
Rogers, Thorold, 151
Rosebery, Lord, 108
Royal Burghs of Scotland, 1
Russell, Lord John, and fixed duty, 93
and sliding scale, 86
his failure to form a government, 99
Russia, 119, 134
Rye, and corn bounty Act of 1688, 1
duty on, 178
production in Poland of, 115

St George's Hill, 143
Salomons, D., 86
San Francisco, 147
Scotland, 63–4
Scott, Samuel, 125
Senior, Nassau, 151
Sheridan, R. B., 192
Shortt, Adam, 131, 133

Sinking Fund, Pitt's, 145
Sliding scale, and Huskisson, 82
details of, 177
Duke of Wellington's, 83–6
its effect on prices, 110
Smith, Adam, and corn bounty, 15–16, 25–6
and corn law of 1773, 2
and importance of agriculture, 7
and Invisible Hand, 9
and liberalism, 142
and rise in price of silver, 19
and taxation, 198
and the Middleman, 135
and wages of labour, 104, 208
Smith, Charles, and consumption of bread, 3
and corn bounty, 16–17, 21–2
Smith, Mr, President of the Manchester Chamber of Commerce, 109
Snell, R., 60
Snowden, Viscount, 142, 147
Socialism, 81
Sodbury Union, the, 204–5
Solly, Isaac, 150
South Sea Company, 27
Speenhamland, 8
Spence, Thomas, 142
and the rent of land, 144–5
Spencer, Earl, 102
Squire Western's Resolutions, 78
Standard Bread Controversy, The, 5
Stanley, Lord, 95, 99, 127
State of the Poor (Eden), 4
Stettin, 201
Sturge, Joseph, 101
Sussex, Duke of, 94

Taylor, Miss Helen, 142
Thackeray, W. M., 107
Thünen, von, 116
Tithes, calculation of, 67, 169, 175
Tooke, Thomas, and bad harvests, 28
and House of Commons, 150
and price of corn, 168
and price of silver, 19
and sale of corn, 71–2
and seizure of neutral ships, 37
as witness before Committee of 1821, 80
Torrens, Colonel Robert, 151
Townshend, Lord, 148
Trevelyan, G. M., 147
Tull, J., 148
Turgot, 10, 138

United Empire Loyalists, 122
United States, the, 131, 158
Unwin (George), 132

Venn, J. A., 70
Vermuyden, Cornelius, 143
Villiers, Charles, and petitions
    against corn laws, 90
    and taxation, 103
    annual motion on corn laws, 92
    member for Wolverhampton, 89

Wages, and price of provisions, 104,
    202–9
    effect of repeal on, 103
Wallace, Alfred Russel, 146
Wealth of Nations, and Lord Gren-
    ville, 43
    and rent of land, 135
    and smuggling, 68
Webb, S. and B. (Lord Passfield
    and Mrs Webb), 147
Wellington, Duke of, and repeal of
    corn laws, 100
    and sliding scale, 83, 117
West, Sir Edward, and diminishing
    returns in agriculture, 137–8
    and price of raw produce, 139

West India Islands, 125
Wheat, and committee of 1813, 39
    and corn averages, 51
    and corn bounty of 1688, 1, 12
    and corn law of 1773, 29–30
    and Ireland, 194
    and Mark Lane market, 57
    and North America, 131
    colonial wheat, 179
    consumption of, 166, 174
    demand for, 115–16
    its export from Baltic ports, 115
    price of, 200–1
    price of, in Scotland, 63–4
    sale by weight of, 73
Winchester bushel, 68–70
Windham, Colonel, 97
Winstanley, Gerard, 141, 143

Young, Arthur, and Assize of Bread,
    68–9
    and consumption of wheat, 6
    and corn bounty, 25
    and expense of raising wheat, 40
    and the villager, 144

Zollverein, the, 162

CAMBRIDGE: PRINTED BY WALTER LEWIS, M.A., AT THE UNIVERSITY PRESS